first expressions

first expressions

innovation and the mission of God

Steve Taylor

scm press

© Steve Taylor 2019

Published in 2019 by SCM Press
Editorial office
3rd Floor, Invicta House,
108–114 Golden Lane,
London EC1Y 0TG, UK
www.scmpress.co.uk

SCM Press is an imprint of Hymns Ancient & Modern Ltd
(a registered charity)

Hymns Ancient & Modern® is a registered trademark of
Hymns Ancient & Modern Ltd
13A Hellesdon Park Road, Norwich,
Norfolk NR6 5DR, UK

978-0-334-05847-2

British Library Cataloguing in Publication data

A catalogue record for this book is available
from the British Library

Typeset by Regent Typesetting
Printed and bound by
CPI Group (UK) Ltd

Contents

To Pop

Much loved grammar fiend
In eternal peace, now no
infinitives split

Acknowledgements

I have lived with this book for a quarter of a century. It began in 1994, when planting Graceway Baptist Church and experimenting with ecclesial innovation. The creativity of that community, along with the isolation of pioneering fresh expressions before there were wider church support structures like Fresh Expressions, was significant for my journey and the journey of this book. In 1999 I took the missiology questions being generated by the planting of Graceway into a PhD and began researching new forms of church. As part of that exploration, I conducted research in the United Kingdom in 2001, interviewing alt.worship communities and various Christian thinkers about new forms of church. However, by the time the thesis was submitted at the end of 2003, the PhD was already 140,000 words. There was not the space to include the UK data. It hurt, but all the UK research had to hit the cutting room floor, in film editing terms.

Free of the PhD, I was keen to find a way for the gift of research in the UK – of people's time and reflection – to be honoured. However, I felt I lacked the language, and the time, to tell the story. At this point the project stalled. In 2012, I began to wonder if a further gathering of data – some longitudinal research – might move the project forward. University ethics approval was granted. Study leave made possible a return visit to the United Kingdom from late in 2012 through to early 2013. Further data was gathered, and I am very grateful to those who participated in this second phase of research.

However, the project stalled again. Work commitments were a major factor. But I was still searching for the language – the words and frames by which to tell the stories emerging from the data. These were people's dreams I was daring to turn into black text on white pages.

A number of presentations, one a research seminar in 2015 at Uniting College for Leadership and Theology, another a lecture in 2018 at Knox Centre for Ministry and Leadership, were important steps in finding words.

A wonderful set of digital coincidences sparked a book proposal, which was generously received by David Shervington in June 2018 and accepted by SCM in September 2018. Outside study leave in 2019 provided the space to complete the project.

Over these years, there are many folk to thank:

My parents, who taught me to hold a pencil and write. More importantly, they raised me in a world where crossing cultures was normal.

Graceway Baptist Church, my first expression, who body-ied forth the Spirit as creative and present in contemporary culture.

John Drane, Mike Riddell and Gregory McCormack who supervised the initial PhD research.

The communities, leaders, individuals and focus group participants who gave me time.

My Taylor family, who supported this research for years but most particularly during the two UK research trips.

Those who funded the trips and the space to write. In particular, I wish to thank Graceway Baptist Church who granted a sabbatical in 2001, Uniting College for Leadership and Theology who granted a sabbatical in December 2012–March 2013 and Knox Centre for Ministry and Leadership who granted Outside Study Leave in March–May 2019. There is a commitment to the kingdom shown by each of these institutions and a generosity of spirit shown by colleagues who picked up extra work, particularly matters in relationship to my role as Principal. My specific thanks to Eloise Scherer, Craig Bailey, Mark Johnston and Geoff New.

Doug Gay and Trinity College, Glasgow who generously invited me to lecture in June 2018 and in so doing became unknowing agents in making possible a face-to-face meeting with SCM Senior Commissioning Editor, David Shervington.

Twitter, which allows strangers – in this case book writers and potential book editors – to connect.

SCM Press, who said yes. Knowing an editorial board believed in the project through the final weeks of writing was a wonderful en-couragement.

Shannon Taylor, who created the images in Chapter 3.

Those who peer-reviewed the proposal, read drafts and provided editorial assistance. All errors remain mine.

My father-in-law, Ian Kennedy, who died in the final weeks of writing. He is greatly missed, and this book is dedicated to him.

Steve Taylor
Feast of Visitation of Mary to Elizabeth (see Chapter 7)
31 May 2019

PART I

Introducing first expressions

To bloom, wild flower
Consider lilies, scattered
So structured for risk

Hand held hazel nut
Maker, Keeper, Lover made
In unique, God is

As yeast ferments, rise
bubbles. So bread now is born
Hands kneaded, needed

I

Definitions and a roadmap

Innovation is nothing new

Innovation is nothing new. *Alternative Church* was published in 1976 by the Urban Theology Unit in Sheffield. Author John Vincent described the 1960s as an era of ecclesial experimentation. Hundreds of Christians poured time, creativity and energy into new expressions of Christian community (1976, p. 9). *Alternative Church* shares in detail the stories of new forms of church which were emerging across the United Kingdom – Corrymeela Community, Open Group, the Eucharist Congregation and the House Church. Each are innovative experiments in new forms of Christian expression.

Innovation is nothing new, and neither are the responses to innovation. Vincent describes how ten years on, by the mid-1970s, experimentation had declined. Perhaps the reasons sound familiar? First, church structures seemed to resource the status quo rather than the emerging. 'The new things inevitably disappeared as survival and maintenance in a time of pressure became unquestionable necessities' (p. 12). Second, a lack of theological reflection from within these experimental communities. This weakened their ability to learn, grow and engage in further innovation in action–reflection modes. Third, a growing realization that what is needed is not only innovation at the grassroots and among experimental communities, but also systematic innovation in which the structures of the church are reordered in mission.

Today, of the four innovative communities celebrated in *Alternative Church*, only Corrymeela remains as a worshipping community. What do we make of the other three? Does the decline of Open Group, the Eucharist Congregation and the House Church make the pursuit of new forms of alternative church a waste of time? Vincent describes the approach of various church leaders at the time: '"We've seen it all before", they say ... "Just a few *entrepreneurs* doing their own thing ..." And soon the ultimate knockout is delivered. "Will they stand the test of time?"' (p. 100). Such thinking suggests that innovation, unless sustained, is a waste of ecclesial time. A fifth mark of the church – that of durability – is added to the historic understandings of church as one, holy, catholic and apostolic.

A contrasting approach is evident as Jesus approaches his death. Following his triumphal entry into Jerusalem on Palm Sunday, Jesus declares that unless the seed falls into the ground and dies, it cannot produce a harvest (John 12.24). What we love must be lost, in order to experience the durability of eternal life (John 12.26). The apostle Paul describes the church as the body of Christ. The weaving of the body of Christ, about to die and rise, with the body of Christ, who in baptism will die and rise (Rom. 6.3–11), suggests that dying and rising, rather than durability should be the fifth mark of the true church. It is a value-inverting, redeeming contrast to a 'seen-it-all-before' waste of time and energy efficiency analysis.

Hence Vincent argues that when approaching alternative church and ecclesial innovation, the 'seen-it-all-before/durability' test approach should be resisted. Instead, argues Vincent, weave the planting of seeds of experimentation with the sharing of stories and close theological and historical analysis. Such an approach will clarify the lessons for the future of faith. It embodies practices that create and sustain the life of the Christian church, not as durable, but as a community sharing stories of death and resurrection, faith and risk, surprise and hope.

Stefan Paas, in his analysis of church planting in Europe, argues that the primary motivation for planting churches is to enable renewal through innovation. 'In our contemporary thinking about the church there must be space for experimentation' (Paas 2016, p. 198). Paas resists the 'seen-it-all-before/durability' analysis. Rather, 'radical renewal will only take place when we do not concentrate on results but on the facilitation of stimulating processes' (p. 225). Like Vincent, for Paas, as we plant, we must share stories, which are subject to close theological and historical examination. Innovative insights emerge from the 'tacit knowledge' embodied in fresh expressions: 'Initiating fresh expressions produces an incredible amount of theological, ecclesiological, missiological, and organizational experience, and, of course, a lot of questions' (p. 235). Alternative is nothing new, but are the seeds which, in dying and rising in innovation, offer 'hermeneutic discoveries' (p. 239).

Defining first expressions

In this book, first expressions are defined as initial experiments in ecclesial innovation. The term prioritizes initial, for first expressions occur in situations in which there are no pre-existing ten-step 'been-there, done-that, learnt lots' books on how to respond. This definition describes the ten first expression communities researched in this book.

As with Croft (2008, p. 15), lower case 'first expressions' is used to refer to new expressions of church, while capitalization 'Fresh Expressions' is used to refer to an organizational initiative as a joint Anglican and Methodist venture. However, using the definition above, Fresh Expressions is a first expression, given it is an experiment in how an organization might engage in ecclesial innovation.

As defined, the first expressions grassroots communities studied in this book are a subset of the term fresh expressions. They are first, birthed and becoming prior to the fresh expression commitments in the *Mission-Shaped Church* report (2004) to proclaim the gospel afresh.

The domain of first expression involves a particular form of loneliness. It assumes that as cultures shift, there will need to be fresh ways for making disciples and offering Christian witness. The nature of being 'first' invites the risk of being misunderstood.

However, using the definition of this book, while the journey in relation to a specific culture is lonely, there have been fellow travellers, other communities in times past who have sought to make disciples afresh. This is evident in the four new forms of ecclesial communities described by Vincent in *Alternative Church*. How to establish a community in a rapidly changing urban context? At other times in history, churches have responded to urban change, but never (as faced the Eucharist Congregation and the House Church) in the particular culture of London and Sheffield in the 1960s. How to break down centuries of religious separatism and histories of clericalism? At other times in history, churches have sought to empower laity, but never (as faces Corrymeela) in the particular context of tension between Protestant and Catholic in Ireland in the 1970s. Hence first expressions involves the shared experience of a particular loneliness. Using the term in this way seeks to name the reality of being first and the particular challenges, while looking to other first expressions communities through time and space for insight (see in particular Chapters 5 and 8).

Every time a culture shifts, there are first expressions. This book examines ten first expressions, each seeking to respond to the cultural changes in the United Kingdom at a certain time in history. In telling their stories, in submitting them to close theological and historical analysis, it seeks 'hermeneutic discoveries' that will guide the church as it seeks to be apostolic and one, holy and catholic.

First expressions are dangerous

Vincent encouraged a range of first expressions during the 1970s. In the same city, as cultures continued to shift some ten years on, a new form of first expression began to emerge. A young ecclesial entrepreneur named Chris Brain began to find in the bass and beats of contemporary dance culture a fresh expression of youth-orientated worship.

The Nine O'Clock Service started in 1986 at St Thomas Church in Crookes, Sheffield. It began with a small group of musicians and artists and, over time, grew to almost 600 members. With an average age of 24 and a membership that drew significantly from non-church backgrounds, it too would produce an incredible amount of theological, ecclesiological, missiological and organizational experience. It is tempting to examine only the stories that embody surprise and hope. Yet as Paas reminds us, we also need to consider the stories that produce lots of questions (2016, p. 235).

The story of The Nine O'Clock Service is not a comfortable place to start a book on innovation.[1] The *Independent* called The Nine O'Clock Service (NOS) a sex cult (McKie and Brown 1995). It carried pain and trauma for individual survivors, who complained about the actions of the then priest of NOS, the Revd Chris Brain. It also carried pain and trauma for the wider church. It shows the dangers of alternative church: whether the 'stand back/will it stand the test of time' approach, or involvement through providing resources and ordaining leadership. Yet a theology of ecclesial innovation needs to offer close theological and historical analysis not only in relation to the potential of humanity to be not only creative and constructive, but also deceptive and damaged. A theologic of first expressions needs to articulate a polity that rightly orders not only word and sacrament, but also discipline. By way of illustration, let us consider the theological, ecclesiological, missiological and organizational questions emerging from The Nine O'Clock Service, followed by the roadmap by which this book will engage those questions.

Here is how the worship of NOS was experienced by one participant:

We enter a round, darkened room where there are forty-two television sets and twelve large video screens and projections around the walls – projections of dancing DNA, dancing planets and galaxies and atoms. The altar is a large round table that, being white, is also a projection screen. Throughout the services, slides are projected over it that vary in colour and geometric form. [first] this was a very friendly place for a generation raised on television and images ... [second] these people are taking television away from the 'big guys' – the networks and government broadcasters and corporate sponsors – and are doing it themselves *and in the center of the city and in the center of their society: at worship itself.* (Fox 1996, pp. 9–10, italics original)

This description of worship for a 'generation raised on television and images' occurred after NOS had relocated to Ponds Forge, an entertainment venue in the centre of Sheffield. Chris Brain had been accelerated through ordination processes, and the Planetary Mass was pioneering multimedia worship, embracing new technologies to explore liturgies of enormous creativity.

NOS was staggeringly successful in mission. In the late 1980s, it held the largest ever confirmation service in the Diocese, with about 100 people being confirmed by the then Bishop of Sheffield. To quote Neil Hopkins: 'thousands of people had had the kind of spiritual experience normally denied to our culture. People were healed and lives were changed, and the gospel was preached' (2014). This also raises questions about the necessity of contextualization in contemporary culture and how to offer witness in a secular world (these will be discussed in Chapters 10 and 11).

NOS would have a significant influence on many subsequent 'alternative worship' groups.

> The Nine O'Clock Service (NOS) was the first worshipping community to combine elements of club culture with passionate worship and create the first truly post-modern church. Between 1985 and 1995, NOS pioneered what is commonly known as 'alternative worship' ... Without doubt NOS has had a huge influence on the church in the UK. Similar groups were established themselves albeit on a smaller scale. (Riley 1999, p. 6)

In 1995, allegations of abuse emerged in relation to Brain's leadership. It is tempting to begin a study of fresh expressions in more comfortable places, with the fanfare of *Mission-Shaped Church* or the theological nous of Archbishop Rowan Williams. But NOS remains the very first expression. It is an icon on to possibility.

The critical and historical questions that need to be asked about the story of NOS include sustainability. NOS – beginning in 1985, ending in 1995 – would not have made the 11-years-on framework for sustainability used in this book. Is 'Just a few *entrepreneurs* doing their own thing ... "Will they stand the test of time?"' an adequate response to the lessons of hope and trauma in the first expression that is NOS? Central to NOS was the Nairn Street Community. It was based on the early chapters of Acts and held to a pattern of holding all things in common. As a result, it generated resources, of money and people, significant in the generation of creativity of the Planetary Mass. How to transition from key leaders, in this case the charisma of Chris Brain, to values-held sustainably beyond the initial pioneering leader? What insights regarding sustainability might emerge from this, along with other stories not only of those who try, but also those who die? (These will be discussed in Chapters 4 and 5.)

Equally NOS offers commentary on the pitfalls of emergence. What is the configuration of catholicity, given what seemed the failure of the ecclesial structures at that time? To be more pointed, would Chris Brain have made it through Pioneer selection panels today? Would a Bishops' Mission Order, with its patterns and processes for accountability, have provided a different ending to the NOS story? What does 'church decently and in order' mean in relation to innovation? In hindsight, was the relentless search for fresh expressions simply a way to cover the shadow side of NOS? What might good governance in the context of ecclesial innovation look like? (This will be discussed further in Chapter 12.)

By beginning with NOS, the honest, albeit uncomfortable question can be asked. The first NOS service included lyrics that fuse mission with a certain view of church: 'Tear down the walls.' What is the place of the old wineskin when someone steps forward claiming to offer a new wine? These questions remain as relevant to first expressions of ecclesial innovation today as they did to the very first expression that was NOS.

Alongside these questions, there is another important reason for beginning with NOS.

In a curiosity of this research project, I would drive past Ponds Forge, snow gently falling, to interview Steven Croft in 2012–13. Steven Croft was the first Fresh Expressions Missioner. In other words, he was a pioneer, not of grassroots ecclesial communities, but in an institution, creating an organization called Fresh Expressions. The innovation of Fresh Expressions, as an organizational response to first expressions, was an essential layer of research that emerged (see Chapters 5 and 6). Now, over 20 years after NOS imploded, Steven Croft was Bishop of Sheffield. It was his predecessor who had ordained Chris Brain and confirmed around 100 people one bright day in the life of NOS.

Researching a church that is one, holy, catholic and apostolic requires paying attention to grassroots ecclesial innovation (first expressions) and to institutional and re-structural innovation (Fresh Expressions). Such are the living complexities of researching contemporary ecclesiology.

First expressions and 'I'

So how does a New Zealand pastor end up researching first expressions halfway around the world, in the United Kingdom?

In 1994, I was training for ministry as a Baptist pastor. In my free time,

I was loving U2's ZooTV, the kaleidoscope of images and engagement with contemporary multimedia. I was reading *Generation X: Tales for an Accelerated Culture* and enjoying the stories of friends, seeking meaning by finding community in the dropping out of institutions. It resonated with stories some of my friends shared with me, of being nourished by faith through popular culture, of having faith but feeling it no longer fitted with church. With a group of colleagues training for ministry, along with our spouses, we started a community of faith (Graceway Baptist Church). It was a first expression. There were no models. There were colleagues, asking similar questions. But there were no ten-step 'been-there, done-that, learnt lots' books.

I faced significant questions. Some were internal, seeking to understand ministry, given the particularity of my unique gift mix. Some were external, driven by controversy. Was this church? asked some parts of the church. Others were external, driven by culture. What was Christian witness in this particular context? What does making disciples look like in an image-saturated world?

The questions were what drew me to the United Kingdom. For a number of years a picture from Visions, in York, was pinned to my desk. I had found it on a website called 'alternative worship'. It depicted multiple slide images projected on church walls. It made me wonder what worship of God that valued body as well as mind and soul might look like. I wondered, intuitively, if these might be fellow travellers in a journey of ecclesial innovation.

Wanting to take the questions raised by mission seriously, I enrolled in doctoral study. I continued to innovate, part-time first expression planting, as I researched new forms of church as contextual expressions of mission in Western culture. This included a visit to the United Kingdom. Finally, I got to participate in Visions worship and interview participants!

During 2001, over a three-month period, as part of my PhD on new forms of church, I focused on what at that time was called 'alternative worship' (Taylor 2004). I participated in worship, from cafes in Edinburgh to church buildings in Bristol. I conducted interviews, in railway stations, vicarages, homes and gardens. I gathered data, heard individual dreams about the emergence of fresh expressions of faith.[2] My doctoral research became a book: *The Out of Bounds Church?* (2005).

In 2012, some 11 years after my first research, I began to wonder what had happened to those communities I visited in 2001. An initial web search was sobering. In the UK, of the communities I researched in 2001, only five – Sanctuary, Foundation, Grace, Moot and Visions – seemed, from a distance, to have survived. Seven – Late Late Service, Host, Bigger Picture, Club Culture Project, Graceland, Vaux and Holy Joes – seemed to be no longer active.

My research questions were again sharpened by my personal story. In 2003, as the PhD ended, I sensed God's call to lead another church in mission. The church I had planted – Graceway – called a new leader and re-formed a leadership team. In 2007, I received news that Graceway had decided to close. The new leader had moved on. Numbers had declined. After two years of pondering, the community sensed the season had ended. In the week following the closure, we received a parcel. Square shaped, it felt like an urn that might hold cremated ashes. Inside were written prayers, offered by those from that church who gathered for a final service. Holding the urn, I realized I was holding not only birth, but also death. How, theologically, might sustainability and fresh expressions be understood? How to understand innovation not only in birth, but in death?

With a period of sabbatical due in December 2012 to February 2013, I decided to research more closely. If I returned to the UK, could I locate the communities I researched in 2001? What, over time, had they learnt about discipleship and pastoral care, worship and mission? What about those communities no longer in existence? While perhaps much more difficult to locate, what insights might they have with regard to sustainability and witness, durability and discipleship? Where are the people in those communities now? Does death of a community mean death of faith?

Such questions shape this book. It is both a personal and theological reflection on sustainability and mission. It emerges from my story – as a church planter of a first expression of church that did not survive – and my research of first expressions over an extended period of time.

Personal stories make for interesting beginnings. But what is the role of lived experience in theological reflection? How to manage subjectivity – mine and those whom I might interview – in the task of research? One place to turn is practical theology.

Managing the 'I' in research: a first expression methodology

Practical theology investigates the concrete actions of the church in the light of the gospel and of church tradition in order to inform how the church might live and act in the world.[3] The actions of individuals and communities (in this case, first expressions) invite theological reflection, given they are theory-laden, value-directed and as such profoundly saturated by meaning. For Swinton and Mowatt (2006), one way to undertake practical theology is by action-research. This involves insiders conducting research with the aim of transformation of the communities they care about (Taylor and Dewerse 2018). These approaches provide ways to affirm lived experience, of researchers and the communities they care about, in the undertaking of research.

The concrete actions of the church are by definition particular. They involve learning from communities. Can this include individual communities? It is an important question, given this research project was seeking to study ten first expression communities. Julian of Norwich, English theologian and Christian mystic (1342–c.1416), provides a response. In *Revelations of Divine Love*, the earliest surviving book in the English language written by a woman, Julian contemplates a hazelnut.

> And he showed me more, a little thing, the size of a hazel-nut, on the palm of my hand, round like a ball. I looked at it thoughtfully and wondered, 'What is this?' And the answer came, 'It is all that is made.' I marvelled how it continued to exist ... it was so small ... 'It exists, both now and for ever, because God loves it'. In short, everything owes its existence to the love of God. In this 'little thing' I saw three truths. The first is that God made it; the second is that God loves it; and the third is that God sustains it. But what he is who is in truth Maker, Keeper and Lover I cannot tell. (Julian of Norwich 1966, p. 68)

She senses God affirming the value in creation, of contemplating what is singular and small. As she does, the activity of God is revealed in the singular reality of the one small thing. God is Maker, Lover and Keeper. In small things lie knowledge that has a Trinitarian pattern (Clark 1982; Soskice 2007). This is a first expression methodology.

The research focus

In this project, I am approaching each community as a hazel-nut. I am wanting, like Julian of Norwich, to hold these communities in reflective gaze before God, looking to see what patterns of God might be visible. How, uniquely in the world today, is God revealed in the birthing of a first expression? This begins, following Julian, by paying attention to individual communities through the gathering of empirical data. The data included interview, focus group, participant observation and online resources. Table 1 shows the research undertaken with each community.

The aim was triangulation, seeking to gain multiple perspectives through hearing from a mix of individuals, groups and personal participation. However, triangulation was not always possible given the time constraints of the periods of research and the logistics of using public transport to travel around the UK (with two children under five in 2001).

Interviews, both individual and group, were extensive, often lasting over 90 minutes. The result was one-off, yet very thick descriptions. All the interviews were recorded, then transcribed. Listening to the interviews again in 2019, a striking feature is the evidence of active listening. This includes rephrasing, in order to check perceptions and enhance the accuracy of the interview process. Finally, thematic analysis, looking for themes and patterns, was undertaken.

Table 1: Research engagement with each community 2001 and 2013

	Interview	*Focus group*	*Participation*
Bigger Picture	13		01 (worship)
Club Culture Project	13	01	01 (event)
Epicentre → Moot	01 13		13 (worship)
Grace	13	01 13	01 (worship)
Graceland	01 13 (email)		
Host	01 13		
Late Late Service	01 (three) 13 (one)	01	01 (AGM)
Sanctuary	13	01 13	13 (worship)
Third Sunday → Foundation	01 13	13	13 (worship)
Visions	13	01 13	01 (worship)

This use of empirical data has particular value in paying attention to the church as concrete. Catholic theologian Nicholas Healy argues that the study of the church tends to become a blueprint 'of what the church should ideally become' (2000, p. 36). It deals with ideals, rather than realities. It obscures the particularity of ecclesial communities in specific contexts. Healy argues instead for the concrete church as an approach which focuses on the 'thoroughly human' and 'grace-enabled activities of its members' (p. 5). It is researched through interview and observation, the study of ecclesial identity 'constituted by action' (p. 5). It values the particularity, the one small thing that Julian contemplates in search of the activity of God.

Longitudinal research: 11 years on

The first research period occurred between May and June of 2001. The second research period occurred between December 2012 and February 2013. This was eleven and a half years later, which for the purposes of this book will be abbreviated as eleven years. The academic term for a return to re-research is longitudinal research. While rare in theological studies, it has significant advantages. These include generating a pool of data over time and offering insight into the impact of transitions, both expected and unexpected. In this case, a key unexpected transition was the development of Fresh Expressions. As a result, I opened up a second trajectory of research, seeking to interview individuals significant in the development of Fresh Expressions (Chapters 6 and 7).

Longitudinal research can be undertaken in three ways. First, a cross-section of people can be sampled. Second, a retrospective study can consider historical information. Third, a cohort study can select a group based on a specific event such as birth or location and follow that cohort over time. My research involved the third method. Despite the advantages, longitudinal research also has limitations. These are perhaps obvious, but for the sake of transparency, let me mention the following.

First, it can only study moments in time. My impressions are shaped by what I observed in one particular service, or the feelings of a group during a particular focus group interview. To use a media image, the empirical data I am analysing is like recording a birthday party by taking snapshots on a camera rather than using a video camera. To continue the analogy, a sudden gust of wind can spoil even the best-planned photo shoot.

Second, the research sample for the longitudinal research is dictated by the research sample from the original research. My initial research in 2001 focused on what were then called 'alternative worship' communities. In 2004, *Mission-Shaped Church* documented 12 groupings of Fresh Expressions, only one of which was 'alternative worship'.[4] Even more diverse expressions of church have emerged since. In what follows, an inevitably limited perspective on first expressions will be presented, based around alternative worship communities present in 2001. To broaden my cohort by exploring these new groupings, while tempting, would have rendered impossible the longitudinal nature of the research. Despite this limitation, it is noteworthy that *Mission-Shaped Church* describes alternative worship as 'one of the most thoughtful attempts to relate worship and culture … they have a profoundly mission-based instinct' (p. 45). This makes them worthy of investigation as 'first expressions'.

Therefore this project utilizes a first expressions methodology. It is a unique study, as it values the empirical, longitudinal, interactional and theological. It examines not the ideals of what might be, but through interview and observation, the realities of what is. It is the first longitudinal study of first expressions. It pays attention to the interplay between first expressions and Fresh Expressions. This provides rich insight into how organizations might partner with grassroots innovation. While empirical, it is also theological, constantly seeking to discern the action of God in the 'one small thing'.

A critical friend

Whatever posture a researcher inhabits has both advantages and disadvantages. As an insider, there are the advantages of connections, background knowledge and a more intuitive awareness of natural categories. There is, however, a temptation to not be as critical as perhaps an outsider. However, an outsider might lack nuance and gain less access to inside conversations. In empirical research, an ideal location never exists.

In undertaking the research, I located myself as a 'critical friend' (Costa and Kallick 1993). I am a friend, in that I have been a practitioner in fresh expressions, a researcher of new forms of church and an educator of pioneering ministers. Through early internet web forums and now through social media, I know many of the participants. I am critical in that I write from a distance, as neither English, Anglican nor Methodist.

The road ahead: in detail

In the pages that follow I will describe the work of God in the world today, as it relates to an empirical study of first expressions in the UK. In Part 1, a theology of birthing and becoming is developed to offer a theologic of first expressions. Part 2 investigates the first expressions 11 years on. Part 3 looks at Fresh Expressions as one institutional experiment in mission, locating it in relation to leadership strengths and the mission history of Great Britain. Part 4 develops an ecclesiology of innovation, in particular what it means to be one and holy, apostolic and catholic in mission today.

Chapter 2 – Birthing first expressions

I begin in 2002 with five first expression birthing stories. Interviews with leaders from six experiments in ecclesial formation – Grace, Epicentre/Moot, Host, Late Late Service, Sanctuary and Vaux – will clarify intent and purpose in ecclesial innovation and in relationship to faith and culture. These grassroot stories are located in relation to a contemporary ecclesiology, an eschatological anthropology of kinship by Janet Martin Soskice. Her work is generative in defining keywords used in researching first expressions, including culture and a theologic of first expressions.

Chapter 3 – Body-ing forth in innovation

Four different understandings of innovation – from commerce, ecology, indigenous (Maori) and craft – are introduced. These are considered in relation to Scripture and used to develop a theologic of ecclesial innovation:

- Does it grow and mature?
- Does it compost in renewable cycles of birth, life and death?
- Does it weave with place and carry forward ancestor wisdom?
- Does it contribute to mending?

Chapter 4 – Tried

Five first expressions communities will be examined 11 years on. Attention will be paid to their experience of God, patterns of growth and understanding of mission. Study of these grassroots communities generates important insights regarding innovation and the factors that contribute to sustainability. These include discerning uniqueness, creating community, growing the whole person and flexible patterns and processes.

Chapter 5 – Tried and died

First expressions have a hidden side, those communities that try and die. Research demonstrates than 50 per cent of first expressions are likely to die. What does this mean missionally and ecclesiologically? What does it mean pastorally, for leaders and participants within those communities? The book of Philippians is examined as a 'first expression' story written to a 'first expression' church. This provides an important frame for the stories of five first expression communities no longer gathering 11 years on, in 2013. It is argued that church is more than gathering. It has layers that include disciple-making, leadership formation and resource production. These are dimensions of body-ing forth and demonstrate ecclesial becoming.

Chapter 6 – An apostle of Fresh Expressions

Ecclesial innovation includes not only grassroots communities but also organizational structures. The birth of Fresh Expressions in 2004 is examined. The role of Rowan Williams, who as Archbishop of Canterbury was a key pioneer of Fresh Expressions, is considered. Analysis of an extended interview with Rowan Williams along with relevant public statements made by Rowan during his time as Archbishop suggest Fresh Expressions is a profoundly theological activity, in complete coherence with his theological method. Williams offered a 'missio-ecclesiology' that emphasizes catholicity and apostolicity as the edges of the church renew the centre. This makes Fresh Expressions a deeply theological expression of ecclesiology today.

Chapter 7 – Birthing Fresh Expressions as an organizational innovation

The becoming of Fresh Expressions is considered, drawing on interviews with key pioneering influencers, including Steven Croft, Stephen Cottrell, Andrew Roberts and Rowan Williams. The development will be analysed through a Leadership Strengths model, seeking to understand Fresh Expressions as a systemic innovation across a denominational system. The development raised important questions for mission. One involves the absence of one leadership strength, that of optimism. Another involves the absence of female voices in the development of Fresh Expressions.

Chapter 8 – Moves in mission

In a continued examination of ecclesial innovation from an organizational perspective, 'first expressions' is used as a frame to reflect on British mission history. A study of four movements in mission – the Celtic patterns of mission into England, the ecclesial renewal engendered by Methodism, the restructuring of modern mission around the voluntary society, the contemporary impact of activist networks – provides a historical, yet distinctly missional, way of understanding institutional innovations like Fresh Expressions.

Chapter 9 – One in authenticity

The Apostles' Creed affirms the church as one, holy, catholic and apostolic. This chapter examines how the trope of authenticity contributes to an understanding of the church as one. The liturgy of a first expression community is analysed to establish the essential role of authenticity in their integration of faith with culture. The impact of a first expression of authenticity is examined in relation to *Mission-Shaped Church* (2004), which drew on the authentic life of grassroots first expressions in justifying ecclesial innovation. The work of Sarah Thornton is used to clarify how creative communities might maintain their sense of authenticity as their body-ing forth is drawn into the mainstream. Different ways by which organizational innovation might encourage grassroots innovation are considered, using different types of environments – free havens, laboratories, incubators. This chapter demonstrates the importance of authenticity in innovation and offers ways for organizations to sustain grassroots innovation.

Chapter 10 – Becoming apostolic in ambient witness

The witness of first expression communities is examined. The work of Charles Taylor is used to clarify the shape of witness in a secular world. Three case studies of contemporary witness are then examined: buildings that breathe in York, angels that hover in Swindon and spirituality as humanization in central London. Each of the case studies is analysed in relation to Taylor's understanding of the nature of conversion in a secular age. Ambient witness is proposed, in which first expressions bear apostolic witness that invite conversion in a secular age. First expressions have found ways to offer witness. In so doing, they resist the public/private dualisms of secularity, invite the pursuit of Christian spirituality and attend to formation in the whole of life.

Chapter 11 – Becoming holy in making

This chapter considers how first expressions form people. Making is defined theoretically, as a way to creatively subvert popular culture, and theologically, as an approach to engaging culture that bodies forth distinct Christian identities. Making as formation is then detailed empirically with an extended analysis of one first expression, the Late Late Service. Using interview data and analysis of liturgy, the significance of making is demonstrated as a way to integrate theology and ethics and offer a becoming holy that is inculturated within, and integrative of, daily life. Two challenges to making are considered, one in regard to transience, the other in regard to the other. This returns us to the arguments of Chapter 9, including the ethical implications of the claims of authenticity.

Chapter 12 – Becoming catholic in sacrament and structure

The dynamic interplay between authenticity, ambient witness and making as formation requires consideration of the possibilities and limits of the church as catholic. Catholicity is examined as a dynamic relationship between innovation and order, through attention to sacraments and governance as particular ways in which the church orders itself. Sacraments are essential to Rowan Williams's theology of first expressions. A notion of patterning is developed, utilizing the four eucharistic actions of take, break, thank and give, in relation to Scripture and the risen Christ. This approach to sacramental practices is argued to provide a becoming of ecclesial life. Similarly, it is argued that governance needs to be understood as a participation in ecclesial becoming. Placing innovation at the edge and governance at the centre results in power imbalances, with innovation at the mercy of governance. Contemporary approaches to governance are examined, as a way of embodying a mutual conversion. Innovation in mission invites a becoming of catholicity. Mission is a converting ordinance that invites reformation at individual, communal and structural levels.

Chapter 13 – Coda

Birth stories must be treasured. In the birth stories that surround Jesus, a significant narrative is that of Mary and Elizabeth. As an older woman (Elizabeth) blesses a younger woman (Mary), the Spirit moves and fresh insights emerge. Through history, God's Spirit continues to move, brooding over the bodies of God's faithful servants, giving fresh insight to those who take risks in faithful obedience. This book provides a theologic of first expressions, the result of a three-way dialogue between the empirical realities of grassroots innovation, organizational innovation and theologies of birth and becoming. The four understandings of innovation – from commerce, ecology, indigenous (Maori) and craft – are suggested as a guide for organizations seeking to support innovation. The hermeneutical discoveries that result from the interplay between the church as one, apostolic, holy and catholic and as authentic, ambient, making and converting are described. Nine implications for ecclesial innovation are offered. Ecclesial innovation is the ants in the pants of the body of Christ, enabling a becoming as one, apostolic, holy and catholic church. Such is the mission of God through first expressions.

With an introduction to first expressions and a roadmap describing the uniqueness of this project, let us turn to the birthing stories of five small things, experiments in ecclesial innovation.

Notes

1 For an extended narrative of NOS, see Howard (1996). For theological analysis, see Rogerson (2006), Till (2006) and Lyon (2012).

2 The word constraints of the PhD thesis meant that the thesis focused on one community in New Zealand with the data from the United Kingdom – the attending of ten alt.worship services and the interviewing of seventeen people/groups – not able to be included.

3 For Swinton (2000, p. 12): 'Practical theology is a dynamic process of reflective, critical inquiry into the praxis of the church in the world and God's purpose for humanity, carried out in the light of Christian Scripture and tradition, and in critical dialogue with other sources of knowledge.' See also Anderson (2001, p. 48).

4 The others include base ecclesial communities, cafe church, cell church, churches arising out of community initiatives, multiple congregations, network-focused churches, school-based or linked congregations, seeker church, traditional church plants, new monastic communities and youth congregations.

2

Birthing first expressions: empirical and ecclesiological

Reality and theology belong together. As described in Chapter 1, Julian of Norwich finds in the reality of the hazel-nut the activity of God. Paying attention to the small and singular is generative. As we approach first expressions, we contemplate singularity, reality and seeking theological language to articulate the activity of God. This chapter begins with five first expression birthing stories. Interviews with leaders from five experiments in ecclesial formation – Grace, Epicentre/Moot, Late Late Service, Sanctuary and Vaux – will clarify intent and purpose in ecclesial innovation and in relationship to faith and culture. Through interviews and participant observation, what is clear are new patterns of gathering, liturgical innovation and a conscious exploration of diverse hermeneutics. As we contemplate these grassroot stories, theological language is provided through dialogue with the work of Janet Soskice and her articulation of an eschatological anthropology in *The Kindness of God* (2007). The grassroots priority of the interplay between faith and culture in the birthing of these first expressions has a theologic in a becoming into the kinship of God. The empirical and the ecclesiological illuminate each other. They result in a theologic for fresh expressions which takes seriously reality and theology, the lived reality of birthing as the generative activity of God.

The birthing narratives of first expressions

During 2001, I sat in railway stations and cafes, vicarages, lounges and gardens, asking leaders, either as individuals or as a team, to describe their 'alternative worship' community.[1] What I discovered was a range of motivations for birthing and a shared theme; that of an interplay between faith and culture. I will describe these motivations, using data from interviews with four individuals and three focus groups.

When asked to describe their values, ethos and story of beginning, a range of impulses was present. First, there was an impulse of **relational**

community. This was present in one leader's description of the birth of their community: 'So early on the kind of vision was very much drawing on the whole relational kind of approach, a relational sort of theology. That whole thing in 2 Corinthians about the reconciliatory sort of work' (Group 10*, 2001). This birthing narrative was about the desire to find a relational, communal way of being human.

Two quite different impulses were evident in Doug Gay's descriptions of the Late Late Service in Glasgow, from 1990, and then Host, in Hackney, London from 1996. Doug Gay (2001) spoke of seeking to be a 'compassionate local presence working for peace and justice within the community'. This could be summed as **loving the local**. Another impulse, which Doug felt was quite distinctive, was also present. This involved 'surviving as Christians and living faith authentically within late-twentieth century London. [This group] needed to keep on trying to understand their faith in new ways. And express it in new ways' (Gay 2001). The birthing has a location in mission, expressed in a concern for the neighbourhood and a faith engaged with contemporary culture.

This theme, of **a faith authentic to contemporary disciples**, was echoed by a leader of Vaux:

> And this year we are still committed … to developing an urban spirituality … You know, you've got a busy job, a long commute, it's noisy, it's all very well going up the mountain every couple of months but hold on, I'm down here, in the city, what the hell is that about? (Vaux, Group 9*, 2001)

This impulse seems highly sensitive to shifts in contemporary culture and the implications for the life of faith.

A further theme was evident in the birthing narratives, that of **creating as a gifted body**. Sanctuary 'worked over the years to try and encourage people in the group to think about their gifts and skills and how they can share those' (Mainstone-Cotton and Birch 2010, p. 142). This involves a commitment to draw individuals' skills, ideas, interest and gifts into what is being created. A Late Late Service focus group (2001) described the most important value as 'creativity … a chance to be involved in creating worship. The planning was almost as good as the service itself. It made it all seem more real, more valuable'. This extended across generations: 'Late Late Service meant for me that our families were totally involved. We did services together as a family. Children got involved a whole lot. The kids loved them because they were so stimulating, the colours, the visuals.'

These offer a particular embodied articulation of these communities. In doing so they provide a discernment of a particular patterning of God's activity. These include

- relational community
- loving the local
- a faith authentic to contemporary disciples
- creating as a gifted body.

It is important to note that these narratives need not be linear. Consider the following from the leaders of Sanctuary, in Bath:

> Sanctuary initially started off as four people ... over time we've tried more and more ... to work out ways in which other people can discover their creativity ... which is how the pub discussion group came up. And more recently other people have been involved in the worship services, so we hope ... that it's an opportunity for people to discover their skills and bring them along. (Sanctuary 2001)

This suggests a spiral, in which for Sanctuary, an initial birthing impulse, **creating as a gifted body**, generated an impulse for **relational community**, which in turn, as people were added to the community, spiralled back into 'fresher' expressions of their initial **creating as a gifted body**.

A similar sense was evident in the interview with another group. 'Everyone always starts with [worship] service and all these other things start happening. Because actually you can't do a sustained [loving mission] service without worship, otherwise it dies. It becomes introverted' (Group 10*, 2001). Again we have a spiral between worship and loving mission. This would suggest that the birth of a fresh expression is not linear, moving from mission to relationships to worship. Rather, different groups start in different places, find themselves engaging with new impulses and in so doing, are changed in this process.

All of the interviews shared a commonality in terms of a constant interplay between faith and culture. For Grace it was expressed as: 'We're reflecting what's around us and trying to draw that into church and trying to take church out into it. Recognize church out in it ... It's an intuitive response to the world around us' (2001). What is fascinating is how this dialogue is being negotiated with multiple postures.

Some parts of culture were being affirmed. Doug Gay, for example, affirmed one artefact of culture: '[D]ance music ... became part of our spirituality in Glasgow ... There was a kind of excitement and a freedom around that. It was part of trying to find a new mode of celebration ... Dance music ... gave ... a new medium of celebration which was strong and physical and ecstatic' (2001). Again we find that culture was being connected, affirmatively, with the spirituality authentic to contemporary disciples impulse. Such cultural connection was considered important to the effectiveness of their mission.

At other times, culture was being rejected. Of a range of examples, perhaps the most interesting was provided by a leader from Vaux (Group 9*, 2001). 'We critique the culture we exist in pretty strongly. I think we subvert it. We use the media, the aesthetic that they understand.' He then provided an example of how Vaux was seeking to help people think critically about the branded culture of contemporary consumption. Finally, he noted: 'But also in a cheeky kind of way. We are always criticized at Vaux 'cos we're quite into our branding. (*Laughs.*) In that we have developed … before we had anything else we had a logo. That kind of cheeky concept.'

So we have this repeated theme, that of the interplay between faith and culture. What is significant is that the two poles – faith and culture – are being negotiated in a way that makes the use of simple dualisms of 'relevant' and 'distinctive' (to use terms by James Hunter (2010)) problematic. In these birthing narratives there is simultaneously an embrace and a rejection of culture, with a conscious awareness of the irony involved when both are done simultaneously.

These are stories of five first expressions. They emerge prior to the establishing of Fresh Expressions. They have a range of impulses – of relational community, of loving the local, of a spirituality authentic to contemporary disciples and of creating as a gifted body – yet all share in an engagement between faith and culture. As a result, these first expressions are pioneering new patterns of gathering, including creative use of physical space and the use of new technologies, including video, digital and artistic. They are developing their own liturgies, including writing their own music and prayers, offering sophisticated visual hermeneutics, experimenting with diverse forms of proclaiming the Word. They are doing this in conscious dialogue with culture, which they define as postmodern. This trope – of a changing contemporary culture – is creating impetus for being a first expression.

Hearing empirical birthing stories has clarified intent and purpose in ecclesial innovation and pointed to the centrality of navigating faith and culture as these first expressions become church communities. These suggest a need for ecclesiology as a theological conversation partner, one that provides ways to engage a complex relationship between faith and culture.

Eschatological ecclesiology and Janet Martin Soskice

Theology is a discipline broad and wide. In order to bring focus, I will place the empirical research in consistent dialogue with one contemporary theologian, Janet Soskice, in particular her eschatological anthropology of kinship articulated in *The Kindness of God* (2007). The book is an elegant exploration of the main loci of Christian reflection, exploring the nature of God and creation, anthropology, Christology and Trinity. Soskice is, like these first expressions, working at the interplay between faith and culture, particularly in the challenges of gender and the examination of power. She is 'an original voice' (McDougall 2010, p. 534), 'a wonderfully creative theological mind' (Ferreira 2009, p. 434), a 'reliable and evocative guide through some classic, yet often ignored, doctrinal topics' (Allen 2010, p. 99), a 'delight to read' with a 'breadth of engagement [that] is astonishing' (Greggs 2011, p. 242) and a model of charity (Rogers 2009b, p. 521). Her engagement with a breadth of theological loci along with her originality and cultural engagement make her a generative theological conversation partner in understanding first expressions.

Central to Soskice's theology is that of kinship – we are interconnected. 'Metaphors of kinship open up for us an eschatological anthropology wherein our constant becoming is our way of being children of God' (Soskice 2007, p. 6). Her theology can be defined through a selection of quotes from her final chapter:

> Kinship imagery is well suited to the 'already now and not yet' of Christian hope ... the Christian life is one in which the believer is 'born again', not into static perfection, but into a new life which must be characterized by growth and transformation ... kinship metaphors contain the mixture of promise and challenge proper to an eschatological anthropology ... God is ... thirsting for ever greater at-one-ment with the created order ... the faithful are, *each one* ... the kin of Christ and members of one another. (Soskice 2007, pp. 181–7)

In what follows, I will explain Soskice's eschatological anthropology through concepts of becoming, body-ing forth and telos.

First, in relation to becoming, Soskice notes the extensive and hugely neglected repertoire of birth images in the New Testament (p. 119).[2] The becoming is a birthing into fraternal kinship that is located in Christ: made possible because Christ is 'continually "in travail", labouring to give birth to humankind in the fullness of its intended being' (p. 150).[3] In this creation, humans are growing and changing (pp. 29, 37).

For Soskice, this becoming is ecclesial. Birth is a type of sacrificial giving and how Christ births the church (p. 91). She draws on medieval religious iconography, which 'associates the crucified Christ with the human female body, both in giving birth and in feeding' (p. 87). The crucifixion is childbirth, with the church being pulled from Christ's wounded side.[4]

This becoming is more than a singular act: birthing is a becoming through time and space. Through time, in becoming, Christ not only births, but continues to feed the church as Maker, Lover and Keeper. Through space and time, this becoming as birthing is continuous, Christ is continually in travail, not only at Pentecost, the 'birthday' of the church. These are significant theological lenses by which to engage with first expressions, believing in the birthing of the body of Christ, not just once at Easter, but in ongoing birthing of new ecclesial communities.

Second, for Soskice, eschatological anthropology is understood not only through the language of becoming but also through the language of body-ing forth, in which the 'God of Scripture attends to each changing thing – in particular. This is the work of the Spirit, this bodying forth of God in history – in our individual histories and in that of our world' (Soskice 2007, p. 33). This phrase 'body-ing forth' will be introduced here and developed much more thoroughly in Chapter 3.

God in love is attending to creation. In being and doing, immanence and economy, God is creativity, reciprocity and generation (pp. 50–1). Hence becoming has a body-ing forth. This body-ing is always expressed in cultures, in the kinship by which humanity in the creation narratives finds language in response to the activity of God the Maker; in the particularity of Jesus, being born of a woman; in the generativity of the Spirit at Pentecost, so that each is hearing in the particularity of their own language (Acts 2.7).

This has resonance with how this chapter began, with Julian of Norwich attending to one small thing in creation and seeing in that the activity of God as Maker, Lover and Keeper. Indeed, Soskice develops Julian (pp. 125–56), calling her work a 'masterpiece' (p. 127). Soskice points to Julian's 'originality' in 'aligning Paul's language of atonement as fraternal kinship, with the second birth imagery of the gospels' (p. 145). This is a body-ing forth in which the 'vision of the fragility of creation bears the inference that God sustains in love each thing in particular, and this forms a way back to the particularity of the … face of Christ' (p. 141). Kinship images of birth, gestation, growth are essential (p. 131), with the aim of Julian's theology being spiritual exercises in order that God's gift and grace might be body-ied forth (p. 155).

Third, for Soskice, the becoming as a body-ing forth of growth and transformation has a telos in Christ. Christ is the image of God, embodying the love and attention of God in the particularity of individual, communal and human history. Humans are the kin of Christ and as such members of one another, individuals distinct and different, constituted by bonds of kinship. 'Human beings are eschatological and teleological' (p. 36). Our telos is in Christ.

In 188 pages, *The Kindness of God* does an admirable job of introducing themes central to theology, particularly God and creation, anthropology, Christology and Trinity. Placing her work in dialogue with the birthing narratives of first expressions invites a natural next step, of considering what might be learnt if we develop her eschatological anthropology of becoming, body-ing forth and telos. What might the empirical realities of birthing allow us to see more clearly in developing a kinship theology in relation to culture, church and innovation? While these are not themes central to Christian theology in general, they are certainly dimensions of the activity of God in the birthing narratives of Grace, Epicentre/Moot, Late Late Service, Sanctuary and Vaux.

Empirical and ecclesiological interplay: faith and culture

In Christianity, culture is a contested term. There is the Nein, issued by Barth in response to Brunner, in which natural theology has no place. In this view of culture, the activity of first expressions in engaging culture is greeted with suspicion, if not condemnation.

There is pragmatism, in which new methods are co-opted in order to communicate an unchanging message. Hence ecclesial entrepreneurs are greeted with celebration mixed with caution, lest a message be polluted.

Soskice's image of humans as God's image bearers provides another way of thinking about culture. Soskice attends to the nature and grace debate, arguing that we may read of God's ways in creation, but God's image – of creativity, reciprocity and generation – is given to human-kind. This provides an open-endedness. 'We may read of God's ways in creation, but God's image is given only to humankind' (2007, p. 37). This affirms natural theology (God's ways in creation), while asserting the distinctiveness of special revelation (God's image is given).

What is helpful in this interplay between nature and grace is how an eschatological anthropology is developed in relation to Christ. Of particular use is the way Soskice draws forth themes from Julian of Norwich. Julian develops her understanding of being human – and thus of culture – from Christ, not from creation. Christ is fully human, predestined as 'our origin and our way to God' (p. 148). In articulating a theology of human growth towards God, Julian draws conceptually on narratives of earthly pilgrimage, rather than ladders of Neoplatonic ascent. Thus the ordinary and bodily will not be left behind in a movement toward Christ. Rather the everyday, including capacities of culture-making, are integrated. They are part of becoming and essential to body-ing forth.

This is for two reasons. First, in relation to Christ, from whom Julian is developing her understanding of being human. To appreciate the uniqueness of Julian's approach, as highlighted by Soskice, it is worth an extended quote:

there is a lower and a higher nature ... and the 'lower' is sensual, [yet] there is no sense that the lower is less regarded than the higher. The Lord himself is at constant work in the lower part of our human nature ... and in God's sight there is no difference, for the same love pervades all. (p. 149, drawing from Julian §52)

This means God is at work in the whole of a human being, including the intellect and our bodily senses. Intriguingly, Christ is pre-eminently in the lower, in what is sensual (p. 149). Culture, as a dimension of human activity, is pervaded by God's love. Whether higher or lower, intellectual or sensual, God is at work. Indeed, following Julian, the more sensual, the more embodied, the more Christ is present. This is a theology located in the grace of special revelation, which is deeply affirming of nature.

Second, in response to the eschatological anthropology body-ied forth in Christ, humans grow. For Soskice, humans are 'destined to become what they are not ... "God-like" in the sense that they are "made in the image of God"' (p. 37). Humans grow as Christ indwells us, leading us amid life's changes. 'In Julian's Middle English, "travails" carries three meanings: Christ labours with us (gives birth), sorrows with us (shares our travails), and, in doing both, "travels" with us on our way' (p. 151, drawing from Julian §91). Again, this is a theology located in the grace of special revelation, yet deeply affirming of nature. Culture-making is thus a human body-ing forth. God's ways in creation – including acts of culture-making – require love and attention.

Applied to culture in general, and first expressions in particular, this provides a theologic in which dance music, new technologies and the role of senses and the rhythms of dance music are part of God's creativity, reciprocity and generation. As humans are becoming in the image of God, who dwells in all of our bodily nature and being, God's image – of creativity, reciprocity and generation – is being body-ied forth.

This is a more embodied theology of culture than a 'Nein' to natural theology or a utilitarian co-opting to find new communication channels, proclaiming an unchanging message in a changing world. Given the hope of a telos in Christ, there is freedom in engaging with culture. Such an engaging is one of love and attention, believing that in the exploring of faith and culture God's patterning – creativity, reciprocity and generation – may be read. Such an approach to nature is entwined with an expectation of God's image being body-ied forth in human becoming, in culture.

Hence Soskice's eschatological anthropology can be developed in relation to culture. This is important, given the interplay between faith and culture evident in the birthing narratives of first expressions. One way to understand how they engage with dance music, or interact with punk, is through seeing God's image bearers as capable of creativity, reciprocity and generation – whether inside or outside the church. My development of Soskice's eschatological anthropology provides a theologic, to which we will return in more depth when we consider first expressions as communities of ambient witness in Chapter 10 and making in constructive formation in Chapter 11.

Empirical and ecclesiological interplay: a theologic of first expressions

As already noted, Soskice works with the doctrines of creation, anthropology, Christology, atonement, Trinity and eschatology. She does not articulate an ecclesiology. However, her phrase 'bodying forth' has distinct possibilities in seeking to articulate a theologic of first expressions. I will explore this by outlining central images of church located in Scripture, along with the dual understandings of church in *Mission-Shaped Church* (2004). I will apply Soskice's eschatological anthropology to both, in developing a theologic of first expressions.

Church in Scripture

Rather than provide concise definitions, Scripture presents a range of images of the church. In *Images of the Church in the New Testament* (1960), Paul Minear documents nearly 100, but he outlines three dominant images: people of God, body of Christ and household of God.

A first significant image of church is that of the **people of God,** an image that includes shepherd and flock. This understanding had Old Testament roots, with the phrase 'people of God' occurring more than 2,000 times in the Septuagint (Driver 1997, p. 127). Israel are the people of God. They have a kinship that is vertical in relationship to God, horizontal with each other and the marginalized, and downward to care for the land which they will be given. Thus their birthing is a becoming into a 'social holiness' (p. 129), to participate in a body-ing forth of God's saving project.

A second significant image of church is that of the **body of Christ,** an image that includes the kingdom of God, new creation and new humanity. This is located in the birthing of Israel as an experience of liberation from oppressive systems of empire and a becoming into relationships of security and well-being, again horizontal, vertical and downward.

A third significant image of church is that of the **household of God,** an image that includes the spiritual house and family of God. This cluster enhances our understanding of the interplay between structure and mission. It begins with God's commitments in the Old Testament to build up and tear down, an activity related directly to the restoration of a new community. The apostle Paul develops these commitments, applying them to God's mission to the Gentiles.

Driver (1997) adds a fourth significant image of the church: **pilgrimage**. This is clustered around images of the way, sojourners and the poor. In Acts, the Christian community is described using the term 'way' (for example Acts 9.22; 18.25). Each of the Gospels draws on the announcement in Isaiah 40.3 of a voice preparing the way for the Lord. This image is drawing on the exodus from Egypt and God's saving acts on a journey of liberation (pp. 50–1).

Having articulated these images of church in Scripture, we can now locate them in relation to the theology of Soskice, in particular her focus on an eschatological anthropology of becoming kinship. In each cluster of images described above, there is now and not yet: they are the people and yet they are becoming the people. In each image there is kinship, as people, as an interconnected body, as a household, as pilgrims on a journey.

Every ecclesial body is located in time and space. They are changing. Households change, as do people and bodies. Pilgrims by definition are on the move. One way they change is in relation to culture. A changing culture is thus an invitation, the opportunity of becoming.

Hence in a dialogue with an empirical body that is ecclesial, we must expect now and not yet. The aim is generativity. This takes seriously birthing, becoming and body-ing forth. How might this apply to first expressions in particular?

Church in *Mission-Shaped Church*

An ecclesiology is present in two places in *Mission-Shaped Church* (2004). First, framed in relation to the classic marks of the church. Thus in Chapter 4, 'Theology for a Missionary Church': 'The four classic marks of the Church, enshrined in the Nicene Creed as "one, holy, catholic, and apostolic", [to] remind the church of its true nature and calling' (p. 96). This use of the classic marks to evaluate Fresh Expressions is similarly employed by LeRon Schults (2009) who concludes that in light of the classic marks, new forms of church 'have a great deal to teach us about reconstructing ecclesiology' (p. 438). In dialogue with the four marks, John Drane (2008) offers an 'eschatological maturity'. His looking forward, rather than looking back, is consistent with the eschatological anthropology of Janet Soskice. The classic marks of the church need to be read as a becoming, a body-ing forth as the telos of Christ's body.

A second ecclesiology is evident in *Mission-Shaped Church*. In the

Foreword, Rowan Williams writes that '"church" is what happens when people encounter the Risen Jesus and commit themselves to sustaining and deepening that encounter in their encounter with each other' (p. vii). This is an ecclesiology located in encounter, dare we say birthing encounter, of people with regard to the resurrected Jesus. Such an ecclesial benchmark resonates with the first expression birthing narratives outlined above. An ethos of **relational community** resonates with Williams's 'deepening that encounter in their encounter with each other'; **loving the local** and **a faith authentic to contemporary disciples** with 'commit themselves to sustaining and deepening that encounter' and **creating as a gifted body** with 'what happens when people encounter'. Hence *Mission-Shaped Church*, while not explicit, points to an eschatological anthropology as a way of understanding the birthing narratives of first expressions.

The work of Soskice is illuminating, given the way her notion of eschatological anthropology locates Williams's 'encounter in their encounter with each other' in relation to birthing, becoming and body-ing forth. Her kinship theology allows us to apply the classic marks of the church in ways that are interconnected and thus generative.

A theologic of first expressions

First, there is a birthing. This birthing is in the context of kinship and the expectation of growth and change. Soskice reflects on how a parent, in attending to a child, must also let the child go. 'The love of the parent, at the best of times, holds the child up without holding them back, for they must grow, and the parents must in gradual but continuous steps "let go" without ceasing to love unstintingly' (Soskice 2007, p. 31). It is hard to imagine a grandparent leaning back at the news of their first grandchild and going, to borrow from Vincent in Chapter 1 – 'Just a few *entrepreneurs* doing their own thing ... "Will they stand the test of time?"' (1976, p. 100). Instead, love and attention (using Soskice) are paid to their development.

When we hear the birthing narratives of Grace, Epicentre/Moot, Late Late Service, Sanctuary and Vaux, the interconnected nature of an eschatological anthropology invites us to be a people of God, a body of Christ, a household of God, a pilgrim people supportive of ecclesial innovation. Kinship images connect the biblical images of church with the classic marks of the church in an ecclesiology of innovation.

Second, there is a becoming. First expressions are a body-ing forth of generativity. In times of rapid change, God has not finished attending to the church. An eschatological anthropology is at work in first expressions. Their exploration of culture – pioneering new patterns of gathering, the use of new technologies, the development of new liturgies and the exploration of visual hermeneutics – is a becoming. It provides 'hermeneutic discoveries' (Paas 2016, p. 239): innovative insights that emerge from the 'tacit knowledge' embodied in first expressions. This becoming is in relation to culture, for as God is at work in the whole of a human being, including the intellect and our bodily senses, then culture is a dimension of human activity in which Christ is in travail. The interplay between faith and culture evident in the birthing narratives is thus a logical place to experience a becoming, as an ecclesial body is encountered by the body that is Christ.

Third, there is a body-ing forth, in which God is revealed as attending the change in creation and in relationship to the people of God. Regarding the former, God is 'attentive to changing creatures … the God of Scripture, attends to every changing thing – in particular. This is the work of the Spirit, this body-ing forth of God in history – in our individual histories and in that of our world' (Soskice 2007, p. 33). Regarding the latter, God attended to Israel, a community in seemingly ceaseless change, called out, established, exiled, freed (p. 32). God's body-ing forth in ecclesial bodies is never static, and God's attentive gaze is the real that is 'a changing reality' (p. 32).

This body-ing forth returns us to a methodology of first expressions. Applying Soskice, ecclesiology is the study of the body-ing forth of changing realities, not a set of ideals. Empirical research is a way of attending to the ecclesial real.

Fourth, the schema of kinship offers a malleability well suited to the constructive task of seeing and articulating the 'hermeneutic discoveries' (Paas 2016, p. 239). It also provides a way, as this book unfolds, to consider the interplay between first expressions and Fresh Expressions. This will begin in Chapter 3, be extended in Chapter 9 and concluded in Chapter 13.

Conclusion

This chapter has outlined a dialogue between empirical research and theology. Reality and theology belong together. In the particular and the singular, the activity of God can be discerned. The empirical illuminates ecclesiology through 'hermeneutic discoveries' (Paas 2016, p. 239), ecclesiology illuminates the empirical that is first expressions as birthing, becoming and body-ing forth.

This chapter began from the ground up, with first expression birthing stories: five narratives of emergence that clarify intent and purpose in ecclesial innovation. Listening to the individual birth narratives of individual first expressions revealed God as active in the motivations to **create as** a gifted body, explore relational community and develop a spirituality authentic to contemporary culture. These innovations were justified on the basis of cultural change, in particular a shift from modern to postmodern.

The theologies of Julian of Norwich and Janet Soskice enable a first expressions research methodology. This emerges from Julian's valuing of the singular as a location in which the activity of God as Maker, Lover and Keeper can be discerned. Theologically, Soskice draws our attention to the priority of birth images in Scripture and argues that birthing is a becoming through time and space. Her eschatological anthropology provides a theology of culture, interpreting the interplay in first expressions between faith and culture. Humans are becoming in the image of God, who dwells in all of our bodily nature, working with us in body-ing forth God's image in cultured embodiments. This provides a theologic of first expressions, first, in the attentiveness to the empirical; second, in the affirmation of birth, growth and change; and, third, in appreciation of a body-ing forth of generativity as God is attentive to every changing thing.

First expressions invite us to discern the body-ing of God. First expressions are a sign of God's attending, in creativity, reciprocity and generation, to a changing world. The task of the next chapter is to consider further Soskice's notion of body-ing forth. How might innovation be framed theologically and applied empirically?

Notes

1 These included Sue Wallace, Visions and Andii Bowsher around York, Neil Elliott, Pip Piper, Ryan Bolger, Jeffrey Stevenson, Barry Taylor, Eddie Gibbs and Gordon Lynch around Birmingham, Graceland in Cardiff, Grace, Vaux, Holy Joes, Bigger Picture, Dave Tomlinson, Stuart Murray, David Hilborn, Nick Mercer, Doug Gay, David Hilborn, Ian Mobsby, Kester Bruin, Peter Graystone, Stuart Murray, Pete Ward in London, Anne Wilkinson-Hayes in Oxford, Resonance, Sanctuary and Paul Roberts around Bristol, Late Late Service and Charlie Irvine in Glasgow, Club Culture Project, Guid Crack Club, Steve Butler and Jolyon Mitchell in Edinburgh.

2 Particularly footnote 34. The footnote extends over two pages, the relevant quote is located on page 119.

3 Soskice points to the way that Julian of Norwich aligns Paul's language of fraternal kinship (Christ, the firstborn of many brothers) with the second birth imagery of the Gospels (2007, p. 145).

4 For more, see Bynum (1991).

3

Body-ing forth in innovation

The Hundred-Foot Journey (2014), directed by Lasse Hallstrom, is a heart-warming romantic drama in which food crosses cultures.[1] Hassan (Manish Dayal) grows up in India. His skills in cooking are shaped by his mother, who passes on to him a care for spices and a passion for food. Displaced from his native India, Hassan settles with his family in a rural French village. His father opens an Indian restaurant, unaware it is 100 feet from and directly opposite an acclaimed French restaurant run by the competitive Madame Mallory (Helen Mirren). Hassan's curiosity and culinary skills catapult him to fame among the avant-garde in Paris. There, the quest for culinary innovation takes a technological turn, into a space-aged future of molecular gastronomy. One night working late, Hassan enjoys a meal brought by one of the cleaning staff, a fellow Indian from Mumbai. Food has memories. Hassan recalls the spice and markets of his birth. It is a reminder that there are other values that can shape the quest for culinary innovation. Hassan resolves to return to his family restaurant. Innovation can be sought through avant-garde technology, celebrity cheffing and the quest for Michelin stars. Innovation can also be a fusion of tradition across cultures.

Innovation is a contested word. In the minds of many, it means *The Apprentice* and *Dragons' Den*. There is competition as wealthy investors listen to pitches. There is critique as individuals and their personal projects are funded (or not); fired (or not). In clarifying our presuppositions about innovation, this chapter outlines four different understandings of innovation, summarized as

- growth
- ecology
- indigenous (Maori)
- craft.

Each understanding of innovation is introduced. What becomes clear is that embedded in each understanding of innovation are assumptions about the shape of growth and development. Different understandings of innovation have embedded within them different evaluative criteria.

- For commerce, does it grow and mature?
- For ecology, does it compost in renewable cycles of birth, life and death?
- For indigenous, does it spiral in place and carry forward ancestor wisdom?
- For craft, does it result in a mending that is effective and innovative?

This definitional work then offers evaluative criteria by which the longitudinal data that emerge in subsequent chapters – of first expressions as grassroots, local innovation and Fresh Expressions as an organizational, institutional innovation – can be evaluated.

This chapter seeks to imagine forward the theology of Soskice. As outlined in Chapter 2, 'Birthing first expressions', her notion of eschatological anthropology, of birthing, body-ing forth and open-endedness, provides a theologic by which to understand first expressions. Her work brings into focus the interplay between faith and culture that is essential in understanding the ecclesial origins of Grace, Epicentre/Moot, Late Late Service, Sanctuary and Vaux.

However, she does not provide an understanding of the shape of innovation and sustainability. It is not her task. Her dialogue with science points to a methodology by which culture might be engaged. She affirms the need for theology to engage with science. She is cautious about offering a 'Christian opinion' when it is framed as one dogmatic view thrown in by an interest group. The result, argues Soskice, is the theologian is reduced to working within the terms of reference assumed by secular moral philosophy and the 'impoverishment almost to the point of extinction of a distinctive theological voice' (2007, p. 57). Instead, Soskice engages science by a reflection on creation and redemption. She argues for a focus 'not so much with what kind of creation it was in the first place as with what kind of creation it was and is *now*' (p. 61, italics in original). Her theology of eschatological anthropology is deepened as she considers the questions raised by other disciplines – in her case, science. Applied to this chapter, a theology of eschatological anthropology with particular application to ecclesiology and innovation is deepened as we consider the questions raised by different understandings of innovation. The understandings of innovation-as-growth, innovation-as-ecology, innovation-as-indigenous and innovation-as-craft enable the eschatological anthropology of Soskice to be taken a step further, in particular in ecclesial innovation.

This frames the second section of this chapter, in which understandings of growth, ecology, indigenous (Maori) and craft are considered in dialogue with a number of biblical narratives. This enriches our understandings of how we might understand first expressions.

A similar challenge was presented to me by Dr Christine Woods, Associate Professor at the University of Auckland Business School. I had approached her for guidance on developing an innovation incubator. She was delighted to assist. In doing so, she wanted to know what theological resources Christianity would bring to the project. It was not enough to apply Jesus as a theological cherry on top to justify innovation. Her challenge motivates this chapter, in seeking to outline an ecclesiology of innovation.

Growth 'S' curve insights

Innovation, as portrayed in the likes of *The Apprentice* and *Dragons' Den*, works with the classic 'S' growth curve. Investors are looking for innovation that will follow a curve of upward growth. Origins rely on a fusion of smart ideas with astute and calculated financial investment. 'Our ideas about innovation come these days primarily from the tech sector and those privileged few with venture capital' (Everett 2019). The telos involves a maximizing of growth by stretching the 'S' curve. Words like scalability capture this, seeking to delay maturity as a plateau by multiplying growth through replicating a successful template (Figure 1).[2]

Figure 1: Stretching the 'S' curve

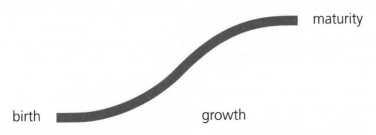

This type of innovation is evident in *The Hundred-Foot Journey*, as Hassan moves to Paris. He is introduced to a city hungry for innovation and hired by a restaurant committed to researching the novel. This is pursued through molecular gastronomy, a style of cuisine that values experimentation in order to develop new ways of cooking. Hassan gains acclaim, featured in culinary magazines and TV talk shows, for the novelty of his creations and his ability to fuse technology and innovation.

The 'S' curve generates expectations in relation to growth. Applied to my research, 11 years on, I would return to find first expressions drawing on technology to produce new and different forms of worship, resulting in ongoing growth, likely evident in numerical increase. If growth was minimal, or if the first expressions were no longer present, they would be deemed a 'failure', with little contribution to make to ongoing reflection on mission in Western cultures.

The growth curve model also invites questions about how the culture of the church responds to innovation. Are there a range of magazines and media outlets eager to promote the novel? Is there a privileging of the 'Hassans' – young leaders, skilled in new technologies, creative and willing to work hard? Are such leaders more likely to attract 'venture capital', to be resourced by an organization like Fresh Expressions?

In reality – and as will be described in Chapter 5 – life tends to be messier and more complex. Not all first expressions grow.

The 'S' curve model also raises interesting ecclesial questions when applied to inherited churches. What is the shape of existence as an inherited church begins to plateau? What does maturity as a plateaued existence say about the work of God in our world? Once mature, how does a church participate in mission life?

The growth 'S' curve is the dominant cultural model of innovation. The pressures on Hassan, and the hype depicted in *The Hundred-Foot Journey*, help us understand the growth 'S' curve. It easily seeps into how innovation is understood in the church, including the expectations that might shape evaluation of first expressions.

Ecosystems insights

The natural life cycle of ecosystems offers another way to consider innovation. Vivian Hutchinson (2011) offers an infinity loop, a figure of '8' with no clear beginning or end. Innovation is affirmed as central to how organizations grow.[3] However, the 'S' curve of growth and maturity is balanced by release and renewal (Figure 2).

Figure 2: Completing the 'S' curve with release and renewal

Hutchinson writes:

> But while we talk a lot in our mainstream culture about the forward
> loop of the birth, development and maturity of our organisations ...
> we don't so easily talk about the backward loop of the destruction,
> or of the incubation of new possibilities. It's the scary, disruptive and
> sometimes mysterious part of the journey. It's all about letting go and
> releasing organisational and cultural resources, and paying attention to
> what is emerging. (p. 5)

Applied to first expressions, this opens up a wider range of expected
possibilities as a result of innovation. We are invited to pay attention not
only to birth, growth and maturity, but also to conception and death.
Eleven years on, I might expect to find first expressions at all four of these
stages. Some would be moving through growth toward maturity. Others
might be moving from maturity to release and renewal.

The ecosystems understanding would expect the culture of the church
to be open to a wider range of trajectories than only growth and maturity.
The role of an organization like Fresh Expressions would include support
– financially and relationally – in growth, maturity, release and renewal.

This would be coherent with inherited expressions, which would be
understood to exist in a wider range of possibilities than either growth
or maturity. A normative ecosystems ecclesiology, both grassroots and
denominational, would include cycles of release and renewal. Inherited
churches would have experience of 'letting go and releasing organizational and cultural resources'. Knowledge exchange, including rituals in
relation to dying and rising, would be gifted to first expressions.

Indeed, all ecclesial systems, whether local and grassroots or denominational, would be in a constant interplay of birth, growth, maturity,
release and renewal. However, when the growth understanding is placed
alongside the ecosystem understanding, in reality the dominant paradigm
applied by the church is that of the growth 'S' curve. The dominant modes
are understood to be either growth or maturity. The closing of a church
tends to be seen as a failure. We expect denominations to continue in
perpetuity. This shapes, and mis-shapes, how innovation is understood
in the church, including the expectations that might shape evaluation of
first expressions.

Indigenous insights

A third understanding of innovation emerges from indigenous culture.
I write from Aotearoa New Zealand. One of our global exports has
been movies. While movies like *The Lord of the Rings* and *The Hobbit*,

showcase New Zealand landscapes, the movie *Whale Rider* (2002) show-cases indigenous culture.[4] The movie, an adaptation of the 1987 novel by indigenous Maori author, Witi Ihimaera follows a young girl (Paikea), seeking to find her place in a changing world.

In a pivotal scene, the teenaged Paikea asks Koro, her grandfather, about their past. Koro (Rawiri Paratene) takes a rope he is using. The strands, woven together, become an illustration for how the past is woven into the present.[5] Koro then uses the rope to attempt to start an outboard motor, only to have the rope break in his hands. He goes to find another rope, only to be greeted by the roar of the outboard motor. Paikea has re-woven the rope and started the outboard motor. This scene, and the use of the rope, provides a metaphor for Paikea's search for ways to re-weave her sense of destiny with the needs of her people. The film ends with a final scene in which a new canoe is launched, the building of which has given their community a new sense of purpose. Sitting in a place of leadership in the canoe, Paikea celebrates 'that our people will keep going forward, all together, with all of our strength'. The interplay between rope and renewed community becomes an understanding of innovation from an indigenous (Maori) perspective.[6]

When Maori voyaged to New Zealand, their ability to innovate allowed them to adapt. They were shaped by a new context and, in turn, they learnt to shape this new context. As Anne Salmond summarizes indigen-ous innovation: 'The life of a people is always shifting, always growing never static, spiralling back to the ancestors, opening up the future.'[7] Examples of their innovation are powerfully documented in *Artefact*, a television documentary series in which indigenous leaders, archae-ologists and historians explore innovation.[8] In a new landscape, Maori dug canals – the largest was 10 kilometres in length – entirely by hand. Natural lagoons were linked with human-made fish traps in order that fish could be trapped, screened and processed. This was an aquaculture industry spread over 10,000 acres of the Wairau Bar area of present-day Marlborough. In a new context, Maori were innovating in response to the landscape around them.

Central to indigenous understandings of innovation are the weaving of past, present and future, in order that the identity and values of the com-munity are taken forward in ways faithful to the past. Ian Taylor, with Maori tribal affiliation, is also CEO of Animation Research.[9] He draws from indigenous culture in creating new digital technologies. Ian sees his indigenous (Maori) ancestors as the real innovators.

Innovation is in my DNA ... inquisitiveness is really important ... it is all about storytelling ... we use this technology to take kids back along those footpaths that bring us to the place we are today. And we start with our ancestors travelling down ... This is natural to them. Being innovative. It is in their DNA. ('Tangata Whenua', *Artefact*, 48.50–50.30)

This is done through 3D visualization technology. Taylor works with an understanding of innovation as a care for well-being of a community, acting in ways that connect with the past and weaving the present into the future.

An indigenous (Maori) understanding would expect innovation, particularly when contexts change. Indeed, adaptation in response to change is expected. This innovation would be shaped by a care for the community to which one belongs, a commitment to see it move forward.

The role of the wider church, for example an organization like Fresh Expressions, would involve providing support, particularly in relation to storytelling. Inherited expressions thus have a crucial role in finding ways for the next generation to explore the 'footpaths that bring us to the place we are today'. Part of the tension of *Whale Rider* revolves around whether Koro, Paikea's grandfather, will recognize her leadership. In order for innovation to happen, Koro needs to innovate by letting go of his inherited assumptions that leadership emerges from certain (male) people.

Indigenous understandings encourage innovation through valuing community, prioritizing knowledge exchange across generations, particularly in the form of storytelling.

Craft

In the *The Hundred-Foot Journey* (2014), Hassan leaves Paris and returns to the French village. He is determined to innovate, but it will come not through technology and the relentless pursuit of novelty (a rejection of innovation-through-growth). Nor will it come from nostalgia, an adhering to life as lived by his parents in India.

Instead, Hassan seeks new partners. This resolves the romantic tensions of the film created by Marguerite (Charlotte Le Bon), who has instructed Hassan regarding the history of French cooking. Together, as partners, they agree to innovate by drawing on the rich culinary history of two traditions – French and Indian cuisine. This cultural fusion suggests an understanding of innovation that is not so much indigenous, but rather what Greg Jones has called 'traditioned innovation'. 'Traditioned innovation honors and engages the past while adapting to the future because it forces us to ask fundamental questions about who we are and what purposes we have for existing' (Jones 2016, p. 49). Jones suggests this is a particular type of social entrepreneurship, 'one that does not force us to choose preserving tradition or leading change, but thinking about them together' (Jones 2009). Laura Everett (2018) applies 'traditioned innovation' to the practice of craft, arguing that quilting and mending 'do not discard the scraps of history, but rework them for both utility and beauty'.

In history, during times of scarcity and decline, craft has offered ways to create beauty in places of limited financial resources. One example is the Master Quilters of Gee's Bend, Alabama. A rural community originally settled by freed slaves, the craft of quilting has been passed down the generations and works now hang in museums around the country, including the Whitney and the Metropolitan Museum of Art. The dedication to 'making something beautiful for themselves, their families and their community' is born out of an 'overarching theme of love – familial love, love of God, and self-love' (Curran 2018). Hence craft becomes a model for Christian innovation. Craft as innovation offers a way of being Christian and engaging in mission: a '"tikkun olam" or "repair of the world." We have the choice to destroy or to become co-participants in repair' (Everett 2019) (Figure 3).

Figure 3: Craft as traditioned innovation[10]

Craft as 'traditioned innovation' is an essential, and innovative, way by which the mission of God is enabled. Such an approach values the creative imagination which sees future potential in what already is and has the patience to work stitch by stitch toward that vision. Eleven years on, I would expect to find a range of creative products, made by the first expressions who were engaged in 'traditioned innovation'. Indeed, the focus is more likely to be on the product, the tikkun olam/repair of the world, than the maintenance of the communities.

The role of the wider church involves providing support, particularly in relation to prior experience. A personal story is illustrative. As part of writing this book, I learnt to knit. I realized that I needed to explore innovation, particularly craft, not only theoretically but also through experience. The craft I chose was knitting. In beginning with a scarf, I made numerous mistakes – a dropped stitch here, a tangle there. I needed help. It came, not from a book or online tutorial, but from an experienced knitter. This was just-in-time learning, guidance in light of the particular tangle I had made for myself. This is how the wider church would provide support in 'traditioned innovation'. This provides a very different understanding of what is maturity: it is those who have practised innovation, learnt by doing what repair of the world might look like, able to apply that knowledge not to their own craft, but to the craft of the first expression. This is what letting go looks like.

These – growth, ecology, indigenous, craft – are four different understandings of innovation. Each has been considered in relation to first expressions as grassroots, local innovation and Fresh Expressions as an organizational, institutional innovation. Each understanding works in different ways, with different values and unique resourcing. These are summarized in Table 2. The words in italics serve to connect Soskice's eschatological anthropological theology of kinship with these four understandings in innovation. Her attention to birthing imagery connects with where innovation is understood to begin; relationship with existing bodies expresses kinship, with a particular focus on mutuality in order to body forth; which is carried by particular embodiments; in order to achieve a certain end goal (Table 2).

Table 2 demonstrates how innovation has different understandings and therefore contains different evaluative criteria. They can be summarized in the four questions:

- For commerce, does it grow and mature?
- For ecology, does it compost in renewable cycles of birth, life and death?
- For indigenous, does it spiral in place and carry forward ancestor wisdom?
- For craft, does it result in a mending that is effective and innovative?

It is tempting to choose a favourite understanding. What is interesting is that all four of these understandings of innovation can be found in Scripture.

Table 2: Understanding innovation

	Beginnings (born again)	Relationship with existing bodies (kinship)	Carrier of innovation (body-ing forth)	End goal (telos)
Commerce	Passion for growth	Funders, inherited church	Idea – stress-tested	Growth to maturity
Ecology	Passion for growth		Attention to rhythms and patterns of ecosystems	Complete cycle, ending with renewal
Indigenous	Ancestors	Community for next generation	Story and connection with past	
Craft	A world needing repair	Fellow menders, particularly 'practised' individuals	Inherited wisdom located in 'practised' individuals	A mended world

Scripture and innovation

I began this chapter noting how Soskice's theology of eschatological anthropology was deepened as she considered the questions raised by other disciplines. This invites an extension of Soskice, drawing on the questions raised by innovation (as growth, as ecology, as indigenous, as craft) to develop an eschatological ecclesiology. One way to do this is to reflect on Scripture in light of innovation-as-growth, innovation-as-ecology, innovation-as-indigenous and innovation-as-craft. This will make clear that each of these approaches to innovation at times has validity. Each provides insight and is likely to be applicable in different contexts. However, Scripture would also suggest that each of these evaluative criteria needs to be applied with wisdom. This is a way to respond to the challenge of neither detaching ecclesial innovation from the wisdom of other disciplines – whether science as per Soskice or innovation in this case – nor of impoverishing ecclesial innovation of a 'distinctive theological voice' (Soskice 2007, p. 57).

Innovation-as-**craft** can be considered in both the Synoptic Gospels and the witness of the early church in Acts. The gospel challenge in relation to craft occurs in the Synoptic Gospels, as Jesus calls for a new wineskin (Matt. 9.16–17; Mark 2.21–22; Luke 5.36–39). 'No one tears a piece from a new garment and sews it on an old garment; otherwise the new will be torn, and the piece from the new will not match the old.'[11] At first glance, this would be seen as a critique of craft, pointing to the impossibility of mending an old wineskin. Better to start anew, rather than work with tradition. Such an approach, however, would in fact serve to take the parable out of context. The parable is placed in all three Gospels after a sequence of conflict stories in which individuals oppose the teachings of Jesus. The parable is not a metaphor with regard to new structures or institutions but with regard to people. Will those who hear be a 'container' of Jesus' teaching? Hence the challenge of mending is the invitation for people to listen to Jesus' teaching with flexibility, compassion and grace. Such a reading encourages innovation. The people of the world can indeed be repaired, as they respond with flexibility, compassion and grace.

Innovation-as-**craft** also appears in the life of the church. Craft – in particular, the making of clothing for widows – was essential to how Dorcas, in Acts 9.36–43, engaged in Christian witness. It is instructive to consider the similarities between the tasks given to the deacons in Acts 6.1–7 and the ministry of Dorcas. Both texts focus on the injustice of widows being neglected (6.1; 9.39) and the need for service (6.1; 9.36). Both the deacons and Dorcas are recognized by the church. Both are affirmed by the Spirit, the deacons directly in the text as 'full of the Spirit' (6.3), Dorcas indirectly as a recipient of resurrection power (9:40–41). Dorcas, like Philip (Acts 8.1–40), becomes a witness through whom 'many believed in the Lord' (9.42; cf. 8.14). Finally, in both cases (8.14–23; 9.32ff.), their ministries are affirmed by the presence of Peter. Dorcas is embodying the diaconal ministry given to Philip, expressing it through craft, making 'tunics and other clothing' (9.39) for a first expression community of widows in Joppa. It is an astonishing story of the diaconal ministry at work ahead of the church; of the power of the Spirit at work among those who stitch and make.

In two other places in the life of the early church, craft is essential in mission and ministry. Paul's use of tentmaking also drew on craft and served as a form of entrepreneurial activity that sustained him financially (2 Thess. 3.8; Acts 18.1–3; 20.33–35). At the same time, it also provided networks. This could well have included Lydia, who welcomed Paul at Philippi and was the first documented convert to Christianity in Europe. She was a dealer in purple cloth, providing craft networks that would sustain Paul's mission (Acts 16.14–15). Everett argues that innovation-as-craft re-centres 'poor people, women and people of color as innovators, design-thinkers and problem-solvers' (2019). This is certainly the case in relation to Dorcas and Lydia, in which widows and women are innovators central to the way the Spirit is at work in the world. Innovation gains a 'distinctive theological voice', as a way in which the Spirit is at work in the world.

Innovation-as-**spiral** is introduced in the genealogies of Matthew 1.1–17 and Luke 3:23–38. God with us, Emmanuel (Matt. 1.23) is placed in continuity with ancestors. I have learnt much when I have read Matthew's genealogy among indigenous (Maori) people. The voyages of Pacific peoples are connected with God's instruction to Abraham to 'Go'. Hence mission is understood as 'the story of ancestors who embark on pilgrimage, crossing borders and cultures, leaving the familiarity of family' (Taylor 2017, p. 33). Mission is freed from colonizing tendencies as the instruction to 'bless' in Genesis 12.1–3 is located as an echo of the creation story of Genesis 1. God blesses creation (Gen. 1.22) before God blesses human activity (1.27). This provides an environmental ethic and a posture of 'divine servant' in which 'human beings are integrally part of the whole created order [with] privileged responsibility ... to attend to [God's creation] both by caring for it and by praising it' (Soskice 2007, p. 62).

Reading the genealogy among indigenous (Maori) people also generated discussion about the way the genealogy provides a 'distinctive theological voice' in relation to inclusivity. The genealogy of Matthew 1 was recognized as respecting not only women, but indigenous women, given that four of the named women ancestors were indigenous: Tamar (Canaanite), Rahab (Canaanite), Ruth (Moabite) and Bathsheba (Hittite). The spiral of God-in-Jesus was inclusive, weaving in different cultures and peoples. A further dimension of inclusion became evident in discussion of names like Zerubbabel, Abiud, Eliakim and Azor, with the spiral of God in history including ancestors more faithful than famous. While genealogies in some indigenous cultures privilege important people and follow patriarchal patterns, the innovative spiral of Jesus was viewed as providing a 'distinctive theological voice'. God's work in the world is a spiral of voyaging in which creation is blessed through the including of stories of indigenous women and the faithful.[12]

Innovation-as-**ecological** can be located in a number of places. First, the instruction by Jesus to his disciples to learn from creation: the birds of the air (Matt. 6.26) and the lilies of the fields (6.28). This makes sense of the multiple parables told by Jesus, which draw on the everyday and created worlds. Second, in Chapter 1 I noted how Jesus in John 12:24–26 described the shape of his mission as a body-ing forth of dying and rising. What we love must be lost, in order to experience the durability of eternal life (John 12.26). This fits well with innovation as **ecological**, in which death and renewal are as significant as birth and growth. This willingness to die is in direct contrast with innovation-as-growth and seems at odds with innovation as a spiral or a mending.

Innovation-as-**growth** is evident in a number of parables in Matthew 13. However, it is interesting that in each case there is a disjunctive space that is created between what is immediately visible and the eschatological end, the telos of the end goal.

In the Parable of the Sower (Matt. 13.1–23), the sower expects a return. Seed sown on good soil bears fruit and yields returns, even up to a hundredfold. Yet growth, while expected, cannot be calculated. Seed is thrown, no matter the rate of return. In the parable, there is no sense of the sower limiting the seed being thrown or experimenting to find more 'growthful' ways to throw seed. The parable expects growth, but establishes a mystery between action and outcome.

The Parable of the Sower is followed by the Parable of the Weeds (Matt. 13.24–30). Again, the Parable of the Weeds opens up a space between what is immediately visible and the telos. Seed is sown and as in the Parable of the Sower, the good soil bears fruit. In this case, that good soil yields fruit that is both seed and weed. This surprises the servants, who are not sure how to manage the 'success' of this innovation, in particular the unintended consequences of weed growth (13.27). The instructions from the sower – 'Let them both grow together' (13.30) – establish a gap between the immediate success and the end goal that is harvest. Growth is expected, but there will be a distinct period of time in which what is visible and is growing will be different from the telos.

The next two parables, of the Mustard Seed and Yeast again speak to growth (Matt. 13.31–33) and again, while growth is expected, there is mystery between action and outcome. The growth of the mustard tree is visible. In successfully growing, the mature mustard tree will yield seeds high in nutritional value and containing selenium, which provides health benefits including anti-inflammatory properties (Times of India 2017). Alongside the benefits of the seeds, growth is affirmed for providing a home for the growth of others, in particular as a nesting place for birds (Matt. 13.32). Yeast is a single-cell organism that multiplies when given ample air and food (carbohydrates) in the dough. The aim of growth is not more yeast, but a loaf of bread. As with the mustard seed, growth is understood to be serving a higher purpose. In both parables, the growth is gradual. It takes time for the mustard bush to grow and the bread to rise. A portrayal of growth as taking time would have shocked the hearers, who were expecting growth to be dramatic and earth-shattering (Ryken et al., 1998, p. 578). Again, we see Scripture affirming an understanding of growth, yet offering a distinctive understanding of how to appreciate such growth.

Hence, in four consecutive parables, growth in the kingdom is expected. Seeds when sown produce crops and provide shelter. Bread rises. The 'S' curve of growth is evident and is affirmed. Yet in each parable, there is a distinctive understanding of how to appreciate such growth. There is a 'yes, but' about applying a commercial understanding of innovation, looking for the 'S' curve of growth and maturity in the parables of Matthew 13.

It is also noteworthy that all four of these parables could be considered not only in relation to growth, but also as ecological. Seeds, mustard seeds and yeast all die, whether through harvest or consumption. This suggests that the church has a number of understandings of innovation from which to draw. The four understandings can be located in relation to Scripture.

Framing innovation in first expressions/Fresh Expressions

Our vision of *telos* is essential in seeking to evaluate innovation. Why innovate? In these parables, not because of rates of return, but because of the value of what will be produced. The emphasis is on the unpredictability of the return (30×, 60×, 100×) and the willingness to risk all.

This broadens the reasons for why the church might innovate. The danger is that the church works subconsciously with only one model. If we work only with the growth model, then we are likely to fund only sowers who guarantee a hundredfold increase and mustard seeds once we've seen the birds.

This broadens the evaluative questions that might then be asked of innovation, including both first expressions and Fresh Expressions. This will become particularly helpful in Chapter 5 (Tried and died) when the first expressions, those that tried and died, will be mapped in relation to these four understandings. This gives dignity in taking risks and enhances reflection on unintended consequences.

Finally, this also provides a 'distinctive theological voice'. Distinctive rather than different. The church is not removed from a world in which the insights of innovation are generative. The location of these four understandings in Scripture offers the church an agility, an ability to work with each of these four. In working with any of these four understandings, however, the church has a distinctive imagination.

- From the growth, we remember to pay attention to the small.
- From ecology, we remember to celebrate compost.
- From the spiral, we remember to include diverse cultures.
- From the craft, we remember to include poor and women.

This is how the church body-ies forth. We learn with and from innovation, while nurturing a 'distinctive theological voice', attentive to the distinct ways that God is at work in the world, attending to the smallness of the mustard seed, the voice of the poor, cultivating communities of diversity. This is consistent with how Soskice offers eschatological anthropology as she engages with science, yet in ways that are nourished by a distinctive theological voice.

Evaluating first expressions

In this chapter I have articulated a theologic of innovation. This extends the work of Soskice, asking what if the notion of body-ing forth could be developed as a theology of innovation. Four different understandings of innovation – from commerce, ecology, indigenous (Maori) and craft – were outlined. These are summarized in Figure 4.

Figure 4: Different understandings of innovation

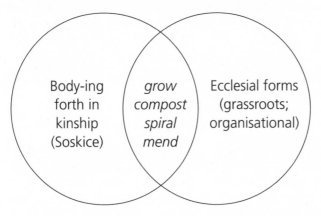

The four understandings of innovation provide a way to reflect on first expressions and Fresh Expressions. They are a bridge between the lived reality and theology, giving concrete shape to Soskice's language of body-ing forth. An evaluative set of criteria are offered, that work with the insights of innovation yet are distinctly theological, being resourced by the biblical emphasis on the lost and the least, diversity and marginality.

- Does it grow and mature?
- Does it compost in renewable cycles of birth, life and death?
- Does it spiral through story in carrying forward ancestor wisdom?
- Does it contribute to mending, whether patch, stitch or remake?

These give concrete shape to the becoming of a kinship ecclesiology. These evaluative questions will be used in subsequent chapters in discussing first expressions and Fresh Expressions, most particularly in the next two chapters (4 and 5). We can return to Grace, Epicentre/Moot,

Late Late Service, Sanctuary and Vaux 11 years on. In exploring each of the four understandings of innovation, we access different dimensions of innovation.

Notes

1 The movie is based on the novel by Morais (2010). For an illuminating interview with the producer, see Morgan (2014).

2 Image created by Shannon Taylor and used with her permission

3 Image created by Shannon Taylor and used with her permission.

4 The movie gained the AGF People's Choice award at the 2002 Toronto International Film Festival and the World Cinema Audience award at the 2003 Sundance Film Festival. Keisha Castle-Hughes, then aged 13, became the youngest nominee for the Academy Award of Best Actress.

5 In indigenous Maori culture, *te here tangata* refers to Maori understandings of how generations connect, backward to ancestors, forward through all future generations. 'All Maori and Moriori knowledge about the past was handed down over the generations in the form of oral traditions attached to genealogies, or whakapapa' (Anderson, Binney and Harris 2015).

6 The world is enriched by countless indigenous cultures, each unique. In order to honour this particularity, I work here with one indigenous culture, that of Maori in Aotearoa New Zealand.

7 'Tangata Whenua', *Artefact*, kindly supplied for research and teaching purposes by Greenstone Productions, Auckland, New Zealand, www.greenstonetv. com/ [viewed 10 April 2019], 51:01.

8 Six episodes hosted by Dame Anne Salmond, one of New Zealand's most distinguished historians, www.greenstonetv.com/our-programmes/artefact/. The information in this paragraph is drawn from 'Tangata Whenua', *Artefact* [viewed 10 April 2019].

9 For examples of the groundbreaking projects by Animation Research, see https://arl.co.nz/ [viewed 20 April 2019].

10 Image created by Shannon Taylor and used with her permission.

11 All scriptural quotations in this book are drawn from the New Revised Standard Version, given the commitment of the translators to draw from biblical manuscripts more ancient than those used in the KJV and their awareness of the impact of the linguistic sexism of the English language.

12 The genealogy of Jesus in relation to indigenous epistemologies is developed in much more detail in Taylor (2017).

PART 2

First expressions 11 years on

Have a go, we try
Sense re-make, first expressions
Every new day dawns

Have a go, we sent
honour seed from Philippi
Bless now the tried, died

4

Tried

any size of community is capable of doing Christian mission
(Roberts 2013)

These next two chapters seek, in the words of Paas, 'hermeneutic discoveries' (2016, p. 239). Applying Julian as a methodology, they value
a theology of the unique and expect to find, in the 'tacit knowledge'
embodied in every first expression, patterns of God's presence, offering
'an incredible amount of theological, ecclesiological, missiological, and
organizational experience, and, of course, a lot of questions' (p. 235).

The journey

In Chapter 2, I describe how, in the middle of 2001, I travelled to Britain
for a three-month period of study leave. Interested in new forms of
church, I found a list of communities on a website: www.alt.worship.org.
Within the confines of an itinerary, the limitations of public transport
and the mixed patterns of worship of these communities, I researched as
many as possible. In pubs, churches, railway stations, cafes, I interviewed
individuals and groups and, as able, attended worship.

   Between 2001 and 2012, I also changed, moved and grew. I concluded
my ministry in a new form of church in 2003. I moved in 2004 to an
established church, planting new congregations that sought, through
listening, serving and discipling, to establish expressions of worship con-
textually appropriate to those being served.[1] This included Espresso, a
cafe-style community that gathered around the questions of those seeking
faith and valued a communal approach to formation. Espresso sparked
a hymn congregation, serving those who found God in choosing hymns
and sharing the stories of why those particular hymns were meaningful. This was followed by a mid-week church gathering that provided
soup, in-depth Bible study and prayers for healing in a local community
centre. In the midst of this, the church community I planted and served
between 1994 and 2003 decided to close. This resulted in a range of
questions about sustainability. Then in 2010, I was called to form leaders

in mission at a theological college. This further sharpened my questions about innovation and sustainability.

At the end of 2012, I returned again to the UK, for another three-month period of study leave. A decade on, much more was happening in new forms of church. I decided to limit my research to the communities I studied in 2001. The logic was simple. This would enable, ten years on, a longitudinal study of sustainability and fresh expressions. Again, I travelled. Again, I sat in pubs, churches, railway stations, cafes. I interviewed and again, as able, attended worship.

In 2012, only five of the eleven communities I researched in 2001 continued. This chapter focuses on these five communities, exploring their spirituality on the road. In seeking to clarify 'hermeneutic discoveries' (Paas 2016, p. 239), three questions are asked. How have they experienced God? What has sustained them? What is their understanding of mission?

The destinations

Each community was warm in their welcome and gracious with their time. They opened their homes, their wine bottles, their hearts and, as appropriate, their beds.

Foundation met in Bristol. In 2001, they were called Resonance. I attended worship (as Resonance), then enjoyed a coffee with a key organizer. In 2013, I attended worship (as Foundation) then, over a focus group at a local pub, interviewed two key organizers.

Sanctuary met in Bath. In 2001, I enjoyed hospitality in an outdoor garden and a focus group conversation with a group of five. In 2013, I enjoyed dinner with a family of four, followed by participation in worship and then a drink with a group of five at the local pub.

Moot met in central London. In 2001, I met a key organizer, in a railway station, to discuss what was then Epicentre. In 2013, I enjoyed coffee in the cafe in the foyer of their church, participated in evening prayer, then interviewed the same key organizer.

Visions meet in York. In 2001, I interviewed two key organizers, followed by participation in worship and a drink with a group from the community at the same local pub. In 2013, I conducted a focus group with seven people over dinner. I then interviewed one of the key organizers from 2001, who in 2013 was offering ministry in another context.

Grace met in the suburbs of London. In 2001, I conducted a focus group over an evening meal with a group of four and later participated in worship. In 2013, I again enjoyed an evening meal, with a group of six.

The spirituality I experienced prioritized hospitality and community. A repeated value in all conversations included culturally connected engagement with God. In worship, I made Trinitarian friendship bracelets, appreciated high quality video mixing, sat on beanbags, listened to punk music, heard honest rants about faith and life and thumbed my way around books of common prayer.

Not only was I blessed to experience their gift of hospitality, extended to me on my road trip. I also gained, through interview, conversation and worship, some insight into the spirituality of their road.

Road lessons

A spirituality of the road is a gift worth opening. Figure 5 indicates a dramatic increase in the planting of fresh expressions. In three Anglican dioceses, in the five years prior to 1999, 12 churches were planted. In the five years between 2006 and 2011, 145 were planted.

Figure 5: Church planting

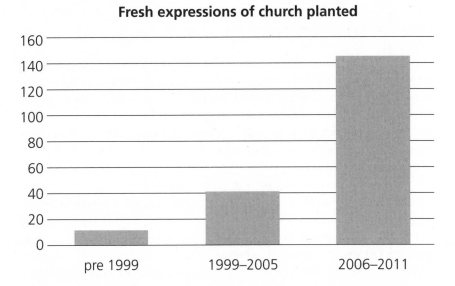

The first expressions that provide the qualitative data for this study were all born pre 1999. As such, they provide a rich data set for those who follow behind. In sun and through rain, these initial pioneers have experienced God. They have undergone transitions – internal, as children are born or a key leader moves; external, as a context unexpectedly changes.

As they follow their call, as they reflect on their journey, they each provide insights on how to sustain creativity, ways to nurture community and wisdom on how to maintain hope in small beginnings. This is a rich fund of knowledge.

> 'Sustainability is more likely to happen when there is a body of experience so that people aren't learning as they go along.' (Paul Roberts 2013, Interview)

Newly planted communities – the 145 noted in the graph above, the many more spread across other dioceses in the United Kingdom, those beginning to think about being newly planted, those in denominational roles wanting to support, those in sending churches wanting to encourage – can learn much from the stories of these early pioneers in innovation and mission.

When the communities I researched in 2001 began, there were very few road maps but plenty of institutional, i.e. denominational, suspicion. While there is now much more institutional encouragement, there are still precious few written road maps of life on the road ten years on.

God, growth and mission

One way to analyse the interviews was to listen for their use of God language. This involved looking for their use of the word 'God' and around that asking a set of questions: How do these communities describe God? How do they discern God being active? Where do they see the actions of God located? The result is 'native categories', a set of phrases and understandings that, rather than imposed externally, emerge from these local communities.

These framing questions emerge from a theology of revelation, an assumption that God is at work in the road trip, in the experiences of life. It is one way to do theology, consistent with a definition provided by Rowan Williams: 'always beginning in the middle of things ... [t]he meanings of the word "God" are to be discovered by watching what this community does ... when it is acting, educating, or "inducting", imagining and worshipping' (2000, p. xii).

Happily for the researcher, not only do these questions ensure native categories, they can also be linked with theological categories: the description of God with images of God, the patterns by which God is active with discipleship, the actions of God with mission.

These can be summarized in Table 3.

Table 3: *Images of God, growth and mission*

	Foundation	Sanctuary	Moot	Visions	Grace
Images of God	Mysterious wind	Sustainer through DIY encounter	Encountering One	Active Agent in experimentation	Engaging One
Patterns of growth	Informality; Creativity ('a great art form')	Participation in 'DIY punk aesthetic'	Experiential orthopraxy made real through a rhythm of life	Adapting to a changing community	'In all parts of life'
Location of God's activity	Blowing on embers; Weekly interactive compline	Community across generations	Hospitality; Relationship; Prayers	In change. This includes within their community, in the wider cultural and in history and tradition.	'jobs and lives'
Under-standings of mission	Closing the backdoor through a thoughtful, wholistic practice of faith	Solidarity in a post-credit crunch culture	Spiritual directors in consumer cultures; Hospitable invitation to a life of prayer	Dancers afresh	Engaging in all parts of life

Foundation: ember ecclesiology

Foundation gather on Sunday evenings, at 8 p.m. in Cotham Anglican, followed by a drink together at the local pub. Ten years on, this first expression had experienced God as a mysterious wind. Central to their spirituality on the road has been the discovery of a pattern of practices, focused on an interactive, creative weekly compline. This serves as embers, on which individual faith remains warm.

At Foundation, **God had been experienced** as a mysterious wind. This was a bringing together of two threads from the interview. First, with regard to mysterious, faith in God had been experienced 'as something more mystical, more numinous' (Foundation 2013). In the journey of mission, a God greater than easy definitions and simple formula had been encountered. This had been life-giving.

Second, with regard to wind, an image used to describe their experience, their spirituality of the road was 'what we've seen is that embers ... can be blown on and they will turn into the next wave' (2013). Foundation today owes life to the embers of what was Resonance, which in turn owes its life to what was Third Sunday Service.

This sense of God's patterning in which they are embers, reliant on the mysterious wind of the Spirit, makes sense of their experiences, in particular in relation to their change of name. Each change of name was related to a reconsideration of what it meant to be church. This included a search for a sustainable pattern and a life-giving structure.

Third Sunday Service offered large events monthly. In 2000 there was a six-month pause. This coincided with the move of Paul Roberts, a lecturer in liturgy at Trinity Theological College and a key initiator of Third Sunday Service, to local parish ministry. Third Sunday Service became a congregation at Cotham Anglican, with a new name, Resonance. But the creativity, both as Third Sunday Service and then as Resonance, proved draining, placing stress on relationships.

The large events stopped. A few people continued to meet weekly on Sunday evenings at Cotham Anglican to say compline together: 'the rhythm of that weekly gathering was very low key, very low maintenance, once a week, small numbers, Sunday night services and those were the embers out of which Foundation grew again' (Foundation 2013).

In 2004, a wind blew on these embers. New people, fresh energy, different networks provided energy for another set of large events.

> There's a great paradox about what big services actually do in terms of mission, or outreach. They are really good at sustaining and renewing a potentially transient regular congregation ... [But] the age groups that tend to go along to things like this, it's by nature transient with people moving to jobs, having children. (2013)

In 2008, the large events stopped. But the embers, sustained by the discovery of the gift of weekly gathering, continue. '[A] weekly community, not trying to be too clever, could work on its spirituality ... we'd survived really by just saying compline together' (2013). My experience as a participant observer helped make sense of this understanding. The worship service was introduced as compline. Alongside the set words, read from the Book of Common Prayer, it involved extensive informal participation. A question asked drew extended, in-depth interaction. It gave space for expression and integration with daily life. There was a dynamic of unscripted participation, cultural engagement and a quest for integration in contrast to patterns of compline, which involve quiet and scripted words.

This provides their **pattern of growth**. God is experienced as at work in the informality: 'I like the ability to talk in the middle of a service' (2013). For educated, thoughtful, engaged people, this is a significant factor in their spiritual development. Mixed with the invitation to be creative – 'I like the artistic and the sensory aspects of it' (2013) – it provides an important way to grow, sustain and deepen faith in a postmodern world.

The **understanding of mission** at Foundation cohered around the assumption that churches have a front door and a back door. Foundation was thus seen as offering a back door, a mission which sustained faith, through the pattern of growth.

> Why not have a church that's the back door not the front door? Not saying people leave by the back door, but it's that part of the journey. So I don't buy the idea that alt.worship is about winning the heathen. I think it's more about stopping people becoming the heathen. (2013)

From the interviews, it seems that Foundation has at least three front doors. One front door was people from larger evangelical charismatic churches. Foundation includes 'disillusioned, well educated, thoughtful, ex-charismatics ... for whom [Foundation] has been a lifeline ... Why not? Because these people need a place to go' (Foundation 2013).

A second front door was 'young people in Christian churches, who were struggling to find a church which they could belong to, which didn't expect them to look and think and act like evangelicals' (P. Roberts 2013).

A third front door was people 'who just happen in on a Sunday night and they'll go, "Oh this isn't the kind of thing I was expecting." These people are very open-minded and they seem quite normal' (Foundation 2013).

At Foundation, these people are resourced, through the pattern of an interactive, creative compline, through a range of spaces that invite reflection on faith and life today. The result is that 'in terms of engaging with their neighbour, maintaining spiritual growth, maintaining an active witness of integrity to the values of the kingdom, they're very strong' (Roberts 2013).

Ten years on, Foundation have experienced a God of mysterious wind. Central to their spirituality on the road has been the discovery of a pattern of practices, focused on an interactive, creative weekly compline. This serves as embers, on which individual faith remains warm.

Sanctuary: DIY punk aesthetic

My first encounter with Sanctuary in 2001 was a rich experience of hospitable community. Gathered around food, in a garden on the outskirts of Bath, I left impressed with an ethic of people and participation.

Sanctuary initially started off as four people ... over time we've tried more and more ... to work out ways in which other people can discover their creativity ... more recently other people have been involved in the worship services ... it's an opportunity for people to discover their skills and bring them along. (Sanctuary 2001)

Ten years on, Sanctuary, while small, continue to remain a hospitable community, in which people and participation are central. Community happens in home gatherings, to discuss, to eat and often to walk together. Worship happens monthly.

At Sanctuary, **God has been experienced** as Sustainer through DIY encounter. The worship service I attended, while small in number, was memorable.

The service began with a Bible reading, the Nazareth manifesto (Luke 4:14–30). This was compared favourably with the protest nature of punk music. An Old Testament reading (Jeremiah 29:4–7) was then offered by way of contrast. Christianity has a tradition of social protest, but also a willingness to act constructively, to live within the empire it seeks to subvert. A number of concrete suggestions, ways to live subversively in a consumer society, were offered.

It is rare for punk music to be used, let alone brought into conversation with lectionary texts. This was a community thinking deeply, culturally, about how to live as disciples of Jesus today.

It made perfect sense of the interviews, in which the worship as Sanctuary was described as 'DIY ... low-tech punk aesthetic' (2013b).

This was linked to their identity and purpose as a community. They described their sense of being grounded 'in reality of post-credit crunch Britain' (2013b).

This introduced **an understanding of mission** as an expression of solidarity with many others in Britain. 'We're financially vulnerable, like so many others in Britain' (2013b). This vulnerability was felt individually and as a community and contrasted with the inherited church, which those interviewed from Sanctuary perceived as cushioned from reality, kept safe by a legacy and a faith insulated from life.

This understanding of mission linked their reading of a context with the Jesus proclaimed in worship, and with their DIY, low-tech punk aesthetic. 'It's not loads of kit. It can't be a lot of cost. So we use what's to hand. We take the ordinary and transform it. There's a down to earth reality' (2013a).

Historically, their **understanding of mission** had been framed as curators of public art. Twice they had partnered with artists and offered a Stations of the Cross. In 2003, they invited 12 artists to participate (Collins n.d.). In 2005, they curated Passion Postcards (Collins n.d.).[2]

Participants included people with no faith. 'They were intrigued. I invited people I work with. Three responded' (2013b).

This DIY worship provided their **pattern of growth**. The input into Sanctuary came from within the group. 'Different persons try different things. I like that. It's really important. You hear different things.' For Sanctuary, this invites a grown-up faith. 'Not waiting for someone to feed us. You have to put stuff in. You are expected to participate' (2013b). In this DIY, low-tech punk aesthetic, God was encountered. 'I'm still surprised to actually encounter God in the context of the worship we've thrown together' (2013a).

> I quite like the edginess of it ... I like the stripped backness of it ... I like being able to have space with children there, to think and reflect and make something. I love that. That's what I've learnt over the 14 years we've been going. It's all right to strip it back and sit and listen ... What are we passing on? What is their view of faith and God and church? (2013a)

This has sustained not only their spiritual journey, but also that of their children. 'As parent I like that our kids get a chance to contribute' (2013a). The results have been impressive.

> At Christmas [the children] did a Station each. They've been doing that for years. When we're doing bigger things, they've inputted there. You kind of take that for granted ... Charlie [a former member of Sanctuary] coming back and seeing them. She's an RE Senior School teacher and she saw what they did and said to me, 'Did the girls do that? That's really good. Do you realize?' And I think we've kind of taken that for granted. (2013a)

Sanctuary feel fragile, confessing that they regularly consider closure. Yet, 'We have survived because we know each other and got deep faith convictions' (2013b). Significant factors have included the emphasis on community and participation, a permission-giving relationship with a local church, a willingness to be flexible as ages and stages change and through irregular larger-scale creative projects, which have given identity, purpose and renewed energy.

Sanctuary is a small group. Yet in an era of overall church decline, for any group to remain stable is a commendable achievement. Further, in a church with declining resources, Sanctuary ask for little. There is no funding required, no paid worker nor vicar needed to perform sacraments. Only a place to offer their DIY, low-tech worship once a month.

'We're incredibly fortunate … [to have a relationship with St Matthew's and St Thomas à Becket Church] … They've been really encouraging. Let us get on with it' (2013a).

In stark contrast to Foundation (and in a reminder of the diversity of cultures within Britain today), individuals at Sanctuary are stable rather than mobile. 'It's quite counter cultural to commit to journeying together. We're geographically settled. Very positive about this. I've grown up with you all. You knew me at 17 and now I've got a 16-year-old … Something really important in that' (2013b).

Sanctuary have experienced God as the Sustainer through DIY encounter. In community, through participation, with a DIY punk aesthetic, faith has been sustained across the years and through generations.

Moot: spiritual directors in consumer cultures

Moot are spiritual directors, cultivating a set of practices which they indwell and which they offer to spiritual seekers in London.

Ten years on, Epicentre had morphed into Moot, a new monastic order, invited by the Bishop of London 'into the mixed economy of the different churches of the centre of London' with a particular mission to the 'spiritual seekers or the dechurched or the unchurched who are not interested in traditional forms of church' (A leader of Moot 2013).

Outside the church, inside their grounds, a cafe was in operation. Portable, with tables and food, it ran as a fundraiser for the mission of Moot.

Inside the church, a cafe also ran. This was permanent, with tables, chairs, sofas and bar stools occupying the first third of the interior. With a countertop in wood, the ambience was warm and inviting, in colours that modernized without clashing with the wood of the interior pews. Wi-fi was free, as was this offer of sitting space in London, clear permission to eat without purchasing, to linger without consuming.

> We've wanted to open a cafe for 20 years and we only did it in September. That's a long wait. So there was a time of frustration but we feel like we've been listened to. It's a bloody miracle, I can't believe still that they trust us with this building. (2013)

On a Wednesday, during a workday, I am warmly greeted but left in peace. Half the tables have people at them, working, phoning. You can imagine a person stepping from outside to inside, from silent prayer to group prayer, through a multiplicity of 'pick and mix' pathways: outdoor cafe, indoor cafe, invitations to silent prayer, to daily prayer, to browse spiritual resources, to attend meditation workshops, to participate in

Lenten justice projects, to think at public lectures or to engage in spiritual discussions in the pub next door.

Their **understanding of mission** is as a hospitable invitation to live this prayer life. 'So our big responsibility with mission here is not to fill people here with facts about God but for people to experience God for themselves' (2013). It is intrinsically tied to their **understanding of God,** as an experience in which 'our lives start to become in tune with God, then God's story becomes part of our story' (2013). For Moot, this involved the discovery of a **pattern of growth** through a rhythm of life and a shared set of lived spiritual practices.

> We realized that we were unhealthy, it was too conceptual and there wasn't the whole integration. A lot of our people were struggling with the separation from head and heart. They weren't integrated people. And then someone just named it one day. When we'd had aspirations about what to do and said 'Well that's the beginning of a rhythm of life.' ... It emerged out of our lives. (2013)

Together, Moot agreed to a rhythm of life and shared set of spiritual practices. It was a fundamental shift from church as gathering to church as a way of praying that sought to receive the love of God within the pace and pressure of life in a modern city.

The result, in the interview, was to listen to some of the most thoughtful and integrated missiology I have ever encountered.

Moot described a transcendental model of contextualization among spiritual seekers.

> The cultural context is that everybody is formed into a consumer society. So everybody is basically addicted to consumption as a way of life. Particularly in London, and United Kingdom, which is now a market society. So actually what we tend to do is find people that come here who are deeply unfulfilled by a society defined by materialism and commodification of life. (2013)

In this, they serve as spiritual directors, offering a relational, experiential pilgrimage. A repeated word was 'orthopraxy', in which is fused together their experience of God, their pattern of growth and their understanding of mission.

> [It] isn't that God is absent from the world, or that God is absent from people's lives. They are just not aware that God is in the details of their lives. So it's ... about trying to help people become more self-aware of the depth of the God who is already there in their lives and they haven't

noticed it … It's much about belief that God is active, catching up with what God is already doing rather than trying to force something. We're not ambassadors for an absent God. We're very much disciples trying to catch up with what God is already doing. (2013)

Their mission is greatly enhanced by having a building. It is conceptualized as 'a leisure centre for mission'. It embodies the wide range of experiential stepping stones that Moot-ers inhabit. It magnifies their mission. Hospitality becomes tangible, relational connections are made possible in a rapidly changing central city.

[T]o open up the gospel in this space by trying to be quite creative about how we create possibilities and opportunities for people to encounter God. So it's not an apologetic approach where we are trying to argue people into the kingdom of God. It's about loving service that we hope that the Spirit will indwell. (2013)

The road trip from Epicentre to Moot began with crisis: 'If we hadn't made it to become a new monastic community, we would've ended. Most definitely' (2013). Their experiences of spirituality have led to significant and extended reflection on the patterns of growth that facilitate mission in their unique context, that of central city London. Moot are spiritual directors, cultivating a set of practices which they indwell and which they offer to spiritual seekers in London. And 'we've had a couple of people just become Christians who were unchurched. That's beautiful' (2013).

Visions: dancing afresh

Visions have been offering alternative worship since 1991. They began as Warehouse, as a mission to connect with club cultures in York. New friendships were born and after the event a small group continued to meet to explore mission, culture and community among club cultures. Two years of praying and dreaming resulted in the birth of Visions: 'we too mixed with the people of York: we did visuals for nightclubs, danced alongside other clubbers, listened to their stories, and stayed open about our Christian faith' (Wallace 2009b, p. 10).

I knew of Visions before I met Visions. I had carried with me from the beginning of my pastoral ministry an image a friend gave me of their worship in the 1990s. It was a picture of multiple pictures, a collage of slide images, projected onto the wall of a church building. It was beautiful, a rich mix of ancient and modern. It was a reminder of the power and potential of sight. That one photo has constantly challenged my under-standing of worship, reminding me of the need to consider in worship all of God's good creation, the eyes as well as the ears, the body as well as the mind.

Over 20 years later, Visions has evolved. Currently they offer Tran-scendence, monthly on the third Sunday, at 7:30 p.m., in various spaces within York Minster. The Eucharist is celebrated with robes, processions, candles, incense and sacred chants, all mixed with modern trip-hop beats, colourful projected images, video loops and creative prayer stations.

On the fourth Sunday, at 4 p.m., they offer worship for parents of young children. This involves story, song and craft, in a multimedia atmosphere.

On other Sundays, there are evening gatherings, a mix of chilled-out dance music, visual images, spoken words, beanbags and space to pray.

When asked what had sustained Visions, the response was a committed community. 'It's the fact that Visions is family. Because there are people you can dip out on but family's not one of them. There's a strong sense of loyalty' (Visions 2013a). This value produces a **pattern of growth**, a transmission of faith through generations. A member of the leadership group at Visions had grown up through the church: 'It's influenced how I've grown up and it's influenced me as a person ... Given me parts of my character, who I am and made me realize some of my abilities and competence and leading skills and creativeness' (2013a).

While some models of youth development assume the need for separ-ated spaces, at Visions this pattern of growth was possible because of a freedom of expression in a community that welcomed diversity and encouraged questions. 'I feel like I was given freedom by being part of it ... Not freedom to step away from it. Freedom to be myself and my teenage rebellious person within doing things within the group' (2013a).

The value of this committed community was a repeated theme through-out the interview.

> Because some of the people within Visions have actually got families of their own, quite young children. We've always made sure they partici-pate quite actively in the service and the services, I really enjoy getting involved in it. I haven't got any kids of my own but I mean they all feel so loved and welcomed and it's an environment where they can express themselves and worship together. It's something for everyone. (2013a)

This pattern of growth can be linked with their **experience of God** as the Active Agent in experimentation. 'We're very keen for God to take us where it seems appropriate and that will mean adapting in some shape or form' (2013a). In the interview with Visions, God language was always related to this experience of finding God in the process of adaptation.

> We're quite experimental. God's behind us most of the time and everything works. So it must say something … How can we adapt to how the community is changing is really important … As the cultural scene changed within society, we also adapted. (2013a)

It almost felt like change enlivened Visions, offered them **a pattern of growth,** became the possibility in which discernment could be practised, creativity could be exercised and further fresh expression might emerge.

Visions ten years on is the story of the multiple birthing of a number of fresh expressions of worship – multimedia worship for families by Visions, Transcendence in the Minster, offering multimedia Vespers as part of Illuminating York Festival.

Hence their **understanding of mission,** dancers afresh. This acknowledges their roots in dance culture. It captures their extraordinary ongoing creativity in birthing new forms of ecclesial life. It arises from their experience of God, as the Active Agent in adaptation. It connects theologically with the image of God the Trinity as perichoresis, the divine dance. Visions are responding to the divine beat they hear in times of change, joining in the movement of God.

What is intriguing about Visions is how they locate God's Active Agency not only in cultural and communal change, but in tradition and history.

Like Grace, Visions appreciate being part of the Church of England. 'We've had the conscious decision that the C of E is what we want to be part of' (2013a). They experience it as a 'broad enough church to accommodate us' (2013a). They also value the possibilities for connection created by this history. The interview included an intriguing phrase, *we can live and breathe* them [historic buildings] well. It provides another window into their pattern of growth and understanding of mission.

> York has lots of old church. It makes sense to use old churches partly because we can live and breathe them well. We can create atmospheres within them well. But also because within the city of York they seem to have a prominent place. And the people relate to them in a different way than you may do in the centre of Leeds. (2013a)

In historic buildings, there is a past to connect with an ever-evolving present. Visions are being invited into a constant dance, a becoming in which what was can be connecting with what is.

A similar pattern was evident in relation to their understanding of tradition. It functions as an invitation

> to explore boundaries, not in the sense of bending of boundaries, but in terms of liturgy and the way you can write within certain parameters and as long as you use this wording, being able to create liturgy within certain formulas and using certain prayers, you can make it, completely different from one church to the next. (2013a)

The past, buildings or prayers, is seen as an invitation to create. Adaptation is an essential **pattern of growth**. It invites the search for connection, a discernment that creates connections between past and present. This is the essence of their fresh expression.

Full of creative people, change offers them the chance to playfully re-create.

Grace: 'jobs and lives'

In September 2005, the monthly Grace worship service began in dramatic fashion. That Saturday evening, a key figure in the community, Steve Collins, picked up a sledgehammer and proceeded to smash a mirror. On it was written the word 'Grace' ('September 2005: Engage').

Grace have, since the community began in 1993, met monthly in 1,000-year-old St Mary's, Ealing, London. Mike Rose, a founder, along with then curate Mike Starkey, wrote of that first service: 'Church was no longer something that happened to me but something I could take responsibility for. There didn't need to be a conflict between the rest of the week and Sunday' ('A history of Grace' n.d.). From the beginning, a faith that made sense to the whole person in all of life was a key motivation.

From the beginning, Grace generated enormous amounts of creativity. A labyrinth service in St Paul's Cathedral led to a cathedral tour and publishing opportunities in the United States. Homespun music led to the *Eucharist* album and performance on the main stage at Greenbelt. A regular zine, followed by early adoption of the internet led to a range of web resources, including the Proost label, which exported a wide range of creative multimedia worship resources.

Yet that Sunday in 2005, Grace lay shattered in the midst of this community, their reflection splintered into a thousand dangerous fragments.

A few minutes later, some explanation was provided. Despite being known internationally for creativity in expressions, despite branding themselves as 'alternative', despite being at the forefront of many things 'fresh' (to quote their website), the community were being challenged to consider new possibilities.

> About 18 months ago in Grace we started a process of exploring who we were, what we had achieved, where we were going ... And as we learned more about Jesus and our community we found that there were new possibilities in an old, a 10 year old, situation. And where we might previously have made an easy, obvious choice, following the rules of our tradition, we became aware of new options in old situations. ('September 2006: New year')

For Grace, the seemingly simple task of turning ten proved significant.

> We'd always said, 'Grace is really fragile, it might end at any moment, its really provisional.' And then we found ourselves celebrating our tenth anniversary ... therefore we'd better start thinking seriously about what kind of community we want to be if it does continue on indefinitely. (Grace 2013)

It generated a sustained period of reflection, a careful discernment of their hopes, dreams and energy levels. Four words – Create, Participate, Engage, Risk – emerged.

They marked a significant shift in the community and offer some important lessons on sustainability.

Regarding the shift, at Grace their **experience of God** had always been linked to their patterns of growth and understanding of mission. God was to be encountered in creative engagement with their contemporary world. Ten years on, their understanding of the word 'engage' needed to change.

> When we talked about our values, some of them like creativity and participation were definitely descriptive of what we were about, what we value. Engage I think when we talked about it, we don't have some outward focus words. It was more of an aspirational value. (2013)

To enable creativity and participation, from the beginning Grace met every Monday as a group to plan worship. This gathering was one of the things that would shatter under the hammer blow in September 2005.

Communally, in order for sustainability to emerge, a new structure was needed. This involved a shift, from 'everyone in the room ... always defaulting to a few people to make things happen' to 'smaller teams, curating different services so not everyone was involved' (2013). Ironically, this would require very different forms of participation, in smaller groups or from individuals.[3]

A further communal restructure was necessary. People at Grace were reading in monasticism.

> Some of the way we developed our thinking about leadership came as a result of thinking about monasticism ... about the ethos needing to be guarded ... which then led to making sure we had three people, whom we call a facilitation group. A group of three, rotated annually, are invited to 'keep an eye on the community'. (2013)

While ancient, Grace were seeking a more participative expression, with a group rather than a lone abbot.

These structural shifts redistributed energy in individuals and in the community. 'What we do monthly on a Saturday night is [now] not the only thing actually. As balanced people and as a balanced community we've also got an outward move' (2013). This is a **pattern of growth**, in which Grace 'compromised some of that creative planning in order to build relationship between both ourselves and to engage in other parts of our life' (2013).

This pattern helped sharpen their understanding of mission. Grace had, from that very first service, wanted to overcome the 'conflict between the rest of the week and Sunday'. But perhaps in the first ten years, the focus had been on engaging through worship. Ten years on, there was a shift to focus on individual application.

Individually, people needed to clarify how their unique and diverse passions and charisms could be the path by which God engaged through them.

> And we'd had conversations several times ... that ... we think that mission is, right, we all need to get together and do something together. But for a lot of people, what they're doing in their jobs and lives, whether that's being an architect or a chaplain or working for a chaplain or whatever, is the main focus of that mission and Grace exists to resource that. (2013)

Ten years on, Grace was more intentionally applying the word 'engage' to their everyday lives.

The result was an intriguing integration of Grace's **experience of God**, their **pattern of growth** and **their understanding of mission**. 'Just the notion that all we do, we all consider to be vocational ... I believe God has put me where he's put me to do a job and something I feel both passionate about and been gifted to do' (2013). Engage was now not only communal, in worship, but individual, in vocation. That founding dream, of a faith that made sense to the whole person in all of life, was now an experienced reality both in community and in individual work and life place mission.

Ten years on, Grace offers some important insights regarding sustainability.

First, regarding where to begin. A simple way to think about church is to consider three circles: one to focus on growth in relationship with God (worship); another, growth in relationships with people (community); a third, growth in relationships in mission.

In the initial structuring of Grace, growth in relationships with people was fused with worship preparation. The Monday gatherings to plan worship also served to build community. Grace came to realize that 'The community is happening, but it's happening by accident, as a result of planning worship. And not everybody who wants to be part of the community actually wants to get directly involved in planning worship ... That was kind of the only mechanism for that' (2013). The restructuring provided place for people.

Second, the importance of shifting identity from selected pioneers to community story. Early on in an innovation, the dream is often embedded in a few key individuals. However, when identity is held in individuals, it can remain exclusive.

> There is a sense of people who've been around for a long time naturally have much longer shared history and in any group or community that creates a dynamic between old hands and new people. There is nothing unique or unusual. It's just something we need to be aware of as a community. (2013)

Hence an important part of sustainability is the shift of a dream from individuals to a community. The story of some first expressions is of the difficulty in transition when those individuals move on. (This will become evident when we explore the stories of Host, Bigger Picture and Late Late Service in Chapter 5.) At Grace, those key individuals have remained. Rather than hold that vision tightly to themselves, Grace have found mechanisms to shift the vision. These have included restructuring their worship planning and their leadership structures and the articulation of an ethos open to interpretation by the community.

These insights are important for sustainability in general in fresh expressions. A number of other factors, perhaps unique to Grace, are also present. First, the long-term presence – 'In an age where most people in their thirties and forties are quite mobile and move around a lot, especially in London, there are a few people here who've been involved in Grace and putting a lot of work in over the majority of the time it's existed ... there's this stability' (2013). Like Sanctuary, albeit in urban

London not more suburban Bath, the longevity of key individuals is seen as important.

Second, a permission-giving church, with Grace noting that 'We hold very dearly to the fact we're part of the Church of England ... we were lucky enough to be in a community here where we were given permission' (2013).

I began with a story of smashing a mirror on which was written the word 'Grace'. It is an intriguing insight into the importance of flexibility in being church today.

Let me end with another story of how Grace became involved in the Mind, Body, Spirit Festival. It is an intriguing demonstration of how four simple words proved so instrumental in the ongoing formation of Grace as a people of God in mission.

I was rang up by this guy Colin who said some alt.worship people should get involved ... Look, one of our ethos words is engage. One is risk. We can't say no. So people got involved. So it was a gentle, but quite strong way of thinking about how that played out. (2013)

Emerging themes

I have begun by telling the story of five first expression communities. Listening to their use of God language has uncovered experiences of God, patterns of growth and images of mission.

Together, these stories start to tell us something about sustainability and first expressions. While further chapters will provide more data and greater clarity, some initial insights are already clear.

First, the diversity of these communities. While *Mission-Shaped Church* (2004) grouped the alt.worship communities studied here into one of twelve different expressions of church, what emerges clearly here is the uniqueness and individuality of each of these communities. What is also evident was the vitality released as each expression found their unique rhythm. The ember theology of Foundation, which requires a building in which to house a weekly saying of compline, with a leadership sensitive to the next wind of the mysterious Spirit. The daily prayer of Moot, in which a leadership acts as spiritual directors in mission, offering experiences of God through patterns of prayer. The cancelling of all-together Monday planning evenings at Grace and the way the discerning of ethos released them into new patterns of trust and clarified their mission. The willingness of Visions to find new expressions, as they innovate multimedia worship for families and establish Transcendence in ancient central city churches.

Helping communities find and nurture their unique life gift is likely to enhance sustainability.

Second, the durability of these forms of church. Apart from Moot, each group requires minimal resourcing, often simply the use of a building, from the wider church. Yet they continue to provide a ministry of the gospel and, through their community ethos, offer significant pastoral care to their participants. These groups would all be considered small in size. The night I attended Foundation, the former vicar, Paul Roberts, was also present. Interviewed afterwards, he was astonished at the changes. 'It's totally changed again. There are only four people in that room who would remember me [from when I was vicar in that community four years ago]. The rest have never met me' (Roberts 2013). For a small community to welcome ten new people in four years is a sign of health and an indication of their durability.

Third, community can be held by different forms of glue. At Sanctuary, it was based around persistence of presence. At Foundation, it was based around a regular weekly pattern of prayer. At Grace, it occurred in the shift from key leaders to a shared ethos. At Moot, it is about the practice of a shared rhythm of life. At Visions, it was the creative play generated by experiencing God in adaptation. In sum, community is not so much a mystical holy grail but can be encouraged in multiple ways through simple repetitions.

Fourth, the importance of these groups for the faith formation of those who participate. A repeated theme in the interviews was comments like 'Grace saved my church going life' (Grace 2013) or 'If Visions wasn't here, I'd have to invent it. Where else would I go?' (Visions 2013). Irrespective of their size, these groups are essential in holding people in faith. The ability to resource growth as a whole person seems significant in this regard. It was intriguing to see how the word 'engage' called Grace into new ways of being in the world. It was a delight, ten years on, to see evidence of the development of children and teenagers. 'We've never had to fight with them to get them to come to church' is not a comment you often hear from parents raising children in churches today (Sanctuary 2013a).

Fifth, the embrace of flexibility. While many inherited churches seem to find it hard to change, all of these groups have been willing to reinvent themselves. These include changing service times to cater for the arrival of children, the finding of a rhythm at Foundation and a rule at Moot, the smashing of the mirror called Grace, and the adaptation at Visions from dance, through chill, to Transcendence.

Sixth, the lay nature of these churches.

Table 4: Leadership

	Visions	*Foundation*	*Sanctuary*	*Grace*	*Moot*
Leadership	Team plus paid worker	Team	Team	Team	Team, with paid worker
Transitions	Loss of key leader	Loss of key leader; Change of name	Move of building	Leadership restructure	Move of building; Change of name
Ordination	Vicar emerging from within	Vicar alongside	none	none	Vicar emerging from within
Structural	Congregation of Anglican church	Congregation of Anglican church	Congregation of Anglican church	Congregation of Anglican church	Anglican church

The majority of the groups were lay led (only Moot had a vicar). The following comment from Grace was typical of the clarity this provides. 'We're a relatively small group, without any full-time or employed staff. Actually if we want to do something, we are the people that will have to take responsibility for doing that. It comes down to what we have energy for' (Grace 2013). Into the future, this will raise some intriguing questions for a church that has historically used ordination as a key structure for accountability and resourcing.

Conclusion

This chapter has offered a spirituality for the road by exploring five communities, all early pioneers in first expressions. Each community and their experience of God, patterns of growth and understanding of mission has been outlined – Foundation's ember ecclesiology; Sanctuary's DIY punk; Moot's spiritual directors in consumer cultures; Visions' dancing afresh; Grace's jobs and lives.

Together, these stories have begun to tell us something about sustainability. While further chapters will provide more data and greater clarity, some initial insights are already clear.

- Discernment of uniqueness.
- Creation of community.
- Growth of the whole person.
- Flexible, adaptable patterns and processes.

This chapter has told the story of the church by telling local stories. The task has been primarily descriptive. I have drawn on interview and focus group data, published literature and, as able, participant observation. Any interviews run the risk of gilding the lily. At the same time, they are consistent with methodologies of empirical research, which draw on lived experiences. In listening, I have sought to articulate God's patterning. This is consistent with an eschatological anthropology, which values birthing as a way of offering theological insight. This chapter has focused on first expressions, which have tried, which ten years on continue to embody ecclesial life. But what of those whom I interviewed in 2001 who no longer offer a worshipping life? That is the task of the next chapter.

Notes

1 These met the criteria that would come to define Fresh Expressions from 2004 onward ('What is a Fresh Expression?' n.d.). Each was fresh (a new thing developing for a particular culture or context), had their own identity (not an extra or a bridge to something else), were for people who don't 'go to church', intended to take them on a journey of discipleship. However, in terms of identity they were not envisaged to be separate church communities. Rather, they were congregations in a multi-congregational model. The theology is articulated in Taylor (2006).

2 Click on passion postcards sanctuary 2005 (Collins n.d.).

3 In March 2006, no preparation went into the service apart from the invitation to participate. The following invitation was issued by email: 'Part of the grace ethos is participation. The next grace puts this to the ultimate test ... Please bring a station with you on the theme of lent and/or a tune on an ipod or CD ... Please don't be shy or think what you do won't be good enough. It can be really simple. Just work with an idea. We value creativity, participation and risk so go for it' ('March 2006: Lent Bring Your Own Station').

5

Tried and died

The focus of this book is on innovation and fresh expressions. I began in Chapter 1 with some of my own story, of how in 1994 I had planted a first expression.[1] A priority was a creative engagement with a changing culture. There were very few other models and plenty of commentary: 'Will they stand the test of time?' Over the years, with creativity, prayer and persistence, a life of mission, discipleship and worship was established.

During those years, I undertook doctoral research, which included researching creative communities in England, Scotland and Wales. Their stories are told in Chapter 2, 'Birthing first expressions', and again in Chapter 4, 'Tried'.

After nine years leading that community, there was a season of transition in which I moved in 2003 to another ministry context. The first expression found new leadership and continued to explore mission, discipleship and worship.

In 2007 came the news that the first expression was going to close. The reasons were complex: the minister that followed us was new to pastoral ministry. Suggested changes proved unsettling for some and divisive for others. The minister moved to another context and the uniqueness of the church impacted on the ability of the church to find another pastor. Mission, discipleship and worship were sustained for another two years, but energy slowly ebbed away.

The news of closure generated grief and provoked questions. First, in terms of sustaining innovation, were there elements of the way I provided ministry and encouraged identity that should have been done differently? Second, in terms of motivations for innovation, was it worth it? I felt responsible for the resources of time and money invested, including of those who participated and the financial contributions of the denomination. To use the frames by Paas, if we planted seeking better churches, then while we had 'flown the Baptist flag' for a period, that denominational presence was no more. If we planted seeking more churches, then while individuals had come to faith, their church was now closing. If we planted seeking renewal, then were the resources that had been contributed a 'good investment'? What are the KPIs – Kingdom Performance Indicators – when it comes to ecclesial innovation?

One place to seek answers was to return to the creative communities I had researched in England, Scotland and Wales during 2001. Had any of them also experienced trying and dying? This would be personal, locating my experiences in relation to their being and becoming. It would also be professional, an experiment in longitudinal empirical research, repeating in 2012–13 the participant observation, focus group and interview research from 2001.

This chapter provides insight into sustaining innovation and motivations for innovation. First, by numerical analysis of the trying and dying of ecclesial innovation. The data reveals that 50 per cent of my first expression UK communities tried and died in 11 years, while 62 per cent of first expressions communities more generally had tried and died.

Second, by reflecting on ecclesiology. An examination of Paul's letter to the Philippians offers a posture of valuing those who try and die and provides an ecclesiology of woven threads, in which church is not only gathered, but is also faith developer, generation nurturer, leadership incubator and resource maker.

Third, by undertaking qualitative, in contrast to numerical, analysis of first expression UK communities. Are there factors that contribute to sustainability, whether internal or in relation to the contexts in which these communities are planted? Lessons in sustainability, including a celebration of church as seasonal rather than church as enduring, will be considered.

This chapter will argue that, in light of the reality of tried and died, a theology drawn from church-as-gathered and church-as-growing is a deficient approach to ecclesiology. The empirical ecclesial reality is that trying generates a rich ecclesial life, in which birthing and becoming make a unique contribution to faith, leadership and ecclesial life, irrespective of the trajectories of the gathered community. At times, particularly in contexts of rapid change, dying is in fact a truer body-ing forth of the activity of God.

The numerical reality: first expressions as signs of failure

Numerical analysis of longitudinal ecclesial innovation demonstrates that the closure of first expressions is relatively common. Over time, across Australia, England, New Zealand and the United States, innovative communities that have been positioned as signs of hope in fact have significant sustainability issues.

Of the first expressions I researched in the United Kingdom in 2001, five of the ten communities (50 per cent) had tried and died 11 years on. Table 5 lists, in alphabetical order, the communities and their status in 2012–13.

Table 5: First expressions longevity

Name	Location	Status 2013
Bigger Picture	London	Died
Club Culture Project	Edinburgh	3-year duration
Epicentre	London	Reborn, Moot
Graceland	Cardiff	Died
Grace	London	Tried
Host	London	Died
Late Late Service	Glasgow	Died
Resonance	Bristol	Reborn, Foundation
Sanctuary	Bath	Alive
Visions	York	Tried; plus planted Transcendence

This analysis is purely numerical, based solely on researching the longevity of communities over time. It is based on a sample size of ten communities.

The sample size can be increased by analysing *The Shaping of Things to Come* and *Threshold of the Future*. In *The Shaping of Things to Come* (2003), Australians Mike Frost and Alan Hirsch outlined their vision of what it meant to be a church in mission in a post-Christendom context. An early chapter, entitled 'Hope of Post-Christendom', presented six stories of new missional beginnings (pp. 17–33). An internet search suggests that 11 years on, three of these communities had closed. In the case of two of these communities, the closure also involved significant financial losses.[2] Of the three that were still alive 11 years on, one had taken a 'nap' for four years.[3] In *Threshold of the Future* (1998), New Zealander Mike Riddell presented a picture of a future of the church in a post-Christian West. A concluding chapter, entitled 'Models to hope on', offered stories of grassroots communities that Mike considered signs of hope (pp. 157–71). Of the five communities listed in that book, 11 years on, none were alive.

Grouped together, across Australia, England, New Zealand and the United States, 11 years on, of these 21 communities, 13 have tried and died. This is a try and die rate of 62 per cent. First expressions might have positioned themselves as signs of hope, but time suggests there are significant sustainability issues.

One of those communities – Graceway Baptist Church – was the community I planted. When it closed, I was deeply saddened. At the time, I was preaching a sermon series through the Old Testament minor prophets.

Then in the afternoon, we offered a discipleship event called 'Stoning the Prophets' as a chance to engage more deeply with the particular minor prophet. Those who chose to participate gathered in an upper room. In the middle was a pile of stones. After a welcome, a prayer of illumination was prayed. The entire minor prophet was then read aloud. Sometimes this was short: the entire book of Obadiah is 21 verses. Sometimes this was over an hour: the entire book of Hosea is 196 verses, Zechariah 210 verses. Once the prophet was read, individuals were invited to choose a stone from the central pile, to share a reflection from what they heard and then return the stone to the centre. Together we shared the Lord's Prayer and heard a simple benediction. It was a powerful experience which deepened engagement with Scripture.

That Sunday, the prophet was Micah. The words of Micah 6.8 became a particular comfort. 'What does the Lord require of you?'

A sustainable community like Graceway, my heart cried. Yet Micah writes to a nation under military assault from an aggressive and expanding Assyrian empire. Entire communities of people – the villages and towns of Israel – had been emptied and sent into exile (for example, Samaria in 1.2–7). Where was God? Could faith survive? In the midst of collective trauma, Micah speaks. God does not require sustainable communities but a life of justice, devotion and humility before God.

It might be that these early expressions are an aberration. A sample size of 21 is small, and perhaps the inclusion of more communities would change the percentages. First expressions are by definition ahead of their time, and perhaps their trail-blazing isolation decreases the chances of survival. It might be that from these early expressions lessons have been learnt, which in turn enhance sustainability. It might also be that the arrival of Fresh Expressions as an organization will provide greater resourcing, which could also enhance sustainability.

A mortality rate of 9.7 per cent was calculated by the Church Army's Research Unit (2013), which conducted qualitative research across ten dioceses. However, this figure was an overall percentage and was clearly impacted by significant internal variation. Fresh expressions planted between 2006 and 2012 had a mortality rate of 5.6 per cent, while those planted between 1992 and 1998 had a mortality rate of 23 per cent. Hence those initially planted (between 1992 and 1998) clearly affected the overall mortality rate.

The reality of try and die percentages can be extrapolated against the development of fresh expressions. This is undertaken in Table 6. A first column, with a sample size of ten, applies the 50 per cent from my research of first expressions communities in the United Kingdom. A second column, with a sample size of 21, applies the cumulative data from three sources (adding in *The Shaping of Things to Come* and *Threshold of the Future* to my first expressions research). A third column uses the Church Army Research Unit figures of a mortality rate of 23 per cent between 1992 and 1998.

Table 6: Numerical realities extrapolated

		50% try and die (10 first expressions extrapolated)	62% try and die (Cumulative extrapolated)	23% try and die (extrapolated from Church Army's Research Unit)
10 Dioceses in 2013	20,863 people; 518 communities	10,431 people; 259 communities	12,935 people; 321 communities	4,798 people; 120 communities
2013 data extrapolated 41 dioceses	85,538 people; 2,124 communities	42,767 people; 1,062 die	53,033 people; 1,316 die	19,674 people; 489 die
Leicester 2030 vision	320 communities	160 die	198 die	74 die
C of E pioneer 2027 vision	6,000 pioneers	3,000 experience try and die	3,720 experience try and die	1,380 experience try and die

Research from the Church Army Research Unit (2013, p. 31) concluded that among ten Anglican dioceses, there were 518 fresh expressions, with 20,863 people in attendance.[4] If in 11 years' time, half of these communities were to be closed (259), then 10,431 ordinary participants could be impacted. Multiplied across the entire nation of England, assuming a hypothetical equal uptake across all 41 dioceses, the Church of England would face the closure of 1,062 fresh expression communities, affecting some 42,767 people. What type of support might they need as they face a forced relocation of their faith? The Diocese of Leicester has a vision to establish 320 fresh expressions by 2030 (Fresh Expressions 2015). Will it matter if by 2040, 160 of them have tried and died? The Church of England has committed itself to having 6,000 pioneers by 2027.[5] How will 3,000 of them feel if they give their energy to something that in time will close?

These are hypothetical figures, intended to demonstrate that the risks inherent in mission have longitudinal consequences; that vision – for fresh expressions and training pioneers – has reality. Alongside these extrapolations, the Parable of the Lost Sheep reminds us that the one lost person matters more than the ninety-nine (Luke 15.3–7). Each individual in every try and die enters a space of risk and experimentation. They will pray, work and give. The closure of their communities is an ending of their dreams, which will generate significant pastoral implications and theological questions.

How do we place the reality of try and die alongside the claims that these fresh expressions are signs of hope, expressions of church that will be fresh, new ways of being God's people on the threshold of the future? Moynagh (2017) argues that sustainability of fresh expressions is a self-referential conversation, 'more about the church than the world'. However, practical and pastoral questions remain. Where will these people go? Will they return to the expressions of church they left? Or will they be like those in some of the communities, who articulated an experience of Christian discipleship that made them unwilling to return to their inherited expressions of church? Ecclesiologically, how might the church respond to the questions regarding worth, time and resource? How to understand the reality of try and die, given an articulation of Soskice's theology of birthing and becoming?

A theology of try and (almost) die: Epaphroditus as valuable

One way to approach these questions is by an imaginative thought experiment. Imagine that I was applying my longitudinal, 13-years-on, research methodology to a first expression, not from the UK, but from further back in history. Imagine that I decided to research the sustainability of first expressions of the Apostle Paul. I begin to map out a travel schedule by which I might visit communities in Corinth, Galatia and Philippi.

The reality is that these original first expression communities have also now closed. They lasted longer than the nine years that NOS lasted and the thirteen years that Graceway tried. But the communities planted by Paul have, in time, closed. Churches are not permanent.

Perhaps it is the shift to buildings and the use of stone in Western cultures that has resulted in the imagination of the church in the West assuming ecclesiology has a permanency. In reality, trying and dying lie at the heart of the early church. In theology, death and resurrection are central to ecclesiology. Paul's claims that the church of Corinth is *aparche* and *arrabon* (Greek), a first fruits (1 Cor. 15.20, 23) and a pledge or down payment (2 Cor. 1.22; 5.5), are shaped by his articulation of a gospel of life, death and resurrection. Christianity lives by a different story. Might this include ecclesiology? Should a permanency of ecclesial expression – an unbroken line of buildings that march into the future – be an aberration?

The Apostle Paul offers a theology of try and (almost) die in his letter to the Philippians. Paul writes of Epaphroditus, who has embarked on a mission, sent by the church to partner, to be a *leitourgos* (Phil. 2.25), a minister, with the pioneer Paul. 'Epaphroditus is equally an "apostle" with Paul, in that both men were commissioned and sent out with full authority to perform specific tasks of service' (Hawthorne and Martin 2004, p. 163). Sickness strikes ('he was ill and almost died', Phil. 2.27). One commentary suggests both homesickness and a nervous disorder (Martin 1976, p. 121).

It would be easy to perceive this narrative as a story of pioneering failure. Using the data collection methodologies of my research, if I was to return in 11 years' time to research the ministry of Epaphroditus, I would record a tried and died. I would also note the impact of his health on the pioneering ministry of Paul, who experienced increased anxiety (Phil. 2.28).

In response to this story of a pioneer leader where vision did not meet with reality, Paul provides a theology of 'tried and died'. First, the very fact that the story is recorded is itself an indication of Paul's theological impulse. Second, Paul not only tells the story, but offers a posture. 'Welcome him then in the Lord with all joy and honour such people' (Phil. 2.29). Martin offers a literal translation: 'regard them as valuable' (p. 122). This provides a posture towards those who try and die. It also provides a rationale for this book, for the longitudinal research is seeking to regard as valuable all those who experiment – individuals and communities – irrespective of their trajectory in ministry. A posture of valuing those who try and die also suggests a theology of partnership is needed, in which sending congregations, already established in ministry, welcome risk-takers, irrespective of the results.

It is significant that the posture in regard to Epaphroditus is recorded in Philippians, a community which meets the definition of being a first expression. As we shift from individual to community, an ecclesial presence made up of multiple strands is described.

A 'first expression' woven ecclesiology

Information about the community of Philippians as a first expression comes from two sources, one in the book of Acts, the other in the letter of Philippians. They have different genres – historical narrative and epistle – and authors – Luke and Paul. Working with both these sources, my argument is that the church needs to be understood not only as gathered, but also as faith developer, generation nurturer, leadership incubator and resource maker. Such an ecclesiology can be imagined as an ecclesiology of woven threads.

The book of Acts provides us with the birthing of a first expression. 'This narrative is an important one for Luke because it shows the mission's encounter with the Roman world' (Witherington 1998, p. 499). The city of Philippi was significant in a number of ways. First, geographically it was located on a boundary between two provinces. Second, culturally, Philippi is 'Rome in a microcosm' (p. 488), a city in which an overwhelming number (85 per cent) of written inscriptions are in Latin (Keener 1994, p. 369). Third, politically, the city was pronounced *ius italicum* by Mark Antony in 31 BC, giving citizens the privilege of Roman citizenship, access to Italian legal and property rights and exemption from poll and land taxes (Bockmuehl 2006, pp. 3–4). 'Luke is at pains to show that the Gospel and its followers can exist within the confines of the place of Roman authority by creating its own space "in house"' (Witherington 1991, p. 148). At Philippi, we are reminded that the gospel crosses boundaries and can take root in Roman cultures.

Missiologically, the narrative of Acts shows a partnership between guest and host. Paul's journey is guided by the Spirit (Acts 16.6) and initiated by a man from Macedonia (16.9–10). Paul seeks out those who pray on the edges of the city of Philippi (16.13) and experiences the hospitality of Lydia, who offers her home (16.15). 'It is hard to express the importance of the welcoming into a home for Christians in such a city ... if Christianity had such a venue it would likely ... not be seen as a dangerous foreign cult' (Witherington 1998, p. 487, n. 68). Paul is the recipient of hospitality, and in that offer of welcome and creation of space an ecclesial body is birthed at Philippi.

The letter of Philippians clarifies the becoming that follows a birthing. In four short chapters, one becomes aware of the complexity of the word 'church'.

An essential strand of the church at Philippi is the **gathering**, the regular worshipping life of the Philippians, presumably at which the letter from Paul to the 'saints in Christ Jesus who are in Philippi' (Phil. 1.1) was read. The 'church' at Philippi – to whom Paul extends 'grace and peace' (1.2) and for whom Paul 'constantly prays' (1.3) – has experienced not only a birthing in 'the gospel from the first day' but also a becoming as God's good work is being brought to completion (1.6). This gathering has evolved from the initial meetings on the riverbank in Acts to the baptisms of households and into a more regular pattern of worshipping life.

Another essential strand of the church at Philippi was **leadership**. These include Lydia (Acts 16.15), who helped birth the community as one who was 'sharing in the gospel from the first day until now' (Phil. 1.5). Epaphroditus is another named leader developed by the church at Philippi, who is sent on mission to give gifts to Paul (4.18). Euodia, Syntyche and Clement are named as 'co-workers' who have struggled beside Paul in the 'work of the gospel' (4.2–3). Co-worker is a distinctly Pauline term, which describes 'associates who work with him in his effort to get the gospel to these places where Christ's name has never been mentioned' (Hawthorne and Martin 2004, p. 163). As co-workers, these three named women and two named men emerge from the leadership incubator that is the church at Philippi. They, along with 'the bishops and deacons' (Phil. 1.1), co-participate with Paul in the mission of God. Philippi is a leadership incubator.

Another essential strand of the church at Philippi is the **faith development** of people. From the beginning in Acts, faith is developed across generations. This includes two households – those of Lydia (Acts 16.15) and the jailer (16.33) – who participate in the sacrament of baptism. There is also the slave girl (16.16). Ann Phillips locates her in relation to the faith development of teenagers and offers a reading of the slave girl in which she reflects on the significance of her spirituality in a time and place of transition and foregrounds the 'ecstatic' nature of her spirituality (Phillips 2017, p. 165). Phillips notes how the slave girl provides 'real insight into the identity of Paul and his companions', a 'revelation' that exceeds that of Legion who, in Mark 5.19–20, became a witness for Jesus (p. 165). Thus the encounter with Paul affirms the shape of her faith development and potential as a witness who like Legion might 'Go home to your friends, and tell them how much the Lord has done for you, and what mercy he has shown you' (Mark 5.19). Turning from Acts to the letter to the Philippians, we see faith development occurring as a 'good work' carried to 'completion' (Phil. 1.6). Faith development involves living a life worthy of the gospel (1.27), for the sake of witness, to 'shine like stars in the world' (2.15).

A further essential strand of the church at Philippi is **artefacts**. These are the material objects that circulate among communities, resourcing spirituality independent of the original gathered community, leaders and laity. In the case of Philippians, first there is the letter itself. Addressed initially to the church at Philippi, this letter as a material object is preserved. It is detached initially from the author – Paul – and then in time from the gathered community at Philippi. As a material artefact, it begins to circulate, shaping and guiding the worldwide church. A second example is the 'pre-Pauline hymnic composition' (Martin 1976, p. 93) that is Philippians 2.5–11. It is a 'hymn of the way' (p. 93), most likely sung by the church at baptism, 'a living medium for the development of christology in the early church' (Thurston and Ryan 2005, p. 78). As a piece of liturgy, it was most likely created by another community prior to Philippi, 'as a teaching tool that expressed christology' (p. 77). As a liturgical artefact, it is thus able to nourish the worshipping and catechetical lives of communities beyond the original creator. Hence the letter and the hymn are artefacts, creativity produced in relation to a community, yet as material objects able to resource ecclesial life more widely.

Finally, an essential strand of the church at Philippi is a sense of **ecclesial interconnectedness**. There is the interplay between the church at Philippi, in which Paul was so dramatically freed from prison, and the prison church Paul describes in Rome (Phil. 1.12–14). There is Timothy (2.19) whom Paul hopes to send as a messenger to embody the connections between Philippi and Rome. There is the sharing in Paul's mission in Macedonia, which the Philippians share through the gifts brought by Epaphroditus (4.15–18). Hence the church at Philippi embodies wider connections, an ecclesial interconnectedness distinct from gathered life.

This is a rich ecclesiology. Philippi is birthed as a first expression outside the city gates and experiences a becoming into gathered worship, leadership incubation, faith development, artefact creation and wider ecclesial interconnectedness. A permanency of ecclesial expression is found not in an unbroken line of buildings but in a gospel of life, death and resurrection, which forms worship, leaders and faith, and generates artefacts and a body-ing forth of wider ecclesial interconnectedness.

This provides a frame by which to consider the empirical research of this book. As we turn in this next section to consider the sustainability of first expression communities, including those who have tried and died, we have a theologically formed first expressions woven ecclesiology to use for analysis. Are there examples of leadership incubation, faith development, artefact creation and wider ecclesial interconnectedness? Might these communities, like the first expression of Philippi, try and die, yet still be 'regarded as valuable' because of a woven ecclesiology?

The lived reality of tried and died: sustainability insights

The quantitative research conducted by the Church Army's Research Unit (2013, pp. 96–9) revealed a range of reasons for mortality among those who try, with no generally recurring reasons. External factors could include moral failure, a new primary leader arriving with different ideas or the changing demographics in a local community. A range of internal factors were also noted. One reason was leadership transitions, whether the founder or key lay leaders. A second reason was a depletion of ideas, although the research found no correlation between mortality rates and resource-hungry types of first expressions (including alternative worship communities, among which the majority of my research was conducted). A third reason was a sense of a season naturally coming to an end. What the quantitative research did clarify was that there was no correlation between mortality and the size of the initial team or the type of first expressions being planted (of which they identified 18 (p. 99)).

Turning to my qualitative research of first expressions, factors that impacted on sustainability were a theme in many of the interviews. As these are discussed, the data will be de-identified. Factors that impact on mortality include mobility, leadership transitions, event management, batteries losing charge and wider connections.

First, **mobility** was a significant factor. Moynagh (2017, p. 376) observes that life 'contains more transitions than previously ... personal identities evolve and change more markedly than in the past'. Mobility can be geographic. For one first expression, 'people moved away [and] we didn't replace the always small numbers' (Group 7* 2013). In contrast, another group observed that 'it's quite counter cultural to commit to journeying together. We're geographically settled ... I've grown up with you all. You knew me at seventeen and now I've got a sixteen-year-old ... Something really important in that' (Group 5* 2013). Mobility is an increasing fact in contemporary life. Groups in which key participants retain employment in the area, or have stable domestic situations, are naturally more likely to be sustainable.

Mobility can also be generational. Many of these communities began among young adults. Sociologically, young adults are at an incredibly fluid stage of life. They face transitions in regard to study and work. They are at a stage of life in which travel is encouraged. This mobility raises significant contextual questions. Does it seek to continue to reach a specific age group, in this case young adults? Or does a community 'age gracefully' with those present, including making adjustments to their communal life? Both approaches were evident in the data. Interestingly, both approaches were also contributing toward sustainability.

For one community

some of the people ... have actually got families of their own, quite young children. We've always made sure they participate quite actively in the service and the services ... the feedback we consistently get is that in that context, the children have an integrated part in the worship they don't have in any other service they've been to around [the city] that theoretically does. (Group 6* 2013)

In contrast, for another community

A lot of people who were key [leaders] about five years ago now have kids ... go along to a nice, probably classical Anglican church with a crèche ... There's a nice sense in which they're still part of the [our] network, the emails still go out. It's another good way of holding people together. (Group 4* 2013)

What is important to note is that the communities being researched were trying to express Christian life in highly mobile settings, a factor which required attention in relation to sustainability.

Second, **leadership transitions** were also significant. Taylor and Nash note that times of transition were 'significant determinates' of sustainability in innovation (2018, p. 13). Leadership transitions can result from change in an external leader. If new leaders have a different focus or are perceived not to understand the particularities of the first expression community, instability results. Leadership transitions can also occur through changes in the personal circumstances of those within the group.

Communities in which key leaders transition, whether internally or externally, are incredibly fragile. When asked what enhanced sustainability, one leader of a failed first expression noted the need to train 'the next generation to lead it. Working with them to help them get my passion for people ... to come to Christ' (Group 1* 2013). The risks around leadership transitions are magnified in first expression communities, which can lack a shared history of navigating leadership transitions.

Third, **event management**. In highly creative communities, there can be a temptation to focus on the artistic at the expense of the organizational. To make the point negatively, here is the experience of one visitor to one of the communities I researched:

there was no indication at all outside ... as to how to get into the building – access was through a poorly lit door in the ... car-park which hardly seemed like public space – two car loads of participants from [a nearby city] never found the way in and returned home disgruntled. (Allen 2007)

To make the point positively, an analogy is helpful. Sustainable art galleries require curators producing fresh exhibitions, along with front-desk receptionists, a well-run cafe and well-maintained facilities. Sustainability of first expressions is enhanced by attention to event management, including communication, hospitality and organizational details.

Fourth, **batteries lose charge**. The depletion of energy that occurs with any initiative was accentuated by the fact these communities were first expressions. This is evident in the reflection from one group, who shared having 'no paid-up people involved and no official links ... we just guessed our way through ... didn't end in catastrophe, just fizzled out' (Group 7* 2013). For another: 'At the time we had no idea. The language didn't exist ... After 6 or 7 years ... I was absolutely exhausted. Worn out because of the pressure of being a Christian leader, intensified when no one else understood' (Group 1* 2013). What was instructive was that in spite of this depletion of energy, participation in a first expression was still considered a blessing. 'It was the price for being in the vanguard. It was prophetic. We shaped what is now happening' (Group 1* 2013). While the isolation of being a first expression took a toll over time, it was regarded as valuable. 'I feel a mix of gratefulness and delight. With wistfulness. But it was all in God's economy' (Group 1* 2013). Economy can imply wealth and saving. Here it is used to speak of God's creation and management of the world, in which birthing and becoming are a sacrifice:

> wherever in the world people give themselves to others or sacrifice themselves for others, these actions will also match the movement in God that is like a Son going forth on mission in response to the purpose of a Father; their acts share in the patterns of love in God, and so in them we can discern the body of Christ. (Fiddes 2012, p. 31)

Fifth, **wider interconnectedness**. In theory, one way to reduce the inevitability of energy depletion is to develop wider connections. Table 7 outlines the denominational affiliations of the first expression communities and provides some detail regarding the relationship.

Two of the first expressions did not have a denominational affiliation, both by choice (Late Late Service, Graceland). While these two did not survive, three of the communities with denominational affiliation also did not survive. Hence wider connections as a way of reducing the inevitability of energy depletion do not guarantee sustainability. In addition, during a number of interviews, a request for confidentiality was followed by a narration of ways that wider affiliations with a denomination could also drain energy.

Eight of the first expressions had some sort of denominational affiliation, six in connection with the Church of England, one in connection with the United Reformed Church and one in connection with the Church of Scotland. The affiliation was expressed in a variety of ways, including

- funding and accommodation but without relational connections (Club Culture Project)
- a building to use (Sanctuary, Visions, Foundation, Epicentre)
- being seen as a distinct congregation (Bigger Picture, Host, Resonance)
- being seen as a distinct entity within a church (Grace)
- being understood as a church (Moot).

Table 7: First expressions denominational affiliations

Name	Status 2013	Denomination	Type of affiliation
Bigger Picture	Died	Anglican	Distinct congregation within a church
Club Culture Project	Funded for fixed three-year term	Church of Scotland	'No one ... was part of the [C]hurch of [S]cotland.' (Pers. comm after interview)
Epicentre	Renewed as Moot	Anglican	Distinct congregation; renewed as church
Graceland	Died	None	No relationship with external church
Grace	Tried	Anglican	Distinct community within a church
Host	Died	United Reformed Church	Distinct congregation within a church, planted by paid clergy
Late Late Service	Died	None	Ecumenical project
Resonance	Renewed as Foundation	Anglican	Distinct congregation within a church; Paid clergy part of leadership team while Resonance
Sanctuary	Alive	Anglican	Provision of building
Visions	Tried; plus planted Transcendence	Anglican	Provision of building

We will return to the role of wider connections in ecclesial innovation in Chapter 12.

We have looked at lessons from churches that have tried and died. There are also lessons regarding sustainability from those communities still alive 11 years on, already discussed in Chapter 4, 'Tried'. Considering this data also allows us to capture the uniqueness of the experiences of Epicentre/Moot and Third Sunday/Resonance/Foundation. These two communities were categorized as alive, yet had each gone through dimensions of tried and died in relation to their names, identity and wider interconnectedness.

Sustainability equation

Comparing and contrasting between communities that remained alive and communities that tried and died suggests a sustainability equation:

Sustainability = sociological stability × evolving group identities × flexibility

The equation suggests that there is no simple reason for sustainability or mortality. Instead a number of elements are at play. Ecclesial becoming is indeed located in a range of relationships, of which three require particular attention. The concept of an equation is used to signify that a decrease in one area can be offset by intentional actions, whether in the same area or in another area. Hence becoming is placed as an active process, in which humans participate with the divine in the ongoing economy of God.

A first element of the sustainability equation is **sociological stability**. This is clearly evident in relation to mobility. For example, being located in a suburb of a city likely to attract graduates seeking work generates a different type of stability than being located in the city centre of a university town.

A leader returning after several years to a first expression in the city centre of a university town observed to me: 'It's totally changed again. There are only four people in that room who would remember me [from four years ago]. The rest have never met me' (Group 4* 2013). To retain the same numerical size, this group needed to attract ten new people over those four years. In contrast, some groups had a core group that was still present 11 years on.

However, intentional action could enhance stability. One community shared about the impact when a key member moved to teach overseas. The use of the internet allowed this person to continue involvement. Even at a distance, they contributed resources to the community, enhancing their individual faith formation and that of the community. Another first expression community maintained active connection while one of their group was at university, including encouraging her to start a similar type of community. When she found work in a nearby city, she returned to her sending first expression with increased confidence.

A second element of the sustainability equation is **evolving group identities**. While sustainability is greatly enhanced by healthy group dynamics, the dynamics are constantly evolving. The impact of an unhealthy dynamic was expressed by one interview: 'when a group is totally overtaken by a kind of reactive agenda ... cynicism and joking and humour and anger and protest are all to the fore. And you become inhospitable to an outsider ... [you] make no sense at all' (Group 4* 2013). Intentional action in this case involved inviting the group to reflect on the weaknesses inherent in their humanity.

While sustainability is greatly enhanced by gifted individuals, their strengths can also have a negative impact on dynamics. One group realized with hindsight how even with an espoused commitment to a flat structure, certain individuals had become more influential than others. Intentional action involved, first, a structural shift to a rotating leadership and, second, group work to articulate values. This provided 'a body of experience so that people aren't learning as they go along' (Group 3* 2013). Another group intentionally acted by providing an anniversary audit at which the values were revisited, considered in light of the evolving community life over the year. This enabled those new to the community to hear the founding story, while at the same time being able to contribute to evolving group identity.

Group identities are decidedly vulnerable during leadership transitions, particularly in first expression communities that have no corporate memory of working through a transition. Intentional action in the form of extra external and experienced support is essential. This could be provided by a denomination, particularly when an incoming leader is not familiar with first expressions. Equally a group not affiliated with a denomination could seek out a chaplain type figure, who might provide an external reference point. Reflecting on the tried and died interview data, including my own experiences articulated at the start of this chapter, would suggest sustainability is enhanced by an accompanier for periods of up to three years.

A third element of the sustainability equation is **flexibility in Christian practices**. It was revealing how many groups had, over the 11 years, acquired new resources, explored new structures of leadership, clarified identities and experimented with new patterns of prayer. This is perhaps consistent with being first expressions. It is also a reminder of the inherent flexibility required of any becoming.

The most intriguing example was Third Sunday/Resonance/Foundation. They began life configured around, and subsequently identified by, large events. Initially, when this declined, their sustainability was brought into question. They ceased large events and instead met weekly, around a simple pattern of prayer drawn from the Book of Common Prayer. This required far less energy, but it provided a gathering point for relationships and prayer. These were the 'embers' – 'low key mode, once a week, small numbers, Sunday night services' (Foundation 2013) – out of which Foundation grew.

When I observed this Sunday night worship, the Book of Common Prayer service was deeply infused by first expression values (articulated in Chapter 2, 'Birthing first expressions') including the value of participation as a community and the interplay between faith and culture. This included spontaneous interruptions that altered what was prayed, along with in-depth engagement with the biblical text, the like of which I have rarely observed in other Book of Common Prayer services in which I have participated. These were first expression embers, gathered in a sustainable pattern of prayer.

Intentional actions do not include a resorting to historic resources, in this case the Book of Common Prayer. Rather they include the commitment to flexible Christian practices based on a realistic assessment of the life of the group. Sustainability is enhanced by flexibility, in this case of Christian practices.

To conclude, there is no simple reason for sustainability or mortality. Instead I have outlined a sustainability equation:

Sustainability = sociological stability × evolving group identities × flexibility

Mobility, leadership transitions, poor event management, batteries losing charge and wider connections all impact on mortality. In response, the first expression communities took intentional actions. These included

- maintaining active connection, particularly the use of technologies to enable participation
- accentuating humanity in group formation
- structural shifts to rotate leadership
- articulation of founding story and community values
- annual values audit conversations
- seeking external support during leadership transitions
- flexible Christian practices
- undertaking realistic assessment of the life of the group.

These actions can be read theologically, as a becoming in which ecclesial life is sustained by human participation in the ongoing economy of God. However, a danger in clarifying lessons regarding sustainability is that permanency is elevated as a virtue and the gathered community viewed as the only indicator of ecclesial presence. The reality is that a woven ecclesiology understands church as not only gathered, but also faith developer, generation nurturer, leadership incubator and resource maker. What does 'regard as valuable' in relation to a woven ecclesiology look like when applied to first expressions?

'Regard as valuable': a woven ecclesiology applied

The first strand of a woven ecclesiology is the **gathering,** the regular wor-shipping life of the Philippians, at which the letter from Paul was read. As already noted, 50 per cent (five out of ten) of first expression communities from my research and 62 per cent (13 out of 21) from a wider study, no longer gather. Thus this strand of the woven ecclesiology is not visible. However, the significant insight emerging from the first expression that was the church of Philippi is that the church that is Philippi is now dead. If I was researching the sustainability of Pauline first expressions today, I would be unable to locate this worshipping community. Yet this community is still regarded as valuable by the church today.

A second strand of a woven ecclesiology is **leadership incubator.** One way to describe the first expression communities, whether dead or alive, is as being like 'vicar factories'. Maggi Dawn calculated that six people from a first expression she was part of were in time ordained. She also noted that following ordination, three of them were involved in 'semi-alt. communities' (13 April 2012, pers. comm.). Even though that first expression no longer exists as a gathering, they have offered a signifi-cant gift to the church more widely. There is thus a multiplying effect, in which the seed has indeed fallen into the ground and died. The original first expression has died. The result has been a harvest (John 12.24). This is the value in looking for a woven ecclesiology, rather than a gathered ecclesiology.

Similarly, Andrew Jones observes that

> although many of the emerging churches/fresh expressions/experimental ministries quite possibly did, in some sense, FAIL – and with that failure … the leaders and in many cases the leadership teams are still around, launching new expressions of church and mission that in many ways are more holistic, more sustainable both financially and in terms of man-power. [P]erhaps the focus should have been on the emerging leaders and not on their projects. (Jones 2014)

Why are first expression communities such vital leadership incubators? One reason is the expectation of participation. For one (now failed) first expression community, 'what was important was that from the moment a person arrived, they could be involved in shaping it. We were creating it together. That's because we were respecting people's spirituality, seeing it as God-given. It was their inner-life coming alive, in a Christian context' (Group 1* 2013). Such an ethos would provide many opportunities for leadership development.

It's influenced how I've grown up and it's influenced me as a person. It has ... given me parts of my character, who I am and made me realize some of my abilities and competence and leading skills and creativeness and things that I was quite shy about before really. I've just been given the opportunity to bring those and to use it in my Christian life. (Visions 2013a)

Another reason is the value of experimentation. Respecting an individual spirituality as 'God-given' suggests a willingness to find ways for the God-givenness of that spirituality to be expressed in worship. Worship is being shaped by the giftedness of those present. The result is a form of enquiry-based learning. What of the music I currently love might fit with the theme of this service? Could I use my graphic design or video editing skills to communicate this lectionary text? This is likely to result in a range of questions regarding the nature of worship and the meaning of biblical texts.

Thus a context of enquiry-based learning becomes a stepping stone towards more formal study, which is often provided by ordination tracks. Hence first expressions become leadership incubators.

A third strand of a woven ecclesiology is **faith development**. The first expression empirical research makes clear the extent to which these first expression communities were invested in lives. Communities were served, for example: 'we were gifted a city centre tenement flat – which we remade as a modern [friary] ... to serve the local club scene, which a bunch of us worked in' (Group 2* 2013). People came to faith, for example: '[m]y friends now I met through [this now dead first expression] and that's how they came to faith' (Group 1* 2013).

What is also clear is that the faith development that occurred in these first expression communities that failed has become a significant blessing for other communities of faith. A former participant of one of the first expression communities commented on how their participation 'transformed my life as I learnt how to seek God, and really build a personal relationship ... I'm now a trustee of a huge Pentecostal church in London ... Funny where God takes you, eh!' (Dorothea Hodge, pers. comm. in Taylor 2012). This was a repeated refrain. For example, '[A]ll of us have gone and pushed into stuff across a spectrum of life ... into pretty challenging areas' (Group 2* 2013). 'Looking back, I look at (almost) every individual who was involved and I see how God has moved you on in life. I see leaders who have gone on to do other things. Everyone has come out well' (Group 1* 2013). These first expression communities might die, but the disciples they generate move on to enrich other faith communities. This is a third strand of a woven ecclesiology.

A fourth strand of a woven ecclesiology is **artefacts,** material objects that circulate among communities, resourcing spirituality independent of the original gathered community.[6] In relation to the first expression communities I researched, artefacts included music, books and online resources. The Late Late Service produced music, including the *God in the Flesh* CD. The liner notes for the album encourage use and creativity. 'This is the 4th album of LLS music. You are free to use any of this music in a worship setting, although our aim has always been to encourage others to do their own thing, rather than becoming consumers of our thing' (Late Late Service 1994). Books like *Alternative Worship* (2003) and *The Prodigal Project: Journey into the Emerging Church* (2000) included interactive CD-ROMs, with rituals, images, music tracks, video loops and animations. Sue Wallace produced *Multi-Sensory Prayer* (2000), *Multi-Sensory Church* (2002), *Multi-Sensory Scripture* (2005) and *Multi-Sensory Worship* (2009), each offering photocopiable resources branded as fresh, innovative and imaginative. Grace provided labyrinths in a range of modes, including as a digital resource (www.labyrinth.org.uk/onlinelabyrinthpage1.html) and as a prayer resource distributed through Group Publishing in the United States. Jonny Baker, from Grace, was one of the creatives who developed Proost as a website (https://proost.co.uk/) to promote the work of poets, musicians, writers, visual artists and creatives. This is a fourth strand of a woven ecclesiology, which recognizes that, while a community might try and die, it can still provide an ecclesial presence through music, books and product that resources spirituality independent of the original gathered community.

A fifth strand of a woven ecclesiology is **ecclesial interconnectedness.** The analysis of first expressions in relation to leadership incubation as vicar factories points to wider church connections. Similarly, the production of artefacts provides ecclesial interconnectedness. Another dimension is that six of the individuals I interviewed, from six different communities, over time moved into significant wider church ministry roles with denominations, mission agencies or theological colleges. This is an important expression of wider church involvement, in ways similar to the first expression of Philippi sending Epaphroditus.

Hence the woven ecclesiology, present in the first expression of Philippi, provides a way to theologically read first expression communities that tried and died. As the research concluded, I found myself pondering 11 years into the future. Gatherings might cease, but the ecclesial value of first expressions as leadership incubators, faith formers, artefact creators and gifters of ecclesial interconnectedness reminds us of the true nature and richness of ecclesial life. Might it be that in time leaders that are incubated become bishops and principals of theological colleges?

Conclusion

And what of my own story, with which I began this chapter? How far might the woven ecclesiology of the church of Philippi and the empirical research from first expressions provide insight into the mortality of the community I planted and served for nine years?

Certainly, that church no longer meets for worship. As **church-as-gathered**, Graceway experienced closure. Regarding **leadership**, Graceway was my first pastoral role after I left theological college. It formed my leadership, profoundly shaped my habits and instincts in ministry. I took those gifts with me into an established church, with expectations generated over nearly 100 years of how ministry would be outworked. The instincts learnt at Graceway enabled me to challenge established patterns and kept me alert to mission opportunities. In preparing to transition out of Graceway, I observed three individuals within Graceway at that time who were themselves training for ministry, with Graceway as their primary context. In other words, this church was an incubator for leadership. In addition, at least four of those in leadership at Graceway in the year I left (2003) can still be found serving as ordained in other churches or mission communities. In conversation, each has indicated how formative their involvement in Graceway as a new form of church was.

A month after the church closed, the church sent a gift. It was the offering jar – hand painted pottery. Inside were letters of thanks from the individuals that made up Graceway as the church closed. All had found homes in other churches, enhancing the overall vitality of the wider body of Christ. A few years ago, I received a Facebook comment from one of the children raised at Graceway, naming those years as formative in her life.

The insights from this chapter are

- maintaining active connection, particularly the use of technologies to enable participation
- accentuating humanity in group formation
- structural shifts to rotate leadership
- articulation of founding story and community values
- annual values audit conversations
- seeking external support during leadership transitions
- flexible Christian practices
- undertaking realistic assessment of the life of the group.

They alert me to things that could have been done differently, intentional actions that might have sustained the becoming of Graceway.

The argument of this chapter is that a focus on church-as-gathered and church-as-growing is a deficient approach to ecclesiology. The woven ecclesiology in Philippians and the first expressions empirical data enable me to see Graceway differently. The empirical ecclesial reality is that trying generates a rich ecclesial life, in which birthing and becoming make a unique contribution to faith, leadership and ecclesial life, irrespective of the trajectories of the gathered community.

As Ecclesiastes 3 reminds us, there is a time for every activity. Seasons are part of life. In nature, Western cultures expect autumn mist, winter frost, spring winds and summer burn. While some cultures have four seasons, other cultures have more. The Bininj Kunwok people of the Goulburn Islands, in Arnhem Land, Northern Territory recognize six seasons. Kinyjapurr is the season of bushfire burning and new shoots. Wumulukuk is the season when flowers are blooming and wild honey and tiger prawns are in abundance. Walmatpalmat is the wet season and the time to enjoy wild plums, bush potatoes and turtle eggs. Can gathered church be seasonal? Can an ecclesiology of permanence – expressed in the expectation of an unbroken line of buildings that march into the future – be replaced by an ecclesiology of innovation that celebrates seasons? Can church synods include a liturgy of tried and died, in which the surprise inherent in death and resurrection is applied to ecclesial life?

That would ensure that all those who try and die are regarded as valuable, not because they sustain and succeed but because, like Epaphroditus, 'for the work of Christ' they 'risked' (Phil. 2.30).

Notes

1 Some of this story is told in Taylor (2005).

2 Elevation Cafe, Melbourne and The Millennia Project, Pomona. For more on Millennia, see http://ichthuspomona.blogspot.com.au/.

3 One Small Barking Dog, from 2007 to 2011. Quote from website, www.osbd.org/. Viewed April 2013.

4 Data was collected between January 2012 and October 2013, roughly the same time as my research. While the ten dioceses were selected to reflect variety in relation to context, the sampling was not representative.

5 Dave Male 2019, pers. comm.

6 Another way to understand artefacts is to apply the notion of spiritual capital as a form of cultural capital shaped by the same laws of accumulation, inheritance and exchange (Verter 2003, p. 152). Guest understands spiritual capital as a positive expression beyond self-interest, 'a liquid flow of ideas and values' that remain 'shaped by the traditions out of which they emerged, traditions that still steer their course, mould their practical expression and infuse the language in which they are affirmed, silenced or challenged' (Guest 2007, p. 198).

PART 3

Fresh Expressions

Rowan's dream, weaving
Wisely worded poet, gift
Centre edge re-made

To live, we die, fine
One bloom, a thousand dreams drop
Petals drift by bold

God kissed cultures past
Celts, Wesley, Carey, NGO dance
Mission bodies make

6

An apostle of Fresh Expressions: Rowan Williams's missio-ecclesiology and the birth of Fresh Expressions

I don't come to this task with a fixed programme or agenda.
(Rowan Williams 2002)

In 2004, three people crossed the Thames, seeking an audience with Rowan Williams. They came with a phrase, 'fresh expressions of church', to suggest a shared mission.[1]

> So a number of senior leaders [in the Methodist Church] literally went across the river from here, Methodist Church House to Lambeth Palace and said; 'We hear you are thinking of developing this team, this mission agency … could we partner with you in that' … Hence Fresh Expressions was born, from the outset as a joint initiative of the Archbishops of Canterbury and York and the Methodist Council, technically of the British Methodist Church. (A. Roberts 2013)

The phrase 'fresh expressions of church' had been named, in 2004, as a strategic priority by the Methodist Connexion.[2] In making this commitment, they were aware of the culture within the church,[3] and expressed their commitment to 'partnership with others wherever possible'.[4]

The clarity of 2004 was generated by a period of consultation, in response to the adoption, in 2004, by the Methodist Conference, of Our Calling. This identifying shared concerns for Methodism in contemporary Britain provided a process for review and encouraged the release of creativity.[5] It was a 'seminal moment' for Methodism in Great Britain (Roberts 2013). Having agreed to shared concerns, a period of consultation resulted in four priorities for the Methodist Church, one of which was to encourage 'fresh expressions of church'.

This chapter will examine the practical ecclesiology of Rowan Williams, the man the three Methodists had come to meet. As Archbishop of Canterbury, Rowan Williams would become a key influencer of Fresh Expressions. I will argue for a 'missio-ecclesiology', a distinctive ecclesiology that emphasizes catholicity and contingency and results in a missiology by which the edges of the church are essential in renewing the centre.

This chapter draws on an extended author interview with Rowan Williams, along with analysis of relevant public statements made by Rowan during his time as archbishop.

Twelve items were relevant. These included two press statements, three presentations to synod and seven addresses, from lectures, special services and public addresses. Interestingly, the material clustered around 2004, the year in which Fresh Expressions began.[6] This material will be read alongside Williams's theology, most particularly *On Christian Theology* (2000), *The Dwelling of the Light* (2003a) and *Ponder These Things* (2012, reprint). What becomes clear is that Fresh Expressions is a profoundly theological activity, in complete coherence with Rowan Williams's theological method. Williams applies 'missio-ecclesiology' not only in thinking theologically and acting organizationally, but also in the specific practices of his leadership as archbishop.

Rowan Williams

This is what I've been watching and what I've been seeing grow. I really want to see how that could impact on the Church of England as a whole. (Williams 2013)

In January 2013, I interviewed Rowan Williams at Magdalene College, Cambridge. Some nine months earlier, in March 2012, Rowan had indicated he would retire. As 2012 ended, he took up an appointment as Master of Magdalene College. Moving was still in process. Books, waiting to be shelved, were piled in various rooms. Rowan led me into his study, surrounded by icons, describing the internet issues caused by an energetic gardener putting a spade through a cable. It was a lovely blend of ancient and modern and an indication of how the interview would develop.

Rowan became archbishop with a track record of supporting innovation. Biographer Rupert Shortt (2008, p. 199) describes him as 'an ardent supporter of church plants – new, extra-parochial congregations – notably in Duffryn, part of Maesglas parish, and in Wyllie, a mining village in the benefice of Pontllanfraith'. Shortt also observed that Rowan was aware of how the church could both obstruct and yet influence innovation. 'Opposed by the local rector, this initiative was led by a laywoman, Marian Barge, whom Rowan later ordained deacon' (pp. 199–200).

Given the focus of this book is on sustainability, it is worth noting the state of these two communities, ardently supported by Rowan. There is evidence of sustainability through an ongoing creative worshipping witness. The Duffryn Community Church is featured in the *Monmouth Diocesan Newsletter* (Batt 2012, p. 3), with an article describing a creative Good Friday service, a form of Tenebrae that included the use of a labyrinth and projected images. Feedback from participants was positive and included comments like 'I felt the meditation was very modern without taking away the emotion of the journey – very moving' and 'A good way to spend Good Friday, giving time to think and pray.'

Wyllie was news for the BBC (2006):

> Islwyn Inn in Wyllie near Pontllanfraith has doubled as a place of worship since the Rev Marian Barge became the village deacon. While no services had been held in the village since the 1970s, Marian Barge, then a lay person, began a Carols service in the pub at the end of 2001, observing this is 'where the people are today – you have to go to them'.[7]

In a radio interview with Sue Lawley, on Radio 4's Desert Island Discs, Rowan was questioned about his strategy for the church. Rowan outlined the seeds of what would become Fresh Expressions.

> His strategy for arresting decline would focus on 'New Expressions' of church alongside the parish system rather than in competition with it. Go and open a community centre on an estate and see who comes, [Rowan] suggested. If pastors made themselves known and trusted in areas like that, the approach would pay dividends. (Shortt 2008, pp. 257–8)

From a purist perspective, Fresh Expressions is certainly about going to the community, although the emphasis would be on beginning by listening, serving and community building, rather than 'see who comes'.

Three themes were repeatedly evident in my interview with Rowan: the experiences of Wales, a theology of church and the patterns of leadership.

The experiences of ministry in Wales

Rowan Williams's discernment begins from the ground up. He describes, in *On Christian Theology* (2000, p. xii), his methodological starting point as 'always beginning in the middle of things'. He considers that the 'meanings of the word "God" are to be discovered by watching what this community does ... when it is acting, educating, or "inducting," imagining and worshipping'. Nicholas Healy points to a theological inconsistency in Rowan, observing that despite this call in *On Christian Theology* for theology to be attentive to what the community does, Williams chooses rather to attend to 'the written forms of a very limited group of Christians – saints and theologians – using them constructively to help our contemporary "common life and language" be more Christian' (Healy 2012, p. 184). However, it is precisely this method, 'in the middle of things', discerning by 'watching what this community does', that shapes Rowan Williams's convictions regarding the nature of the church in response to fresh expressions.

First, as Bishop of Monmouth, he observed new shoots in his parishes. These included a youth project in the council estates of East Cardiff, a healing centre in a valley parish and an informal afternoon worship service in a country parish. Observing these ('watching what this community does'), he discerned some patterns. First, a flexibility with regard to the time and pattern of worship, arising, concluded Williams (2013), out of pastoral sensitivity attuned to the 'natural affiliations and networks people had'. Second, a mutual, reciprocal movement. New shoots found themselves needing to be 'plugged into something' (Williams 2013). The inherited church experienced fresh life as they found themselves, to continue Rowan's colloquialism, being plugged into.[8] This caused a rethink in his ecclesiology (Williams 2013), in what he saw as 'possible for the church'.

Second, this experience, gleaned from observation among the communities in the Diocese of Monmouth, 'just being alongside people doing this stuff in Wales', shaped his priorities as he began as archbishop (Williams 2013). 'That meant that when I was asked initially "What are your priorities for Canterbury?" I said, "Well, this is what I've been watching and what I've been seeing grow. I really want to see how that could impact on the Church of England as a whole."' It was what Rowan saw, and his resultant discernment of what this meant to be the church, that sparked the development of Fresh Expressions. Fresh Expressions began with first expressions.

Thirdly, this experience shaped his communication as archbishop, as he spoke with clergy and on the topic of fresh expressions (Williams 2013). 'Whenever I spoke about this, I would begin by saying, "This is what I experienced as a bishop in Wales. This is what changed my perspective upon what is possible for the church."' Again, we see the place of experience, expressed now in narrative in the pursuit of change. To persuade, Rowan Williams begins 'at the ground level personal', with his experience of being changed, with the renewal of his ecclesiology.

Four threads are worth teasing out. First, the similarity between the theological method of Williams and that of *Mission-Shaped Church*, which has an entire chapter (Chapter 4, 'Fresh Expressions of church') that describes various forms of church.

This chapter has recorded a number of different styles or types of church that have emerged in the last decade. They are ways in which the Church of England has sought to engage with the variety of diverse cultures and networks that are part of contemporary life. They reflect our Anglican instinct to be 'how' and 'where' people are. (*Mission-Shaped Church* 2004, p. 80)

The entire chapter is based on 'watching' 'ways in which "church" is being expressed' (p. 43). While similar in method, both seem to have been developed independently, based on the interview with Rowan Williams (2013): 'I wasn't really aware of what was happening in England. I barely knew Graham Cray. Just a tiny bit. I didn't have any networks in England at the time really.' In other words, both draw on a practice of discernment of watching the church.

Second, this approach, of paying attention to the lived practices among new forms of church, would also be crucial in the development of the entire Fresh Expressions project. Steven Croft summarized his first year as Team Leader of Fresh Expressions as one of listening, travelling 'to every Diocese and Methodist District' (Croft 2013). This structured approach to the action of listening was repeated again several years down the track. 'So I would go to an area and invite maybe six or seven people together for an evening in a pub. We'd have a meal together and they would tell their stories to each other and to me' (Croft 2013).

Third, this approach will also find expression in the fresh expressions model. In the *Mission Shaped Ministry* course, fresh expressions is idealized as a four stage model. It begins, just as Williams did, with listening. It moves to serving, then to community building, then to discipling around the story of Jesus, before the evolution of contextual worship. In other words, both prioritize listening and relationships.

In sum, Fresh Expressions begins with first expressions. It is based on a clear and distinct theological method. This is consistent with Rowan's observation (2002), at his first press conference, that the gift he is most likely to bring to the role is that he is a 'theologian by training'. There is no evidence of it being rooted in concern about the decline of the church, a desire for managerialism and restructuring or a search for relevance. Rather, by deciding to be located 'in the middle of things', in the life of churches, and by a practice of discernment which 'watches' ecclesial life, an innovation has taken shape.

This method, of discernment from the ground up, raises two questions, one regarding the nature of Williams's ecclesiology, the other regarding his practice of leadership.

A theology of church

When I interviewed him about his discernment,[9] Rowan Williams appeared to draw upon a missio-ecclesiology, although with an emphasis more on the ecclesiology than the missiology.

Regarding mission, Rowan Williams spoke of looking at the new shoots in order to uncover 'the capacity to make some sense of the gospel to people who have no cultural affiliation with church'. At his first press conference (2002), he described the growth in his ecclesiology, specifically shaped by his experience in mission and ministry. 'Recent experience in Wales ... has taught me a great deal about how the Church engages with and serves the life of a whole national community.' This experience includes both fresh expressions and 'the Church's relation with government at every level'. This provides an important corrective to the notion of an ecclesio-centrism in which the church exists for numerical growth, rather than the shalom of the kingdom.

Discernment is shaped by his understanding of the life and ministry of Jesus. In Rowan Williams's words (2002), 'the way Jesus' conversations and encounters map out in the gospels'. This includes baptism, in which he 'maps' a missional ecclesiology.

> Baptism brings you into the proximity of Jesus. You go down where he is under the water so to speak. And when you're in the proximity of Jesus you are in the proximity of the people he is in proximity to. And who are those people? Well they're the ones who get left out. (Williams 2013)

The life of Jesus was lived in proximity to those on the margins. Hence a way to discern a fresh expression is to notice the ways they 'make some sense of the gospel to people who have no cultural affiliation'.

What is intriguing is how Williams locates this in baptism, not in ecclesial roles. By inference, it means that all who are baptized are expected to participate in this mission of God. What Williams did, as bishop and as archbishop, in paying attention to the edges of the church, to those working in places with 'no cultural affiliation with church', emerges as a consequence of his baptism. It is a vocation for all the baptized. Further, when considered corporately as well as individually, fresh expressions are in fact giving proximity, enabling an inherited church, one with no edge, to attend to cultural affiliations.

One way to theorize this is in categories in which God is the One who 'makes room in God's self for us to dwell' (Fiddes 2012, p. 27). This takes fullness of expression in the Incarnated One, who in incarnation, resurrection, then ascension makes room in God's self for humanity to dwell.

By imitation, and by ontology, the church being the body of Christ, it is invited to make room in itself for those 'people who have no cultural affiliation with church'.

Hence Rowan Williams's missiology becomes a missio-ecclesiology. For Rowan Williams (2013), 'the second thing comes in quite importantly. It's to have a theology of the church.' This arises because of a desire for a mutuality in relationships. The edge needs the church, in order to be more fully the church. 'It's looking at these groups understanding that they need to be rooted in something more than just a charismatic personality, more than just a successful programme.'[10] Equally, the church needs the edge, in order to be more fully the church. 'A theological reading of church history might suggest that the church always gets renewed from the edges rather than the middle.'

His ecclesiology is shaped by two postures. First, in a provisionality. 'Every particular way we crystallize [the church] is going to lack something.' The church 'is not captured by any one institutional expression … Of course it changes. And of course it's diverse. Always has been' (Williams 2013). In his address to the 2003 General Synod, he noted that 'the Church is renewed (as it so often is) from the edges, not the centre' (Williams 2003b). Although not expressed, there was a sense of an eschatological horizon in which the very prayer 'Thy Kingdom come, Thy Will be done', is a realization of the need for the church to proclaim faith afresh.

Second, an attention to the rear-view mirror, to church history. 'The history of the Church of England, the history of the whole church, is a lot more diverse than we think' (Williams 2013). For Williams, church history reveals a diversity of expressions of church. Again, although not expressed, this suggests an eschatological horizon in which the God who acted the same yesterday, might act, afresh and in diversity, today and forever.

This missio-ecclesiology found expression in Williams's understanding and practice of leadership.

Fresh expressions of church? Or mission?

It leaves one question, regarding the relationship between church and world. To put it simply, is Rowan Williams's theology overly church-centric? He concluded his first synod presidential address by hoping that the synod would 'be newly aware of what God is already doing in our Church' (Williams 2003b). There are a number of places to seek discernment, including with individuals within the church and within the world.

Let us consider this through a Trinitarian lens.

Regarding Jesus, while Christ is the body of the church, he is also the wandering one, inviting his disciples on a journey. At times he is ahead of his disciples, at times behind, in a disruptive rhythm in which they are always confident that they have yet more to learn. He invites his followers to consider creation, the birds of the air and the lilies of the field to reflect upon the signs of the times (Matt. 7.26, 28; 18.3). All of this points to the importance of discernment in places other than only the church.

Regarding the Spirit, Anglican theologian Sarah Coakley (1998) argues that in our understandings of God, the Spirit is primary. She argues this on the basis of Romans 8:22–27:

> We know that the whole creation has been groaning in labour pains of childbirth until now; and not only the creation, but we ourselves, who have the firstfruits of the Spirit, groan inwardly while we wait for adoption, the redemption of our bodies ... the Spirit intercedes for the saints according to the will of God.

Discernment is present in the groans of both creation and those who are first fruits. Hearing both becomes a participation in what God is already doing. Such listening assumes an 'incorporative pneumatology' (Rogers 2009a, p. 44) in which the Spirit is at work in all creation, in spaces and places both inside and outside the ecclesial. Put simply, we are invited to be aware of what God is doing in both the world and the church.

Theological activity

Finally, let me note a number of consistencies between Rowan's theological method and fresh expressions. This adds further weight to the argument that fresh expressions and Fresh Expressions are in fact intentional acts of missio-ecclesiology.

Having argued that theology needs to be 'always beginning in the middle of things ... watching what this community does ... when it is acting, educating, or "inducting," imagining and worshipping' (2000, p. xii), Williams then proposes a threefold typology of theological activity.

First, a celebratory style. For Rowan, this type of theology is nourished and nurtured in the language of hymn and prayer. Examples include the theology of the Psalms, the sermons of Gregory of Nyssa, the icons of Orthodoxy and the writings of Hans Urs von Balthasar. Theological activity as celebratory occurs because of the intention not to argue but rather to 'evoke a fullness of vision – that "glory"' around which theology circles (Williams 2000, p. xiv).

Second, a communicative style. 'Theology seeks also to persuade or commend, to witness to the gospel's capacity for being at home in more than one cultural environment' (p. xiv). Examples include Clement or Origen, engaging Stoic and Platonic thought with 'enough confidence to believe that this gospel can be rediscovered at the end of a long and exotic detour through strange idioms and structures of thought' (p. xiv). Or more recently (for Williams), the use of Marxist categories in liberation theology and theological readings of feminist theory.

Third, such experimenting often leads to a degree of crisis. As Williams (2000, p. xiv) describes it, 'is what is emerging actually identical or at least continuous with what has been believed and articulated?' This becomes the critical style of theological activity, a self-reflection on continuity and coherence. It can be conservative or revisionist and has two ultimate directions, one a nihilism, the other a rediscovery of the celebratory.

Are these three styles of theology present in fresh expressions? Williams observes that each of these styles of theological activity has a different public. **Celebratory** is for a believing public. **Communicative** is for those to whom Christianity, in both vocabulary and grammar, are strange. **Critical** often occurs within the academy. Certainly, a consistent pattern in fresh expressions is **celebratory** activity. Williams notes that the problem with a celebratory approach is how, over time, it becomes so 'densely worked that the language is in danger of being sealed in on itself' (2000, p. xiv). Experimenting with hospitality and film, making friendship bracelets in a Trinity Sunday service, a conversation between the origins of punk music and the Old Testament prophets, the remixing of ancient forms with modern beats and contemporary lighting, all of these can be viewed as celebratory theological activity motivated by a desire to overcome liturgy 'sealed in on itself' (p. xiv). Hence, fleshing out Williams's typology of theological styles, fresh expressions is a profoundly theological activity.

Williams posits an ordering, seeming to suggest that **celebratory** leads to **communicative**, which leads to **critical** and so 'the cycle begins again'. Williams (2000, pp. xv, xiv) does not view this ordering as a kind of hierarchy, but rather a mobility brought about by an 'essential restlessness' in Christianity. This provides another way to understand fresh expressions, that the Spirit of God has been 'restless' in the dawn of a new millennium.

In sum, this section has argued that fresh expressions and Fresh Expressions are not only theological, but exist in complete coherence with Williams's theological method. This is evident in his missio-ecclesiology and his attentiveness to the celebratory–communicative–critical.

By initiating Fresh Expressions, Williams set in train a process by which a **critical** style of theological activity would become not simply a conversation within individual communities and between individual critics within a denomination. It became catholic, allowing the wider church to conduct a critical conversation. To quote Steven Croft:

the Church of England … was such an inherited organization that … you didn't think about ecclesiology at all. You just imbibed it … until 2000, the Church of England has done its ecclesiology in ecumenical dialogue. And really hadn't affected practice at all. Suddenly [with Fresh Expressions], it began to … deal with ecclesiology in mission dialogue and that raised a whole different set of questions. (Croft 2013)

This is coherent with a theology that begins 'in the middle of things'. It is an important part of being one, holy, catholic and apostolic.

In doing this, it is important to note Rowan's intention, in *On Christian Theology*, that this typology, 'allows for some clarity about appropriate methods but does not embargo the delivery of believing utterances until the methodology is wholly clear' (2000, p. xiii). There is something both refreshing in the willingness to act, educate, induct, imagine and worship, while still engaged in theological reflection. It is consistent with the development of Fresh Expressions, as noted by Steven Croft.

A pattern for leadership

In moving to be archbishop, Rowan Williams was moving into leadership. He understands this also in missio-ecclesiological terms, 'If you're very much in the middle, then your responsibility for attending to the edges is intensified' (2013). It is a rich, challenging perspective on leadership, a practical, embodied outworking of his missio-ecclesiology.

It is evident in how time is allocated. As bishop, Williams considered he had endeavoured 'to spend a certain amount of quality time with people on the edge, in and out of worship' (2013). In his first press conference as archbishop, Williams noted how much he had 'valued conversations over the years with those rather on the edges of the church' (2002). As archbishop, regular diocesan visits were designed to include time with those on the edges of the church.

A sort of regular, routine part of how I've done archbishopping has been, two or three times a year, to go to a Diocese. To spend three or four days there … I built this in every time, some engagement with the new or experimental that's going on in Diocese. And sometimes that's meant bishops or others discovering there's more going on than they realized. (Williams 2013)

It also seemed to shape how Fresh Expressions engaged with voices both absent and critical. With regard to absent voices, Williams offered the following: 'as [Fresh Expressions] evolved once again it became quite important to say, this is ... something about the church itself. It's not a kind of tribal slogan for this bit of the church rather than that' (2013) Because of missio-ecclesiology, because this is 'about the church itself', deliberate attempts were made to bring voices not present into the conversation. Practically, this involved conscious attempts to build relationships and create conversations of breadth and inclusion.

With regard to critical voices, Williams was gladdened by the way that he perceived the leadership of Fresh Expressions responding with engagement, not defensiveness, when concerns were raised. 'Yes, we have heard those anxieties. And they're not stupid. But now come, let me walk you around a couple of projects and see what it looks like on the ground. And then perhaps we can see where we go with it' (2013). This is a leadership that listens ('we have heard'), that builds relationships, without outcome ('we can see where we go with it'). It is important to note that once again, we have an 'experience' methodology at work ('let me walk you around a couple of projects and see what it looks like on the ground').

Conclusion

This returns us to where we began. This chapter has considered the theology of a key influencer of Fresh Expressions. The birthing of Fresh Expressions was portrayed as a top-down, archbishop-initiated, response to a ground-up process of discernment about what it means to be church. I have argued that this is the result of a clear theological method, a missio-ecclesiology emerging from that method, embodied in practices of leadership. There are levels of consistency between theology and practice in the birthing of Fresh Expressions. Once begun, how did this innovation develop through an ecclesial system? How did it body forth? Addressing these questions is the task of the next chapter.

Notes

1 'The phrase now used in the priorities – fresh expressions of church – better expresses the commitment both to new ways of being Church and to the refreshment and renewal of the traditional. Indeed one of the urgent challenges is the networking between the two, to mutual advantage' (*Priorities for the Methodist Church* 2004, 5.4 vi p. 9).

2 'The five priorities were: Underpinning everything we do with God-centred worship and prayer; Supporting community development and action for justice, especially among the most deprived and poor – in Britain and worldwide; Developing confidence in evangelism and in the capacity to speak of God and faith in ways that make sense to all involved; Encouraging fresh ways of being Church and

Nurturing a culture in the Church which is people-centred and flexible' (*Priorities*, p. 1).

3 'People with energy, enthusiasm and vision, who want to experiment and take risks in developing new forms of worship and mission, regularly report that the traditional church structures are fearful of change or discouraging, curled in on themselves and able to consider only the faithful maintenance of the way things have always been' (*Priorities*, 5.4 ii, p. 7).

4 'In respect of "ecumenical partners", much reference is made to developing rapidly and consistently the implications of the Anglican-Methodist Covenant signed with the Church of England on the 1st November 2003. The joint pastoral strategy with the United Reformed Church is also important' (*Priorities*, 5.4 i, p. 7).

5 'Our Calling: The Church exists to: increase awareness of God's presence and to celebrate God's love; Help people to learn and grow as Christians, through mutual support and care; Become a good neighbour to people in need and to challenge injustice; Make more followers of Jesus Christ' (*Priorities*, p. 1).

6 Available at http://rowanwilliams.archbishopofcanterbury.org/ [viewed April 2014]. Single items were from 2002, 2003, 2005, 2009, 2011, 2012. Two items were from 2010 and five items from 2004.

7 Marian is also mentioned in relation to ministry to schools in *Monmouth Diocesan Newsletter* (2011, p. 3).

8 'My vivid memories, a lady from one of the very, very poor, very depressed valley parishes. Which five years earlier had been on the verge of closure. Lucky to get into double figures. They'd had a big revival ... And an elderly lady from that parish. Typical valley's lady. Getting up and saying, I never thought I'd be talking in public like this but, let me tell you what things he has done for my soul. This is what we've been doing' (Williams 2013).

9 The specific question was: 'What was the discernment process by which you decided these things were worth investing in?'

10 For Williams, this was both a conviction but also (again) his experience as Bishop. 'Here were all these rather marginal and unusual people in the church coming and saying, "I want to be connected somehow"' (Williams 2013).

7

Birthing Fresh Expressions as an organizational innovation

Reality and theology belong together. Fresh Expressions was an innovation within an organization, a structured attempt to nurture the grassroots innovations that were first expressions. It was a birthing and a becoming within an existing ecclesial body – birthed in response to the already birthing of first expressions – a re-form-ation that sought to nurture further birthing and becoming.

As an organizational innovation, as a 'hazelnut' of particularity, it is deserving of contemplation. The activity of God can be considered 'In this little thing … God made it … God loves it … God preserves it.' In the empirical reality, what are the 'hermeneutic discoveries'? How does an organization – a denomination – seek to partner with grassroots innovation? What might other organizations seeking to innovate through re-form-ation learn from the birthing and becoming of Fresh Expressions?

Groups under pressure can be tempted to look for simple solutions. A common belief is that one silver bullet, fired by one golden person, will bring about the needed change. So the search begins for the one leader packed with the requisite dynamism and energy. Peter Cammock (2003, pp. 29–30), a lecturer in leadership at the University of Canterbury, Christchurch, Aotearoa New Zealand, offers a very different approach. Leadership is based not on a silver bullet, but on three commitments: first, the ability to awaken parts of a person previously dormant, second, the willingness to serve, and third, the ability to listen and respond.

This has three important implications. First, given it takes time to awaken, to listen, to journey, to serve, the focus shifts from a silver bullet to a process. Second, the focus on actions, of awakening, listening, serving, suggests that change is a verb rather than a noun. We look for the actions, over time, that when practised bring about innovation. Third, given that acts of awakening, listening and servicing involve a range of people, who contribute different strengths and at different times, leadership in change is actually plural, not the singular silver bullet fired by a golden – dynamic, charismatic – person.

Each of these three implications is evident in Scripture. In the words of

Paul (1 Cor. 3.4–6), 'For when one says, "I follow Paul," and another, "I follow Apollos," are you not mere human beings? I planted the seed, Apollos watered it, but God has been making it grow.' As Paul reflects on the 'hazel-nut' that is the Corinthian church, the focus is on the process, of growth over time. The contemplation is of actions, in this Scripture the verbs of planting and watering. Leadership is understood as shared, coming not from one person, but located in Paul, Apollos and the Corinthians.[1]

This chapter will trace the development of Fresh Expressions as an organizational innovation. I will consider process, using a Leadership Strengths framework for analysis. I will focus on actions located in the empirical realities. This chapter will draw on interviews with key pioneering influencers, including Bishop Steven Croft, Bishop Stephen Cottrell, Revd Andrew Roberts and Archbishop Rowan Williams and examine the role of two objects (*Mission-Shaped Church* and Fresh Expressions DVD).

The contemplation of the 'hazel-nut' that is lived ecclesial reality provides insight into the activity of God. In turn, the insights invite growth. In particular, this chapter invites growth by reflecting on the absence of female voices in the development of Fresh Expressions. As part of inviting growth, a number of feminist theological resources will be considered. What might it look like in the birthing and becoming of ecclesial innovation to value women's experience, create relational spaces, foreground imagination and value silence and paradox.

Leadership Strengths as a frame

In order to focus on process and actions in the birthing and becoming of ecclesial organizational innovation, a Leadership Strengths model will be utilized.[2] The Leadership Strengths model was developed by the National Church Life Survey (Australia). It draws on large-scale longitudinal quantitative research in Australia since 1991.[3]

The Leadership Strengths model theorizes that 12 strengths are needed for effective change. These are as follows:

- Listen: deeply.
- Connect: build mutual connections.
- Envision: together.
- Explore: options creatively.
- Inspire: heart commitment.
- Empower: people to contribute.
- Structure: create clear positive structures.
- Communicate: develop reliable communication.

- Optimism: build a culture of optimism.
- Act: move to action.
- Resolve: maintain through challenges.
- Learn: and grow from experiences.

Each strength as an action contributes to a process, depicted in Figure 6.

Figure 6: Leadership Strengths

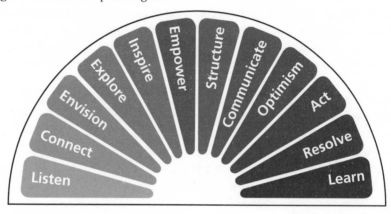

The research found that individuals tend to be strong in three or four of these areas. The research thus critiqued the one-silver-bullet-fired-by-one-golden-person approach to change. Instead, a plurality of leadership is needed in an innovation. The focus on actions supports Cammock's argument that leadership is a verb. The implication is that leadership can be learnt. While individuals can contribute from their strengths, they can also commit to contribute by acting in areas they are weak in, acting for the sake of the whole.

Telling the Fresh Expressions story using this frame enables us to pay attention to the plurality of leadership in the innovation that was Fresh Expressions. While the previous chapter focused on the theology of Rowan Williams, this chapter widens the focus by paying attention to the birthing and becoming of an organization over time. This chapter will demonstrate that, for example, Archbishop Rowan Williams brought strengths in listening deeply, Bishop Graham Cray brought strengths of envisioning, Bishop Steven Croft brought strengths in strategy and resolve, Norman Ivison contributed strengths in communication and the Lambeth Partners gave structure and acted to ensure learning.

Hence the use of the Leadership Strengths model allows Fresh Expressions to be analysed as a 'first expression', a systemic innovation across a denominational system. This de-mystifies birthing and becoming. Innovation becomes a set of actions, taken by a range of people in a process over time, rather than a silver bullet fired by a hero leader. In addition, a number of insights into systemic ecclesial innovation are clarified. These include the importance of diverse gifts embodied in diverse people, the significance of materiality and the value of poetic language.

Leadership Strengths and the innovation that is Fresh Expressions

This story begins with Archbishop Rowan Williams, who **listened** deeply. This has been observed in the previous chapter. It is obvious in his work as Bishop in Monmouth, as he listened to the edges, listened to God and in this discerned that God was at work, calling forth new ways and understandings of being church.

Listening deeply was also how Bishop Steven Croft would begin. He spent his first year as Team Leader of Fresh Expressions travelling 'to every Diocese and Methodist District' (Croft 2013). His aim was to listen to practitioners. This structured approach to the action of listening was repeated again several years down the track. 'So I would go to an area and invite maybe six or seven people together for an evening in a pub. We'd have a meal together and they would tell their stories to each other and to me' (Croft 2013).

Listening deeply was evident in an object, a book, *Mission-Shaped Church* (2004). Bishop Steven Croft (2013) observed that the book 'had done what the report said it did, which was listen, describe what was happening'. A key element in *Mission-Shaped Church* is the way it told stories of God at work, in the creation of new ways of being church. The use of a storytelling methodology ensures a project begins with listening.

As a result of this initial listening by Archbishop Rowan Williams and through *Mission-Shaped Church*, two people began to **envision** together something new. For Williams: 'I still remember sitting in my study in Canterbury with Graham [Cray] and saying, "Oh, I've been thinking of this, that and the other." And Graham ... handing me over the report' (2013). Thus the acts of listening – by Archbishop Rowan Williams as Bishop in Monmouth and in *Mission-Shaped Church* – shaped the envisioning.

Williams described this **envisioning** as the actions of searching for an 'unlocking' project: 'a very specific project ... something that can unlock what we're talking about ... that's got to be quite focused ... well-resourced ... medium term, not just a flash in the pan' (2013). The act of envisioning has a strategic dimension, focused on unlocking the organization that is the church.

Envisioning is a process, and this is evident in the role played by ecclesial meetings. For Williams: 'What you need is ownership ... you get that through synods and the bishops. So that got us going on getting the [*Mission-Shaped Church*] report discussed in synod and preliminary discussions in the house of bishops' (2013). It is tempting, particularly among grassroots innovations, to become cynical about church meetings. However, if structured carefully, meetings offer space in which envisioning conversations can be encouraged. In the case of Fresh Expressions, the envisioning involved structuring time for conversations about new ways of being church in mission. This engaged church leaders with the listening documented in *Mission-Shaped Church* (2004) and invited their consideration of the implications for awakening of the wider church.

Already, even after discussion of two (listen, envision) of the twelve strengths, a pattern is emerging in which the development of Fresh Expressions is due to a range of people and objects, each working together to achieve a greater degree of effectiveness.

Connections deepen engagement and nurture conversations. This is clear when we compare the type of conversations we have with friends in contrast to conversations at the check-out counter. Connections are cultivated through care, commitment and time. With regard to Fresh Expressions, connections were built in a number of ways.

One was structural, the deliberate use of a position of influence. Williams observed, 'I'd have to say also, although it's an awkward thing to say, in terms of ownership, the fact that Archbishop Rowan Williams says he thinks it's a good idea is probably a factor' (2013). A leader is invariably asked about their priorities. Williams used that curiosity as part of building **connections** to Fresh Expressions. Consider the following example. Visiting Singapore, the role of Archbishop Rowan Williams had positional influence. It attracted media attention, and the archbishop was asked about the most critical things he wanted to focus on. His response was to point to Fresh Expressions (2007): 'In the Church of England, the biggest most positive focus is the project that we call *Fresh Expressions* … That's constantly in my mind, in my prayer, that's what I want to focus on.' The archbishop used the media attention to create connections to Fresh Expressions.

A second connection came in the person of Bishop Steven Croft, who as a theological educator provided connections into training institutions.

> appointing a theological educator to the role … [who] knew the inside of theological education … the two worlds of the missioner and the training for ministry are quite separate worlds within the Church of England and missioners don't find it very easy to access the formal world of theological education. So actually having that set of skills was really, really important. (Croft 2013)

This echoes the intentional **envisioning** of the search for an 'unlocking' project, with a careful reading of the organizational dynamics inherent in a denomination, seeking to enhance **connections** through careful recruitment.

A third dimension in the building of mutual **connections** was what Bishop Steven Croft described as grace.

> A whole range of mission agencies … just said, 'We want to be part of this. We don't want to pursue our institutional agenda.' … They just all said, 'Let's make this work. This is a particular moment of opportunity.' There was great grace in that really … Which I think was of God but also depended on lots of people being generous to it. (Croft 2013)

The grace described by Bishop Steven Croft involves connections. Time is taken to connect with mission agencies and in return, the participation of each agency builds the capacity for innovation.

A fourth dimension of mutual **connections** came through the ecumenical DNA laid at the beginning. This demonstrated a commitment to connections that were inclusive and generous. The willingness to connect ecumenically built capacity, including enhancing theological riches and missiological resources. Andrew Roberts believed that the Methodists added a number of distinctive dimensions to Fresh Expressions. Specific examples were, first, 'Methodist Connexional Ecclesiology … one of mutuality and sharing together', second, the 'identification of support and release of lay leadership'[4] and, third, discipleship, given that 'there are things within Methodist history and practice … the whole class meeting system it's taught in MSM for example' (A. Roberts 2013).

Innovation in inherited systems of church is not easy. The 'separate worlds' of an institutional culture and a 'range of mission agencies' can be overcome by the building of **connections**. In the innovation that was Fresh Expressions, this included the leverage provided by utilizing positional leadership influences, the strategic appointment of people into recognized roles and the increasing of capacity through collaboration. In each case, connection is possible as people **listen** deeply and conversation is used to *envision* shared futures.

Inspiration came from two sources. Again, Archbishop Rowan Williams was an important factor. Inspiration came through his positional power, mixed with his own piety and theological reputation. Regarding positional power, for him to state, as archbishop, that 'the biggest most positive focus' was Fresh Expressions provides a positional inspiration which is enhanced by piety – 'constantly in my mind, in my prayer'. Regarding theological reputation, a reflection by Bishop Stephen Cottrell is insightful:

[Archbishop Rowan Williams] giving it theological credibility has had a huge impact. Because there are some people who, rather sniffily, want to refer to all this as the shallow end of the church. And you can accuse [Archbishop Rowan Williams] of many things. But shallow isn't one of them. And so when he's on your side adding real heavyweight theological credibility to what you're doing, that helps enormously. (Cottrell 2013)

It is tempting to locate inspiration in relation to charisma. Here inspiration is provided to Fresh Expressions through theological credibility.

Inspiration also came from first expressions, in particular as they shared from their grassroots innovations in mission. Bishop Steven Croft describes the personal impact of meeting leaders of first expressions from around the United Kingdom and his experience of their passion for mission, their trust in God and the depth of their engagement in the community as being Christlike. 'These are truly inspiring and wonderful people and it's humbling to spend time with them' (Croft 2013). The inspiration of personal impact was similarly important in relation to the training of leaders, in particular the providing of ordained pathways for pioneering leaders in first expressions. Croft made the following observation in relation to a Senior Selection Secretary for the Ministry Division. 'And the thing that converted ... was meeting candidates ... they were brilliant candidates, God genuinely was calling them and the church needed them. And from that moment [Senior Selection Secretary] was turned from a sceptic to an advocate for pioneer ministry' (2013). Again we see the inspiration embodied in lives, in the Christlikeness of those in fresh expressions. This 'Christlike' inspiration was also an important factor in engaging with the Lambeth Partners. 'We started to make some headway with Lambeth Partners presentations when we brought in practitioners to tell their stories ... it was the Christlikeness that was coming through the stories' (2013). Bringing the inspiration embodied in first expressions to the innovation that was Fresh Expressions proved to be a significant contributor in the change process.

The already birthed first expression communities provided another strength, that of **exploring options**. This is evident in *Mission-Shaped Church* (2004). Not only did it tell stories of God at work. It also grouped these stories in 11 different new ways of being church. Each was endorsed in *Mission-Shaped Church*. This diversity affirmed the exploring of a range of options and critiqued any sense of there being one way, whether stylistic or theological, to birth as a first expression. This diversity freed people into further creative exploration. Croft spoke of 'a deep learning process ... [involving] important connections between how you do a fresh expression of church and how you encourage fresh expressions of church' (2013). What was happening institutionally, through Fresh Expressions, was shaped by what was happening from the ground up through first expressions. As first expressions explored mission, this provided a methodology for Fresh Expressions, including the importance of listening, the priority of discernment and the willingness to go on a journey in which the way forward was not yet clear.

However, with hindsight, in the formation of Fresh Expressions an unintended trajectory was set in motion, one that would work against the exploring of options. This featured in many interviews, often in relation to the word 'branding'. Croft described the process of naming:

> I've heard every fresh expressions joke under the sun really ... Too little branding and no one knew what we were talking about and it could be anything. Too much branding and it started to become off-putting, both to the very radical and to the more conservative. So pitching that right was hard. (Croft 2013)

While from the ground up, first expressions were inspiring in their diversity, the use of Fresh Expressions as one name, served to limit the invitation to diversity. One organization, gathering diversity into one brand, would work against the exploring of options, so essential in a rapidly changing culture. We will explore this in much greater detail in Chapter 10, 'One in authenticity'.

Bishop Steven Croft was instrumental in providing another leadership strength, that of creating clear positive **structures**. Bishop Stephen Cottrell (2013) observed that Croft's 'greatest gift is that kind of clear-headed, strategic thinker'. Fresh Expressions began with little structure. The invitation by Archbishop Rowan Williams was 'Pick your own team. Name your budget ... there was no strategy at the beginning for how to do that. We had to make that up as we went along really' (Croft 2013). When approached by Archbishop Rowan Williams, Croft had initial misgivings. 'My response – I didn't dare say it to him – was "Are you sure that's wise? Do you really think it's wise to really back this horse to that degree?"' (2013). The strategic thinker that was Bishop Steven Croft needed convincing. So what changed his mind?

> When I first read *Mission-Shaped Church* ... I thought 'They've put everything they know about in here. They've used all their examples.' I didn't think it was going to be that widespread. It was only after the report was published and I spent the first year travelling the country ... And it became clear that this was genuinely a nascent movement of mission and ... the challenge now was how to resource and deepen that movement and connect it. (Croft 2013)

Again we see the repetition of a methodology. Innovation begins with listening and discerning. The new shoots, from ground up, provide new learnings. From the top down comes a further listening, seeking re-formation of structures in order to resource, deepen and connect. Fresh Expressions becomes an organizational innovation. The structuring of strategic planning, while essential, comes after the birthing.

The structure that would emerge from this listening is found in the Fresh Expressions Five Year plan. It outlined four key strategies: to renew vision, to gather news, to resource growth, to develop training.[5] The verbs in the strategy are instructive. Fresh Expressions would gather news, rather than create news. It would resource growth, rather than create growth. This points to the differences between first expressions and Fresh Expressions. First expressions are orientated towards cultural engagement, while Fresh Expressions is orientated towards organizational innovation, helping 'the whole Church to catch and live this vision', sharing 'what is happening where, what is working and what is not', supporting through 'a national network of skilled coaches or accompaniers', providing training 'for lay and ordained ministries'.[6] This was a structure that **empowered**.

A second key player in the enabling of clear, positive structures was Chris Smith, Archbishop Rowan Williams's chief of staff. The value of both the person and the role was described by Croft: 'Chris Smith, his chief of staff, was a key hinge person ... and whenever I needed anything I'd just email Chris and he sees Archbishop Rowan Williams everyday' (2013). Around a busy person, appropriate access is essential, and through the skills of Chris Smith, a structure was possible in which the strengths of Archbishop Rowan Williams could be appropriately meshed with the needs of Fresh Expressions.

A third key player in the creating of clear, positive structures, was a funding body, the Lambeth Partners.

> the Lambeth Partners who were supervising ... were senior business people. And although they were exceeding generous in terms of fund-ing, which is a different culture than the church, they were extremely demanding in terms of rigorous strategy, results and outcomes. And I found that a very good discipline ... we would have massive, fierce conversations with them about what the outcomes were and whether we were achieving enough, whether we had the right strategy. And that was quite a good, rigorous testing of what was happening. (Croft 2013)

It is tempting to see funding in purely monetary terms. In this innova-tion, those who provided funding also provided the leadership strength of **structure**. In their willingness to be 'extremely demanding' of 'rigorous strategy, results and outcomes', they gifted a 'good discipline'. The result is a clarity in strategy, but also in communication, that enhances the development of Fresh Expressions.

At this juncture, let me note that I have now explored seven of the twelve suggested leadership strengths. A number of themes are emerging. First, the impact of Fresh Expressions in the reforming of an existing structure. Second, how existing organizational realities, including the positional power of roles and ecclesial gatherings, were utilized in innovation. Third, the vital role of first expressions in legitimating and guiding Fresh Expressions. Fourth, that the birthing and becoming of Fresh Expressions was due not to one gifted individual, but to a number of gifted people, each with different strengths, working together to achieve a greater degree of effectiveness.

A fine example of this pattern is in the eighth leadership strength, that of reliable **communication**. In the innovation that was Fresh Expressions, three different modes of communication are meshed together; a video (Fresh Expressions DVD), a video maker (Norman Ivison) and a poet (Archbishop Rowan Williams). Bishop Steven Croft recounted the unexpected way in which the Fresh Expressions DVD was birthed.

> This was a really interesting divine intervention I think. We appointed Norman Ivison as a senior member of the team. The job he was appointed to was Director of Training. But he was appointed to it from a background of BBC producer. And we didn't appoint him for those skills at all ... At my first meeting with Norman after he was appointed Norman said, 'Well rather than pay £30,000 to a company to make a DVD, why don't we spend £10,000 on gear? Then I'll go and film it.' ... And that was a transformative moment. We made the first DVD ... twelve five-minute stories ... That was even better than bringing in people to tell their stories [to Lambeth Partners] ... people wanted to back this because those kinds of people were involved and doing it. (Croft 2013)

A video allowed a form of communication in which people connect directly with first expression communities. *Expressions: the dvd-1*[7] was followed by *Expressions: the dvd-2*[8] then *Sanctus: fresh expressions of church in the sacramental tradition.*[9] In creating the DVDs the story was freed from the storyteller. While I have noted above the danger of branding, in which Fresh Expressions as one name gathers diversity into one brand, the videos provide momentum in a different direction. By interviewing first expressions communities, they re-present the diversity possible, **communicating** inspiration and demonstrating the **exploring** of options in mission. Accessibility is increased, as stories are freed from the limitations of times to visit a first expression and made available in the lounges, church halls and church leadership meetings of the wider organizations. Anyone, anywhere, at any time could connect with the story. The technology of a DVD was a significant mode of communication.

Another mode of communication was language. One of the developments distinctive to Fresh Expressions was the coining of new phrases like fresh expressions, the mixed economy, pioneers and Bishops' Mission Orders. The innovation that was Fresh Expressions was supported by innovation in language. New phrases have the potential disadvantage of being obscure and communicating an elitism. At the same time, they signal change, create curiosity and provide new windows on current realities.

Central to this innovation in language was Archbishop Rowan Williams. He is a noted poet, and these linguistic gifts graced the innovation that was Fresh Expressions.[10] This poetic ability was part of Williams's communication. As archbishop, he considered that an essential part of his role was communication, the 'making sense', both ecclesiologically and practically, of a change project (Williams 2013).

Consider one phrase that he gifted to fresh expressions – that of 'mixed economy'. Williams utilized the term 'to make sense to my Diocese of things that were happening in parallel with the inherited patterns' (2013). The phrase originally emerged in relation to politics in the United Kingdom in the 1930s, as an attempt to describe a system in which both public and private sectors direct the economy. Applied to the church, the use of the word 'mixed' encouraged diversity and endorsed both existing and new forms for ecclesial life. Economy might point to a relationship with business, yet it is also a theological term, related to the Trinitarian activity of God in the world. It thus points to diversity in the work of the divine.

Archbishop Rowan Williams is a noted poet. A collection of his poems, *The Poems of Archbishop Rowan Williams* (2002), was longlisted for the Wales Book of the Year award. When asked to contribute to *Sense Making Faith* (2007), he responded with the poetic gift of seven haiku.[11] It is intriguing to see him offer this gift to the task of **communication** in leadership. 'I have seen my job as from time to time just to try and find a phrase or an image that will give people something to chew on' (Williams 2013). He affirmed the power of metaphor to capture imagination and generate conversation.

In order to communicate Fresh Expressions, Archbishop Rowan Williams needed to allay the fears that first expressions might be 'religion lite' or an 'evangelical takeover'. We have already noted his theological reputation. Hence it is interesting to examine his Foreword to *Mission-Shaped Church* (2004, p. vii). How does an incoming archbishop communicate theological depth? The answer is – poetically. Archbishop Rowan Williams defines the church as 'what happens when people encounter the Risen Jesus and commit themselves to sustaining and deepening that encounter in their encounter with each other'. The articulation of ecclesiology is poetic in the threefold repetition of encounter, set alongside the fourfold verbs, inviting action around encounter, commit, sustain, deepen. It is an ecclesiology freed from much explicit theological language, in which church is a verb, not a noun, understood as a birthing in divine grace ('encounter with the Risen Jesus') and a becoming in relationality ('encounter with each other').

Hence the innovation of Fresh Expressions involved actions of communication, carried through the production of DVDs, which made accessible first expressions, and through poetic gifts, in which new language, metaphor and image were used to 'make sense'.

A ninth leadership strength is **optimism**. This strength involves a hope regarding the future, a confidence in a successful outcome. **Optimism** was the only one of the twelve leadership strengths that was harder to discern in the empirical data, despite a number of readings. Rather than optimism about a better future, those interviewed seemed to locate hope in obedience. A deep faith in Christ was present in all the interviews. This was expressed in the priority of following what God was up to and the belief that fresh expressions and Fresh Expressions were an important contemporary expression of the Spirit's work. However, this faith did not translate into a ready optimism about the state of the church. Energy for the innovation was found in an obedient following of the Spirit, rather than numerically quantified in forms of church, people finding faith and, as a consequence, a reversal in church decline.

A number of explanations for this lack of **optimism** are possible. One possible explanation relates to the NCLS data, which suggested that individuals tend to be strong in three or four of these areas. Thus the key individuals I interviewed might have strengths in areas of leadership other than **optimism**. There might have been a person providing the strength of optimism who was not interviewed. A second possible explanation relates to cultural factors. The NCLS research is focused on Australia, and it might be that optimism as a strength is expressed differently in Australian contexts than in English contexts. A third possible explanation is that optimism was lacking in the development of Fresh Expressions. If so, what is interesting is how a lack of optimism need not result in the failure of innovation.

What was evident in the empirical research was how a lack of optimism was overcome by a set of theological commitments. Consider the following extract from an interview with Rowan Williams, reflecting on the development of Fresh Expressions.

Of course the history of the Church of England, the history of the whole church, is a lot more diverse than we think ... Go back 600 years. You'd have monasteries of different kinds. You'd have the enclosed orders. You'd have the friars, the preaching orders. You'd have local guild churches and parish churches and chantry chapels and cathedrals and minsters. You'd have an incredible variety of church life. What you wouldn't have is just the parish church. And we've airbrushed that variety out of the picture ... That's just part of the historical amnesia that we all give way to ... as the thing evolved once again it became quite important to say, this is ... something about the church itself. (Williams 2013)

In the face of challenges, described as historical amnesia, rather than turn to an optimism about the future of Fresh Expressions, the turn is to reflection on the nature of the church. Hope is maintained by theology rather than confidence in a successful outcome.

A tenth leadership strength is a **move to action**. An important contributor to this strength was the ecumenical nature of this innovation. Bishop Steven Croft observed how the different denominations involved in the project acted to spur each other on.

The Methodist Church coming on board was really important. It was enormously helpful from the beginning to work across both denominations ... [T]here were key points at which the Church of England did not want to be behind the Methodist Church and the Methodist Church did not want to be behind the Church of England. (Croft 2013)

This move to action was sustained not only by the presence of birthing partners, but also by the addition over time of (becoming) partners.[12] This allowed the energy and momentum needed in moves to **action** to come from multiple places. In other words, sustainability is enhanced when it is spread across a number of groups.

Any move to **action** involves an inevitable reaction. This resulted in the need for an eleventh leadership strength, that of **resolve**, maintaining action through challenges. Fresh Expressions encountered strong opposition. One way to understand this is to imagine a boat setting sail. In identity, the boat is made for the open seas and watery horizons. To set sail requires a dream (envision), a route (explore) and a logistical plan (structure). As the boat sets sail, progress is easily hampered. This includes the incoming tide, which slows progress through the quiet, relentless push of water. Another is the breeze, which blows sometimes unexpectedly, often increasing in strength the further the boat progresses away from the shore.

Let us apply this image to analysing the reactions to Fresh Expressions. With regard to incoming tides that steadily slow progress, there was 'institutional inertia' (Williams 2013). Any organization develops particular understandings of itself, expressed in habits, practices and postures. These tend to reinforce the status quo. These incoming tides include church polity. Archbishop Rowan Williams (2013) diagnosed the Church of England as 'a profoundly uncentralized organization'. Bishop Steven Croft (2013) observed that 'the takeup of the ideas at institutional level is significantly dependent on dioceses and the views of the bishop'. What was intriguing about the leadership of Bishop Steven Croft and Archbishop Rowan Williams was – continuing the image of a boat setting sail – their willingness to tack.

When interviewed, Archbishop Rowan Williams affirmed the way that those leading Fresh Expressions responded to reactions not with defensiveness, but through engagement. Engagement involved invitation: 'come, let me walk you around a couple of projects and see what it looks like on the ground. And then perhaps we can see where we go with it' (Williams 2013). Again, we see the value of first expressions and a listen and discern methodology ('let me walk you around a couple of projects and see what it looks like on the ground'). Such a response is a practical, embodied outworking of Archbishop Rowan Williams's theology, described in the previous chapter. For Williams, 'If you're very much in the middle, then your responsibility for attending to the edges is intensified' (2013). This is a theology which sees in first expressions the innovative possibility of re-forming the whole of the church, while working at relationships which seek to take the diversity of the entire body of the church on the journey of innovation.

A central provider of the strength of **resolve** was Bishop Steven Croft. Bishop Stephen Cottrell described him as tenacious: 'He can take criticism and not be knocked back by it. So it's a spiritual quality. Blessed are the meek, they will inherit the earth. That's him. There's a meekness to him' (2013). The strength of **resolve** emerges from character and spirituality.

Resolve is also enhanced when it is shared. Bishop Steven Croft noted his strength in building teams: 'The thing I did most was build a team ... I think that was why they appointed me, because of my track record in building teams and I think that was a particular challenge in building something from scratch, a team that would work nationally and a community of people who would work nationally' (2013). Maintaining action in the face of challenge is enhanced through a community of collective purpose.

A final leadership strength is the ability to **learn**, contemplating the activity of God on the journey of innovation to date, in order to gain insight for the future. The Lambeth Partners provided an unexpected surprise in relation to this leadership strength, in relation to the discipline of knowledge management.

> It's very interesting how the Lambeth Partners ... proved very key intellectually. They were praying, they were giving, but I'd also pitch to them every few months, different sections. And after one of the presentations this guy came up to me and said 'I'm an expert in this discipline of knowledge management and what you've been describing to me sounds like that. And you really need to know about it.' (Croft 2013)

Bishop Steven Croft described the value of these insights to the Fresh Expressions team. 'It was absolutely what we needed to know because it was about the harvesting of wisdom from a new discipline. And shaped a lot of what we did.' The harvesting of wisdom is evident in the Fresh Expressions Five Year plan and all four key strategies – to renew vision, to gather news, to resource growth and to develop training. Gathering news is a harvesting of wisdom from innovation which renews vision, resources growth and is needed to develop training. The *Mission Shaped Ministry* course, which was an essential training strategy, has a module on learning networks which encourages peer learning in the actions of innovation. Hence the strength of learning was woven into Fresh Expressions.

In summary, the becoming of the innovation that is Fresh Expressions has been described using a twelve strengths model. In order of appearance, Archbishop Rowan Williams brought strengths in listening deeply and connecting, Graham Cray brought strengths in envisioning. Bishop Steven Croft brought strengths in structure, a strategy that empowered resolve. Norman Ivison brought strengths in communication, while ecumenical partners helped move to action, and Lambeth Partners gave of their strengths in structure and in learning.

Sustaining organizational innovation

With very few written understandings of denominations engaging in innovation in mission, the courage of the Church of England and the Methodist Church in opting to pioneer as an institution is a significant gift to other denominations. What insights regarding organizational innovation might be gleaned from the innovation that is Fresh Expressions?

First, the need for a range of strengths. This is liberation from the search for a hero leader. It is an invitation to look for others with strengths different than yours, who can play to their strengths.

Second, the value of collaboration in organizational innovation. This includes not only immediate team members, but in this particular innovation, I see the value of ecumenical partners and external funding bodies.

Third, the potential of material objects in the innovation, in this case books and DVDs as carriers of communication.

Fourth, the gift of poetic imagination. The search for metaphors and the articulation of new phrases can be important in processes of communication.

Fifth, the need for, and the value of, working with existing organizational realities. Every organization has realities that can be levered in seeking innovation. In the case of Fresh Expressions, I see the value of the positional power of roles and the way that ecclesial gatherings can be utilized in innovation.

Sixth, the vital role of first expressions in legitimating and guiding Fresh Expressions. This includes the living experience of pioneers, their testimonies of courage and risk.

Seventh, the value of hard questions. It was the funders who kept inviting the work that would provide the communicative clarity. Matters of structure, accountability and strategy are not always welcomed in ecclesial innovation. Yet the innovation that is Fresh Expressions suggests that the hard questions of strategy should be welcomed.

I have considered what insights we might glean from the innovation that is Fresh Expressions.

Learning from Fresh Expressions: institutional innovators as research and development

The analysis of the becoming of Fresh Expressions has also clarified the differences between first expressions and Fresh Expressions. Fresh Expressions draws from the birthing of first expressions and is an innovation seeking to re-form an existing structure. It is, to use the frames from Cammock (2003), an expression of a commitment to awaken parts of an organization previously dormant.

This provides insight regarding the motives for ecclesial innovation. Stefan Paas (2016) analyses church planting in Europe and outlines three reasons for church planting – planting better churches, planting more churches and planting new churches. Each of these motives results in different criteria for assessment. If your motive is purity, you look for reproduction of denominational values. If your motive is growth, you look for growth. If your motive is new churches, you look for diversity.

When Fresh Expressions is seen in relation to purity or growth, different trajectories emerge. If you fund for purity, then preservation of your denomination is the aim. Annual budget lines set funds aside for projects that look distinctly like 'your denomination'. If you fund for growth, then assessment is based on growth. It is anticipated that in time, funding will no longer be required, for success is sustainability.

Fresh Expressions is best seen as research and development. In order to innovate, organizations set aside resources to develop new product. The greater the times of change, the greater the need for research and development, for the testing of new ideas. These innovations are essential because changing times require institutional renewal. In the church, research and development need to be embodied in ecclesial life. Theoretical ideas have a place, but require embodying in ecclesial practices of discipleship, worship and mission. This was the unique gift of first expressions and the genius of Fresh Expressions.

First expressions were research and development embedded in ecclesial life. In grassroots communities, experiments in innovation occurred. Annual budget lines set funds aside in order that a range of experiments can be conducted. Levels of funding are sustained not by the hope of denominational growth but by a commitment to research and development.

One approach to assessing innovation in a research and development model is provided by the Innovation Horizons model, also called McKinsey's Three Horizons Model (Coley 2009). It assumes that innovation takes years to develop and requires activity in three different areas. Horizon 1 (H1) activity seeks to invigorate and extend the existing core activities. Horizon 2 (H2) activity seeks to develop new opportunities in similar areas of activity. Horizon 3 (H3) activity seeks to create entirely new options. Activity in each of the three horizons is needed. Trying and dying is as important as trying, for there is learning in life and death.

For example, innovation that exists as research and development in faith formation of young people might include experiments in improving existing Christian education programmes (H1), a different programme at another time (H2) and entirely new approaches to faith development (H3), for example experiments in digital community. A research and development model funds ecclesial idea generation across all three horizons. In addition, it looks to

- fund experiments across the cultural and theological diversity of the ecclesial body
- display an increasing depth of local community involvement
- demonstrate commitment to deepening relationships across the church.

Such an approach pays attention to the differences that have emerged in this chapter between first expressions and Fresh Expressions. Fresh Expressions lives in complementary partnership with first expressions.

Grassroots experiments are funded for research and development. Sustainability is focused on ensuring the ongoing generation of ideas. Organizational innovation is funded to build networks, ensure diffusion of innovation and synchronize training in which the wider church draws from the emerging insights of grassroots innovation. Sustainability is focused on ensuring vital relationships, in order that innovation might be spread across the breadth of the body that is the church. The aim is renewal through innovation, a partnership between grassroots innovation and organizational innovation in which the church is awakened through a weaving of birthing with becoming.

As well as asking what can be learnt by clarifying the differences between first expressions and Fresh Expressions, we can also learn by asking what could have been done differently.

Learning from Fresh Expressions as institutional innovators: a gendered perspective

What is striking about the innovation that is the becoming of Fresh Expressions is the absence of female voices. While among first expressions, I interviewed women, when it came to Fresh Expressions the key leaders were all male. This invites the question, what might organizational innovation that included women look like in denominational contexts?

The question is consistent with my initial dialogue with Janet Martin Soskice, for whom gender is a major concern in *The Kindness of God*. As described in Chapter 2, 'Birthing first expressions', a theology of eschatological anthropology is birthed in relationships. The reality of the theology of these relationships is that they are gendered. These relationships are also contingent, given that becoming is an invitation to growth. Hence any becoming includes the invitation to consider gender and the impact of difference on growth.

While what follows is in many ways imaginative, there are a range of theological resources from which to draw. Recent research on the becoming of women shows that growth and formation is gendered. Nicola Slee observes that formation has tended to be researched by 'male theorists whose models of development are androcentric' (2004, p. 32), while Ann Phillips (2017) observes that most theologies of childhood faith development have been written by men. Slee researches the faith development of women and highlights the importance of processes of suffering, wonder and relationality which the church can nurture through providing imaginative play, mentoring and providing contexts of relational intimacy as solidarity. Carol Hess has argued that while communities of faith play a crucial role in the development of faith among women, this is not inevitable: 'Churches are too often girl-denying institutions' (1997, p. 14).

Phillips (2017) argues for a 'wombing' theology as an approach to faith development. It **protects** and so cultivates the need for a 'home space'. It enables **play**, in which the one being birthed is free, away from adult control, to work at their identity. It **connects** across generations. Regarding church, 'membership of a cohort was not enough for the girls to feel a sense of belonging. Intergenerational sharing was named as a significant feature in their attachment to the environment ... Girls [interviewed] regularly spoke of the impact on their faith of older people ... Most participation was initiated by adults' (p. 160).

A 'wombing' theology provides a way to reflect on innovation as a birthing and becoming and in relation to the Leadership Strengths. Applying a 'wombing' theology to innovation becomes a way to understand **envision, explore** and **empower**. When we watch children play, we also witness moving to **action** and **learning** in cycles of risk and experimentation. A 'wombing' approach is a way of understanding **listening, connecting** and **communicating**. A 'wombing' approach protects new forms of life, and this could be a way of understanding **structure** when it comes to innovation. In watching parents work with children at play, we see the importance of **optimism** in the encouragement to risk. Optimism is closely linked with **inspiration**, the encouragement to try and the giving of **resolve**, to not only try, but try again.

What emerges when applying a wombing theology is the importance of the interplay between caregivers and children. Fresh Expressions is immediately placed in relation to first expressions, an innovation that makes the interplay of relationships essential. Play becomes central, with first expressions invited to take risks, expecting to fall over. It is in the willingness to make mistakes that learning is most likely. Structure and optimism are located in relation to the protection of what is becoming.

A 'wombing' approach to innovation is most clearly evident in Luke 1.39–45, a text in which birthing and becoming are central. The text suggests an ecclesiological reading, for in Mary is the body of Christ, the One who is birthed that we might be birthed, who in life calls disciples to become friends in a new family in mission, who in death and resurrection births the church[13] and in ascension creates space for the birthing and becoming of the church, through the power of the Spirit. In this ecclesiological birthing and becoming, embodiment is central, as Mary 'hurries' (1.39) with the body of Christ, while Elizabeth feels the baby leap in her womb (1.41). Reality and theology are interwoven, the filling activity of the Spirit named in response to these embodied movements.

Elizabeth's response to the potential of new life is one of double blessing, both the body of Mary and the body of the Christ she bears (1.42).

Elizabeth is older and in the narrative is firmly located in relation to Zechariah and temple obedience. Mary is younger and arrives with the mystery that is a virgin birth. Elizabeth, connected with tradition and history, does not respond with question or rebuke but with blessing, a word repeated three times (1.42, 45). In the blessing, Elizabeth offers significant theological work. The aim of the entire Gospel of Luke is to provide 'an account of the things that have been fulfilled among us' (1.1). The shape of this activity is discerned by Elizabeth, who declares that God's activity is fulfilled in the body of Mary (1.45). Elizabeth is the theologian of the inherited church who articulates God's unfolding activity in the reality of birthing and becoming.

Applying Phillips, in Luke 1.39–45 there is protection: both women carry life, while Mary stays with Elizabeth for three months (1.56). There is play, in the offer of blessing and the 'baby in my womb' leaping for joy (1.44). There is connection, in the embodied interplay between Mary and Elizabeth.

Applying Slee, in Luke 1.39–45, the interactions between Mary and Elizabeth demonstrate relational intimacy ('favoured', 1.43; 'the mother of my Lord', 1.44; 'the baby in my womb leaped for joy', 1.44). There is mentoring, as Elizabeth blesses, offers theological reflection and hosts Mary for three months. There is imaginative play, most powerfully evident in what follows, in the Magnificat. Biblical scholar Walter Brueggemann writes that in handling the Magnificat, one must prioritize the imaginative and poetic. 'In handling such literary form … one should also see liturgy and all artistic acts as crucial for mission' (1989, p. 405). The research of Phillips and Slee and the biblical narrative of Luke 1.39–45 provide helpful insights into how to respond to birthing and becoming.

Applied to first expressions, the first response of an existing denomination would be to embody Elizabeth. Mary arrives in a hurry (Why such a rush Mary?) and with news that invites question (How did you get pregnant Mary?). Yet Elizabeth blesses, offering theological reflection on the activity of God.

Applied to Leadership Strengths, **listening** and **connecting** would be understood in relation to developing relational intimacy; **envisioning**, **exploring** and **learning** would be practised as imaginative play; **empowering**, moving to **action** and **resolve** would occur through mentoring; **communication** would be imaginative, in forms that prioritize poetry, hymnody, craft forms and popular piety (Slee 2004); **inspiration** and **optimism** would be sustained by wonder. **Structure** would come through domestic patterns in which household budgeting and organization sustain family life.

Continuing an imaginatively theoretical approach, the Fresh Expressions Five Year key strategies would be

- to create wonder by sharing God's embodiment in ecclesial life (*renew vision; gather news*)
- to protect birthing and becoming through advocacy and resources (*resource growth*)
- to connect by creating networks and gatherings through which the vulnerability and joy of mission is shared (*resource growth*).

Alongside the essential role of Lambeth Partners in providing structures of accountability, there would be an imaginative application of the protecting dimensions inherent in 'wombing' theology. Bradshaw, Hayday, Armstrong, Levesque and Rykert (1998) argue that governance in stable conditions is different from governance in conditions of innovation. They propose a typology of governance possibilities that include

- entrepreneurial model – board and CEO of a unitary organization working in a context that is adaptive with a focus on effectiveness
- emergent cellular model – a small yet flexible core board, able to draw in others as needed in a pluralistic organization working in conditions of innovation.

It would be easy for Lambeth Partners to adopt the entrepreneurial model, providing funding only in relation to effectiveness. This would run the danger, discussed above, of criteria in relation to growth rather than diversity. A wombing theology would understand the type of governance as emergent cellular rather than entrepreneurial. It would celebrate the Leadership Strengths of **structure** provided by the Lambeth Partners in particular in relation to allocation of resources, including accountability and fiduciary responsibilities. However, it would understand stewardship of the vision and values of the organization as including funding for diversity. As such, it would allocate *ex officio* roles like Elizabeth's to bless and theologize in relation to grassroots innovation. This maintains the ambassadorial, legitimating and learning functions essential to **structure**, while **empowering** in relation to funding for diversity.

My approach in this section has been both theoretical and imaginative. I write as a male, responding to the absence of female voices in the organizational innovation that was Fresh Expressions by reflecting on the wombing theology of Phillips, the formational work of Slee and the interactions between Mary and Elizabeth. The result is 'hermeneutic discoveries' (Paas 2016, p. 239).

Mary and Elizabeth provide another way to consider a mixed economy. They invite the inherited church to bless innovation by enacting embodied theological reflection that pays attention to reality and theology, to the infilling of the Spirit as a baby leaps in a womb. They prioritize playful imagination to explore, inspire and communication. They encourage relational networks to empower, learn and enable, offer and resolve alternative imagination regarding structure. For Soskice, theology is gendered, and this section has developed this in relation to the birthing and becoming of organizational innovation.

Conclusion

This chapter began with leadership. It suggested that it is unhelpful to seek one silver bullet, fired by one golden person (often perceived to be male), to bring about a desired change. A model – of Leadership Strengths – was used to analyse the development of Fresh Expressions. Organizational innovation occurred through a group of people contributing different strengths. In order of appearance: Archbishop Rowan Williams who brought strengths in **listening** deeply; Bishop Graham Cray who brought strengths in **envisioning**; Bishop Steven Croft who brought strengths in **strategy** and **resolve**; Norman Ivison who enacted **communication** and the Lambeth Partners who gave of their strengths in **structure** and in **learning**. All the Strengths were present, apart from optimism.

This provides important lessons for institutional change, for all those who contemplate an organization innovating as a first expression. In particular, first the importance of diverse gifts embodied in diverse people that together enable a project to bring about change. Second, the value of things like books and videos. Third, the vitality provided by poetic language. Fourth, the value inherent in the hard questions around strategy.

The analysis using Leadership Strengths invited reflection on the differences between grassroots innovation and organizational innovation. Seeing innovation in relation to research and development clarified the role of Fresh Expressions as awakening innovative dormancy in an organization. A gendered analysis clarified another dormancy and argued for the possibilities of a wombing theology in encouraging protection, play and connection.

Notes

1 For a comprehensive examination of the collaborative approaches to innovation in 1 Corinthians 3 and 4, see Taylor (2016).

2 Lead With Your Strengths by NCLS team. Available at www.ncls.org.au/default.aspx?sitemapid=6307 [viewed 10 March 2013]. Image used with permission.

3 The NCLS involves a large-scale survey, every five years since 1991, of church life in Australia. Large scale as in more than 300,000 people, from over 6,700 congregations, across 19 denominations. In addition, more than 6,000 church

leaders have completed a Leaders Survey, exploring leadership roles, priorities, foundations and experiences. A profile has emerged regarding church leadership life and practice.

4 'Methodism began ... [primarily] as a movement of lay disciples supported by a few ordained people' (Roberts 2013).

5 In Year One, every diocese and district would be visited. In Years Two and Three, national training would be developed, communication would occur by gathering news and holding a national conference. In Years Four and Five, nine national regions would be identified and in each of them a major conference would occur. In addition, patterns of training and accompaniment would be developed. Provided by Steven Croft as a photocopy during the interview. Dated 6 January 2005.

6 Steven Croft, Fresh Expressions Five Year plan, 6 January 2005, p. 8.

7 Norman Ivison, *Expressions: the dvd – 1: stories of church for a changing culture*, London: Church House Publishing, 2006.

8 Norman Ivison, *Expressions: the dvd – 2: changing church in every place*, London: Church House Publishing, 2007.

9 Norman Ivison, *Sanctus: fresh expressions of church in the sacramental tradition*, Fresh Expressions, 2009.

10 When interviewed, he described this observation as 'very interesting' (Williams 2013).

11 'To guide our thoughts and ideas we asked the Archbishop of Canterbury, Dr Rowan Williams, if he would offer us a creative meditation for each of the chapters on the senses. He has responded by sending us six haiku' (Richards 2007, p. vii).

12 Examples include the United Reformed Church, the Congregational Federation, the Council for World Mission Europe, the Ground Level Network, Church Missionary Society and Anglican Church Planting Initiatives.

13 'Medieval religious art was often explicit in its representation of the Crucifixion as childbirth. We see the church (*ecclesia*) being pulled from Christ's wounded side' (Soskice 2007, p. 87).

8

Moves in mission

My father taught me to drive. Keep checking the rear-view mirror, he repeatedly reminded me. At the time I was young, impetuous and thought I knew everything. This chapter checks the rear-view mirror on mission, in particular as it relates to the history of Christian Britain.

'Mission' is a key word in *Mission-Shaped Church* (2004). For John and Olive Fleming Drane, Fresh Expressions is 'one of the most significant missional movements in the recent history of Christianity in these islands' (2010, p. 11). Drane and Drane locate origins that go back to 1945 and argue for a 'legacy of sustained and serious theological and ecclesiological thinking that has enabled Fresh Expressions to find such ready acceptance' (2010, p. 11). However, while *Mission-Shaped Church* outlines a changing Britain, offers stories of innovation, provides a theology for mission and proposes reformation of denominational structures, it provides little by way of appreciation of the history of mission in Britain. If mission is 'finding out where the Holy Spirit is at work and joining in' (Dunn 1998, p. 72), then an important place to look, to begin to trace what God is up to, is to explore the fingerprints of the God of mission in British history. Particular attention will be paid to the structures by which mission has been organized. This continues the work of the previous two chapters, which described the birthing and becoming of Fresh Expressions as an organizational innovation.

Looking in the mirror, how previously in Great Britain have innovations in mission been organized? Three mission structures in British history will be described – the monastery and pilgrimage patterns of Celtic mission, the 'bands' and connexional systems initiated in early Methodism, and the voluntary mission agencies of the modern missionary movement.

How is mission organized? What are the 'first expressions' of organizational structure? Looking sideways, what other possible ways for organizing innovation in mission are possible? A contemporary structure used to organize innovation – the non-governmental organization (NGO) – will be outlined.

Such exploration enables us to attend to Fresh Expressions as a first expression of organizational innovation. In each structure, we find particularity. God is acting in innovation in mission, but God is acting uniquely, in ways particular to that time and place. These mission-ecclesial descriptions have theological implications. They enable us to appreciate the church's historical continuity as apostolic in structure and visibility. Organizational approaches to innovation have been contextual, as the church in times past has structured itself in response to mission in changing times. Hence the becoming of the church in relation to structuring for mission finds an ecclesial shape. We are thus able to locate Fresh Expressions as a missionary structure, in critical conversation with contextual innovations in missiology, both historical and contemporary.

Celtic mission moves: monastic and pilgrim

A few years ago, I was privileged to be able to retreat to Lindisfarne. Along with time to walk and pray, I took the opportunity to read, to immerse myself in early Celtic writings, with a particular concern for the structures of mission that underpinned the Celtic mission to Great Britain. Essential to Celtic mission was the interplay between the structure of movement and the structure of the monastery.

In terms of **movement**, Celtic Christianity framed the Christian life, both in witness and discipleship, in 'metaphors of journeys, frontiers and goals to be reached which are off in the distance' (O'Loughlin 2000, p. 44). Harrold notes that a novelty of Celtic mission was 'the highly mobile apostolic team that could pack up and move out, much as the nomadic people it sought to reach with the gospel' (2012, p. 32).

A notable example is St Brendan (484–580), an 'intrepid' example of 'the early Irish *peregrini pro Christo*' (O Donnchadha 2004, p. 21). St Brendan spent most of his 94 years 'travelling, mainly by sea, founding monasteries in Ireland, Scotland, Wales and Brittany' (p. 18). His motivation was missionary, to preach to all the world. Brendan's story includes the 'legend' as told in *Navigatio Sancti Brendani Abbatis* (*Voyage of Saint Brendan*) of a journey to the 'Isle of the Blessed'. Some details – for example, the ice floes of the north, the fog of Newfoundland, the exotic birds and flowers of the Caribbean – suggest this was America, thus making an Irish pilgrim the first European to set foot in America, over 1,000 years before Columbus. Tim Severin (1977) built a replica of Brendan's currach and using only *Navigatio Sancti Brendani Abbatis* as his guide, sought to repeat the voyage. Severin ended up in Newfoundland, a journey of 7,200 kilometres, an adventure told in the documentary *The Brendan Voyage*. For Irish academic Gearoid O Donnchadha, while it is 'not possible to prove that Brendan himself experienced the events of the *Voyage*, yet it is most likely, such was his reputation as a navigator' (2004, p. 14).

Another notable example of movement is Bishop Aidan. Bede offered the following observation of Aidan, in which movement in witness and discipleship was essential.

> He was wont to traverse both town and country on foot ... as he went, he might turn aside to any whomsoever he saw, whether rich or poor, and call upon them, if infidels, to receive the mystery of the faith, or, if they were believers, strengthen them in the faith, and stir them up by words and actions to giving of alms and the performance of good works. (*Bede's Ecclesiastical History* 731, III.5)

We are presented with a portrayal of mission as movement. This involves both words and action and an orientation towards people, in witness and discipleship.

Alongside the structure of movement was the structure of the **monastery**. The Celtic church developed around monasteries rather than parishes. Monasteries were places of prayer, discipleship and community. They were built not as a way to retreat from society, but as a place of 'dedication to God and to his service in a community set in the midst of the larger community of the Church' (O'Loughlin 2000, p. 70). Out of this pattern of ecclesial life a broad view of Christian life and mission emerged. Prayer and study were interwoven with a concern for justice and community development. These commitments were expressed by vocations that included *peregrini pro Christo* or education and spiritual direction. Hence monastery and movement were entwined: two distinct structures around which Celtic mission was organized.

A notable example is Adomnan (627/8–704), an abbot at Iona. Located in a monastery, he had a 'theology of Church and society' with 'a broad vision of the place of our community in these islands and the wider world' (Bardsley 2006, pp. 39, 45). Adomnan was a 'champion of peace, reconciliation and right relationships' (p. 141). Inspired by the vision of shalom in the Scriptures, drawing from texts including Isaiah 61.1 and Luke 4.18–19, he developed in the monastery a law (*Cain Adomnan* or Law of Innocents) to protect women and non-combatants in time of war. He then moved from the monastery in order to go 'before kings to intercede for captives [as] a central part of his own task of being Christ's minister to all' (O'Loughlin 2000, p. 74). Mission, structured through movement and monastery, was for the good of all. For Adomnan, conversion includes the whole person and should change the entirety of a person's relationship with God, with their village, with their enemies and with creation.

This understanding was woven through mission, discipleship and worship. Thus Thomas O'Loughlin analyses the Stowe Missal, a description of liturgical practice from around AD 750.

The common theme running through these texts is that of communion: communion with one another, communion with the first Christian meals, communion with the whole Church on earth and in heaven, communion with Christ, and the final future communion of the whole Christ. (O'Loughlin 2000, p. 144)

I was reading these texts, studying the early Celtic church, while on retreat at Lindisfarne. This wholistic vision surrounded me. It was present in the ruins of the monastery, developed by St Aidan around AD 635, rebuilt as a Benedictine house in AD 1093 as a place of worship and discipleship. Lindisfarne and the monasteries present were accessed by the Pilgrims Way, with poles marking (structuring) the journey. These monasteries provided artefacts, most notably the Lindisfarne Gospels, an exquisitely decorated copy of the Gospels of Matthew, Mark, Luke and John produced during the early 700s. Taking a break from reading one day, I walked to find in one particular bird hide an inscription: 'This body of water ... was probably created by the first monks of Holy Island in the 7th century to provide a ready supply of water and fish. Covering an area of approximately four acres, it is home to a variety of birds, animals and plants.' This 'monastic' faith had an environmental legacy. Lindisfarne is famous not only for location and history but also for its bird life, being landfall for migratory birds from across the oceans. The monastic pattern at Lindisfarne was reached by movement and expressed a care for the artistic and the environmental.

Looking in the rear-view mirror of mission, the Celtic is one expression of mission in British history. It was an innovation structured around movement and monastery, which offered a wholistic understanding of conversion, through words, acts and the beauty of the Lindisfarne Gospels, in the concern for all of creation.

Methodist mission moves: bands, connexional systems and means of grace

A second move in mission occurred in the birth of Methodism. It is important, as part of looking in the rear-view mirror, to consider the formation of Methodism, given the role of the Methodist Church in forming Fresh Expressions as a shared denominational venture (as outlined in Chapter 6). Methodism in Great Britain was one part of widespread religious revival across Europe in the eighteenth century.[1] Methodism did not emerge as a distinct denomination until after John Wesley's death. It took structural shape initially as a 'missionary society growing into a Church'. To quote Henry Rack: 'For some years after the death of Wesley

(1791), Methodism had to grapple with problems which may broadly be described as those of a missionary society growing into a Church' (1965, p. 19). What makes Methodism in Great Britain intriguing from the perspective of this book is the way that in Britain it took fresh forms – structural and liturgical – within a denominational context.

An important feature in the development of John Wesley's faith was banding together with other Christians. In 1729, the 26-year-old began a 'Holy Club' while at the University of Oxford. It was 'an organized life of piety' (Rack 2002, p. 83), with regular meetings for purposes of devotion and social work. Initially it was a 'shifting network' (p. 87), shaped by the context of university life and the energy and changing enthusiasm of participants.

Wesley's bands gave social shape to Wesley's innovative insight that 'Christianity was essentially *social* in nature' (Harrold 2012, p. 43). Ward calls them 'cells of religious virtuosi' (1992, p. 340). Historian Henry Rack argued that the 'bands' emerged from a perception that inherited church structures were unable to reach all of the community. The bands were not an innovation unique to Methodism in England, but were adapted from elsewhere in Europe, in particular 'the revivalists in Germany and Switzerland' (Ward 1992, p. 340). As 'little devotional cells ... [they] aimed quietly to revitalize' the Anglican church from within (Walsh 1986, p. 280). For Rack, this was a 'response to a situation where the conventional parish system and parish ministrations had failed to satisfy ... it created a religion of the laity, an organized religious and moral life which the conventional system had been unable to effect' (1965, p. 16).

One of the questions this 'missionary society' within a denomination then faced was how to connect the 'bands'. The result was a '**connexional**' system of linked societies run under the superintendency of Wesley with lay help: 'a kind of halfway house between a Religious Society and a Church' (Rack 1965, p. 17). Rack describes this as developing 'piecemeal' (p. 17). It involved a new way of thinking ecclesiologically, in that oversight (*episcope*), was shared, 'the ethos was societary' (p. 17). There is an intriguing interplay at work here between new forms that emerge at grassroots, and then over time a new form – 'connexional' – that emerges to connect the grassroot new forms.

Rack suggests two patterns – one settled, the other experimental – as a way to understand the development of Methodism. He calls the beginnings of Methodism experimental and includes both the new 'bands' and the 'connexional' ordering. They are both experiments in structural innovation, a demonstration of the 'Wesley emphasis on mission as determining order' (1965, p. 20).

Another innovation involved new worship practices. These included love feasts, watchnights, covenants, the writing of new hymns and new mission practices such as field preaching. The love feast was borrowed from the Moravians (Rack 2002, p. 410). The watchnights were an example of 'spontaneous creation from below only later sanctioned by Wesley himself' (p. 412), first mentioned as occurring in 1733, but with no evidence Wesley experienced one before 1738. The Covenant service was developed by Wesley. It applied the Puritan pattern of individual self-examination and renewal of vows and applied it collectively (pp. 412–13). The hymns, collected in *Hymns for the Use of Methodists* (1780) were not structured around the Christian Year but were to nurture piety, both within Methodist gatherings and in private meditation. Rack (1965, p. 18) groups these new worship practices together and terms them 'means of grace'. A priority is an emphasis on emotion and experience, including 'feelings as evidence of conversion' (Rack 2002, p. 290). However, a 'full Methodist adaptation of the church service ... was [not] possible nor indeed desirable on Wesley's plan, since it would undermine the subordination of Methodist devotion to attendance at church' (p. 416).

Wesley worked with the tensions generated by a commitment to mission and a desire to reform the church from within. He wrote of his desire 'to reform the nation, *particularly the Church*' (Rack 1965, p. 16).[2] This is a mission in which reforming, particularly the church, is a priority. At the same time, 'Wesley's course of action was decided more by the expediences of mission than by ecclesiastical niceties' (Rack 2002, p. 294). Mission was the overarching passion for Wesley, who wrote: 'What is the end of all ecclesiastical order? Is it not to bring souls from the power of Satan to God, and to build them up in His fear and love? Order, then, is so far valuable as it answers these ends; and if it answers them not it is nothing worth' (Rack 1965, p 79).[3] For Wesley, the church exists for mission. Ward concludes that Wesley 'created a non-denominational religious society ... as an effort to revive the smouldering embers of religious faith in the absence of the ordinary ecclesiastical mechanisms' (1992, pp. 350, 353). Research has demonstrated that many of Wesley's converts had a 'marked religious background' (Rack 2002, p. 424), with parents who had a Christian upbringing.

This is an innovation from within. The use of 'means of grace', bands and being connexional is a restructuring intended to revive the smouldering embers of religious faith that already exists within an ecclesial structure. This Methodist move of mission is thus a clear contrast with the Celtic move of mission. One was seeking to renew a structure, the other was seeking to establish a Christian presence.

This is clarified when the Methodist mission moves are analysed in light of the theory of innovation proposed by Joseph Schumpeter. One of 'the theoretical forefathers of entrepreneurship study' (Tapsell and Woods

2010, p. 536), Schumpeter argued that innovation could be understood as the combining and recombining of resources, in contexts of resistance. These new combinations result in new forms of community, what Schumpeter calls 'cooperating groups'. This analysis seems to describe the Methodist moves. 'New combinations' are drawn from Moravian love feasts and Puritan Covenant services. They are practised in new forms of 'cooperating groups', in meetings described as 'domesticated, democratized folk Eucharist' (Walsh 1986, p. 288).

For Schumpeter, innovation is enhanced by resistive tension. Change occurs through leaps and discontinuities rather than continuous change (Tapsell and Woods 2010, p. 541). Hence the tensions between a commitment to mission and a desire to reform the church from within that were experienced by Wesley can be generative of innovation.

Looking in the mirror at the particularity that is mission history in Great Britain, we have considered two organizational innovations: the monastery and pilgrimage patterns of Celtic mission and the 'bands' and connexional systems initiated in early Methodism. Placed side by side, we see that God works differently, distinctly. Innovation can occur through risky pilgrimage and by living within generative tensions. Recombinations are 'means of grace' that can play an important role in revitalization, generating new structures within existing ecclesial bodies.

Modern mission moves: voluntary societies

A third mission move occurs with the modern missionary movement. Walsh describes 'the astonishing proliferation of Evangelical-dominated voluntary societies' (1986, p. 301). While Wesley drew on the potential of voluntary societies to structure for mission within Great Britain, others drew on the potential of voluntary societies to structure for mission as part of the modern mission movement.

Missiologist Andrew Walls documents how 'the voluntary societies have been as revolutionary in their effect as ever the monasteries were in their sphere' (1996, p. 254). In the eighteenth century, none of the existing forms of church structure had the capacity to undertake the tasks of a missionary society (p. 247). The average Christian thought only in terms of parish church. However, embedded in William Carey's passionate call to mission in 1792 was not only a call to mission, but an outline of a new way for the church to structure itself. In *An Enquiry into the Obligations of Christians to Use Means for the Conversion of the Heathens*, William Carey drew on the analogy of the secular trading companies from the commercial world of his time, to suggest a voluntary association.

> Suppose a company of serious Christians, ministers and private persons, were to form themselves into a society, and make a number of rules respecting the regulation of the plan, and the persons who are to be employed as missionaries, the means of defraying the expense, etc etc (Carey 1792, para. 25 of 27)

This is a mission move, the birth of a new way of structuring the church in response to tracing what Carey discerns as a new particularity, a call to world mission. By the time of Carey's death, there were 14 missionary societies in Britain alone, with others also in Continental Europe and America (Tindall 2011, p. 11).[4] The voluntary society, as a structure for mission, was to become a significant and important gift from Great Britain to the world.

Walls documents the factors significant in the innovation that was the voluntary mission society (1996, pp. 247–51). First, voluntary societies could undertake tasks that existing ecclesial structures could not. Second, voluntary societies were ecumenical, allowing people across previous denominational divides to participate in mission.[5] Third, voluntary societies empowered lay people: 'The society took a local embodiment, developed a broad spread of participants, gave scope to lay commitment and enthusiasm' (p. 251). This involved providing new ways for lay people to express their vocation, including in publication, promotion and fundraising.

This mission move, arising in Great Britain, was a revolutionary restructuring of the church in light of mission

> assisting its declericalization, giving new scope for women's energies and gifts and adding an international dimension which hardly any of the churches, growing as they did within a national framework, had any means of expressing. After the age of the voluntary society, the Western Church could never be the same again. (Walls 1996, p. 253)

Carey drew on trends in commerce. The voluntary society was 'like a trading company' (p. 245). 'It is significant that Carey – a man of the provinces and of humble station – takes his analogy from commerce; organizing a society is something like floating a company' (p. 246). For Carey, this part of *the Obligations of Christians to Use Means* involves borrowing from a business model.

This presents as another form of recombination. Drawing again from the analytical frames proposed by Joseph Schumpeter, the voluntary society as a way of structuring for mission is an innovation. It emerges because of resistance. 'The simple fact was that the Church as then organized, whether episcopal, or Presbyterian, or congregational, *could* not effectively operate overseas. Christians had accordingly to "use means" to do so' (Walls 1996, p. 246). So Carey recombines: he draws from the trading company, a new cultural form emerging in modernity as a way to promote a cause, to collect funds towards that cause and to hold regular (annual) shareholder meetings to maintain accountability in relation to that cause. What results is a new form of 'cooperating group', the voluntary society.

When we place the mission moves of the modern missionary movement alongside the mission moves of Methodism, we again see God working distinctly. Methodism offered a recombination in relation to liturgical resources. The voluntary society offered a recombination in relation to the trading company. One drew from the church; the other drew from the culture. In birthing his innovations, Wesley sought to remain within existing organizations. In birthing his innovation of the voluntary society, Carey sought to establish a parallel structure, alongside but distinct.

The voluntary society as a structure does raise ethical questions. Shareholders are more likely to be influenced by growth mentalities. This returns us to the work of Chapter 3, 'Body-ing forth in innovation', and the classic 'S' growth curve (in contrast to compost in renewable cycles of birth, life and death, spiral through story is carrying forward ancestor wisdom and mending through remaking). Share investors in a traditional company are expecting to fund innovation that will follow a curve of upward growth. To use this means generates expectations of multiplying growth through successful mission.

In addition, this 'particular period of Western social, political and economic development' (Walls 1996, p. 253) now goes by the name of colonization. The strategies embedded in trading companies and investment portfolios certainly fuelled the making of Britain Great. Yet the wealth generated came from the lands of colonized countries and an expanding Britain was complicit in the destruction of indigenous cultures' ability to carry forward ancestor wisdom. There are consequences when innovation is framed solely as investment in growth strategies.

Walls suggests this innovative structure of mission was pragmatic, lacking a theology.[6] *The Obligations to Use Means* was a must. Others disagree. Stanley Skreslet has argued that mission structures are 'enfleshed demonstrations of a theoretical orientation to the world ... windows that allow one to peer closely at the underpinnings of a given theology of mission' (1999 p. 2). Drawing on Skreslet, a voluntary mission structure that increases lay participation, gives women voice, enhances a sense of catholicity and allows a participation in apostolicity is good news. The danger is not in the 'S' growth curve, but in the framing of innovation as only growth, detached from innovation as compost, spiral and mending. As established in Chapter 3, each is framed in Scripture in relation to an ethic of justice.

I have looked in the rear-view mirror that is mission in the history of Britain and have outlined three different structures. The Celtic mission move was an innovation structured around movement and monastery. The Methodist mission move was an innovation structured around 'bands', connexional systems and 'means of grace'. The modern missionary movement utilized an innovation that was the voluntary society. Placed side by side, particularity is evident. God has worked differently, distinctly. In each move of mission, structural innovation is evident. The becoming of the church is altered. The ecclesial body finds a different shape. This shape is driven by apostolicity, as the church uses means.

The work of Schumpeter has provided analytical frames to understand these structural innovations, particularly in relation to the Methodist and the modern mission moves. Living within tensions is generative. Recombinations play an important role in revitalization, generating new 'cooperating groups'.

We have looked in the rear-view mirror that is mission in Britain. However, when teaching me to drive, my father reminded me not only to check the rear-view mirror. He also kept reminding me to look sideways. What is happening not only behind us, but beside us? Are there trends in organizational cultures today that might offer potential recombinations and thus innovative structures? How might these help us understand the birthing that was Fresh Expressions?

Looking sideways

Missiologist Stanley Skreslet observes that in the history of mission, a new mission vision has often been accompanied by new structures (2012, pp. 153–9). '[A] new model of mission would also have its own distinctive organizational structure' (1997b, p. 310).

As the church is apostolic, the becoming of the ecclesial body is re-formed. Skreslet (1997a; 1997b; 1999) examines contemporary culture, looking for new ways of organizing that, like the trading company a few hundred years ago, might more fully enhance the participation of the whole church, in a wide variety of vocations, in mission partnership. For Skreslet, theology is contextual not only in relation to liturgy, but also to ecclesial structures.

Skreslet argues that NGO networking is a culturally appropriate model that should be shaping mission structures today. Using examples of Greenpeace and Amnesty International, Skreslet charts the rise from the 1990s of NGO groups. NGO models enable action outside control of states and governments. They are created by citizens to encourage grassroots participation. They are structured as local chapters, which are networked together, yet are strengthened by central co-ordination.

This has significant advantages. Networks can be built globally. They can also be built locally. Networks are flexible, egalitarian and wholistic in orientation. They allow multiple partnerships, at local, regional, national, global levels. Skreslet argues that networking as a mode of action contrasts with the worst parts of colonial mission.

Skreslet wonders what a networking structure might look like for mission societies. 'To be truly suitable, mission structures must also be culturally appropriate and right for their age' (1999, p. 2) For Skreslet, this is not 'sacralizing a secular process' (1997b, p. 314). Rather, it enables ecclesial structures to embody qualities essential to the gospel, particularly partnership and the interplay between an identity that is both local and global. For mission structures, the NGO model would mean prioritizing smaller expressions, with a premium put on the ability to be nimble, to cultivate networks and communicate. Skreslet also applies the NGO model in reimagining the structure of the local church. He argues that the NGO model offers 'the local church a new opportunity to articulate a theology of the public square' (p. 314).

Skreslet examined contemporary organizational developments, rather than contemporary mission structures. As such, his suggestions were speculative. However, his work does enable us to look sideways, as well as in the rear-view mirror, to consider what is going on in the world around Fresh Expressions, as well as what has happened in the particularity of the history of mission in Britain.

Framing Fresh Expressions

In seeking to understand Fresh Expressions as an organizational innovation, this chapter has examined a range of mission structures:

- monastic and pilgrim
- bands and connexions
- voluntary societies
- networks.

Placed side by side, they allow us to reflect on the structures of innovation of first expressions as outlined in Chapters 4 and 5, and Fresh Expressions as outlined in Chapters 6 and 7.

Most first expressions seem to be structured as localized expressions of the voluntary society structure. They were localized in that they were not international, yet added a dimension of mission which existing local churches did not have means of expressing. They were voluntary in that they were a local embodiment that gave scope for lay commitment and enthusiasm. This included finding new ways (particularly in technology and the arts) for people to express their faith in relation to culture.

Hence voluntary society seems to capture the way most first expressions ordered their life, whether as a community that existed as a congregation of an existing church (Bigger Picture, Epicentre, Foundation/Resonance, Grace, Host) or in some sort of stand-alone configuration (Graceland, Late Late Service, Moot, Visions). Club Culture Project certainly had elements of the voluntary society, particularly in finding new ways (particularly in technology and the arts) for people to express their faith in relation to culture. However, it is better described as a monastery, with an intentional focus on practices of spirituality and artistic production in relationship to culture.

In locating these first expressions organizationally, consideration was given to an ordering more akin to a band. This would have made sense of the reality that a band has dimensions of a voluntary society, particularly in being a local embodiment and expressing lay commitment and enthusiasm. However, a band as structured in the Methodist mission move lived in strong synergies with already existing congregational forms of life. In contrast, these first expressions tended to see themselves as standing alone.

What is interesting is that in the voluntary society model, the priority is the identity and activity of a centralized body. To illustrate, Carey did not envisage multiple *Particular Baptist Societies for the Propagation of the Gospel Amongst the Heathen*. Rather he imagined one voluntary society with multiple local chapters.

Turning from first expressions to Fresh Expressions, the organization seemed to be structured as a network. This is evident in the Fresh Expressions Five Year plan. As outlined in Chapter 7, 'Birthing Fresh Expressions as an organizational innovation', the Strategic Plan had four planks:[7]

- Renewing vision. Helping the whole church to capture and live this fresh vision through stories, publications and advocacy.
- Gathering news. On what is happening where, what is working and what is not, where to find help and support through research and through the website.
- Resourcing growth. By developing a national network of skilled coaches or accompaniers for fresh expressions of church life.
- Developing training … for lay and ordained ministries and made available in every region through the new Regional Training Partnerships.

These four planks can be placed alongside using the NGO network model outlined above, particularly the values of nimble, networks, multiple partnerships and communicate. Nimble is evident in 'Gathering news. On what is happening ... and what is not'. Networks is evident in 'Resourcing growth ... developing a national network of skilled coaches or accompaniers' and also in 'Developing ... Regional Training Partnerships'. Partnerships is evident in 'Developing training ... through the new Regional Training Partnerships'. Communicate is evident in 'Gathering news. On what is happening ...' and also in 'Renewing vision ... through stories, publications and advocacy'.

However, what is interesting is that the NGO network model, while having centralized co-ordination, places a priority on the identity and activity of local chapters. It is local chapters of Greenpeace and Amnesty International that organize and recruit and through which advocacy happens. In contrast, Fresh Expressions' primary identity and activity flowed out of a centralized group. In addition, Fresh Expressions was not a voluntary society, in that it retained significant denominational identity.

Such a configuration by Fresh Expressions is consistent with its purpose. Indeed, setting up local chapters might have been seen as challenging existing church structures, along with the already established first expressions.

What it does mean is that organizationally the innovation that is Fresh Expressions was structured as a network, albeit centralized, while first expressions were voluntary societies, albeit localized. Hence both are distortions of organizational structures as already conceived. In addition, both are working out of different structural understandings. We will examine this more carefully in the chapters that follow, particularly Chapter 9, 'One in authenticity'.

Conclusion

This chapter has considered organizational structures for mission. Organizations allow vision to be brought into being. As such, they are empirical carriers of theology. Organizations are a becoming and their configurations express commitments regarding relationships. Hence the reality of structures invites theological reflection.

In this case, the focus has been missiological. Fresh Expressions and first expressions have been considered in relation to the empirical activity of God in mission, in particular in the history of Great Britain. This honours the participation of Methodists in Fresh Expressions, as described in the introduction to Chapter 6. It provides another view of church history, not as a subset of Christendom, but as a set of missionary encounters.

As Skreslet observes, when looking at organizational structures for mission, 'one quickly discovers that this is an area of missiology in which theological convictions may be observed interacting with powerful social dynamics' (2012, p. 153).

Looking at organizational structures for mission is an important part of the systematic study of all aspects of mission. Moves in mission located in the history of Great Britain have been considered.

This analysis is possible through a look in the rear-view mirror and then sideways. Moves in mission have been considered. England has been 'missioned' before, most notably in the Celtic pattern. England has been a sender before, most notably in the modern mission movement through the pattern of the voluntary society. England has been renewed before, most notably in the Methodist movement, which through mission resulted in changes in church life, both within Anglicanism and within what would become Methodism.

A range of innovations in mission structures have been identified:

- monastic and pilgrim
- bands and connexions
- voluntary societies
- NGO networks.

Placed side by side, we see that God works differently, distinctly. In each move of mission, structural innovation is evident. The becoming of the church is altered. The ecclesial body finds a different shape, sometimes monastic or voluntary, other times band or NGO network.

This shape is driven by apostolicity. The becoming of the ecclesial body is being formed by mission. A dynamic engagement with society, a recombination, is vital for ecclesial reform. Innovation can occur through risky pilgrimage, by living within generative tensions and by creating parallel structures shaped by contemporary society. When we look to the past, we are reminded of the need to look sideways, for the contemporary in the past has inevitably shaped the history of our present.

The innovations of the past have been applied to the structures of the present. Voluntary societies help describe first expressions; NGO networks help describe Fresh Expressions. What happens when these different structures meet? The realities of structure inevitably invite us to consider theology, the Creedal affirmation of the church as one, holy, catholic and apostolic. How might innovations working out of different structural understandings embody the unity and diversity of being one and catholic? Can culture be engaged in ways that inhabit being apostolic and enable being holy? It is to these questions that we turn in Part 4.

Notes

1 For a European perspective, see Ward (1992). For an Anglo-American perspective, see Noll (2004).

2 Rack is drawing from *Minutes of Several Conversations ... Works*, edited by T. Jackson, 11th edition, 1856, vol. VIII, p. 288. The emphasis in italics is mine.

3 Rack is drawing on *Letters* II: 77–8, 1746.

4 Tindall is drawing from S. Pearce Carey, *William Carey*, edited by Peter Masters (London: Wakeman, 1923).

5 'However it is far more important to note that the foundation of the LMS demonstrates at the end of the eighteenth century something that would have been inconceivable at its beginning: a common ground of action for Episcopalians and Presbyterians, Independents and Methodists' (Walls 1996, p. 248).

6 'There never was a *theology* of the voluntary society. The voluntary society is one of God's theological jokes, whereby [God] makes tender mockery of ... people when they take themselves too seriously' (Walls 1996, p. 246).

7 Provided by Steven Croft as a photocopy during the interview. Dated 6 January 2005.

PART 4

Becoming in ecclesial innovation

Colours on canvas
Etch faith on creative edge
Authentic ethic

Ambient witness
Public private, mystery
Old stones. Lit. Breathe well

Pearl of what. A price?
A lustre of construction
Clammed tight; a hinge

Decently ordered
Take, break, bless, give, body shape
Governance move, make

9

One in authenticity

The use of the term *authenticity* in the social science literature can be rather eclectic at best and unscrupulous at worst. (Vannini 2011, p. 74)

In 1996, Grace made national TV. *God in the House* was a series of six programmes shown on Channel 4. Each one featured a 'radical alternative Christian service' and the final one was Grace. The producer of *God in the House*, Dave Hill, was upbeat. 'For believers and non-believers alike this is a true reflection of Christian spirituality in 90s' Britain. I hope viewers will check their preconceptions at the door as this series shows a new era in religious history' (Cummings 1996). A new era of religious history is a striking commendation.

The Grace service begins with ambient dance music.[1] In a church stripped of pews, people dance to the repeated chorus, 'Dancing to a New Expression'. The introduction relates faith and culture and suggests a contextual expression of faith. 'We're here to worship in ways and in forms that we can relate to, but without losing the essence of the story' ('Grace' – *God in the House* 1996, 2:10–2:17). The service involves original music, storytelling, video capture, mixed with centring prayer and the Apostles' Creed, 'a version of the Creed, updated a little bit' ('Grace', 7:32).

The TV episode concludes with an interview with Jonny Baker, one of the leaders at Grace. This returns again to the relationship between faith and culture.

> We're into the music. We love all the visuals. It's not like we're putting it on for someone else. Having said that, we are keen to do something that people outside the church can relate to. It's worship and mission. It's the same. It's about what's authentic and flies for us. ('Grace', 18:50–19:13)

This contextual expression of faith is about authenticity. Contextualization is not about crossing into another culture. Rather it is about the commitment to express faith in the music and visual of what 'flies for us'. For a participant at Grace, interviewed for the *God in the House* TV series, Grace was a 'service for young people. It is different. It is not like a normal boring service. It is lively. I enjoy going' ('Grace', 13:20). For another, Grace meant 'freedom and the ability to bring your own self where God is' ('Grace', 12:45). The affirmation of bringing one's own self suggests an authenticity that is personal and integrative and in which God can be experienced. Such an approach to contextualization is needed because the culture has shifted, but the forms of the church have not.

A number of other thinkers have drawn on authenticity to describe contemporary ecclesiology. Steve Rabey applies the term authentic to the emerging church. He describes an emerging generation of 'young people who feel that most traditional and contemporary churches fail to touch them' (2001, p. 11). What is emerging are communities of faith that value authenticity in relationships and in connection with culture. Similarly, Bielo (2011) argues for a new Christian movement in which authenticity is at the heart of the interaction with culture. These new forms of church have coalesced around the idea that culture has shifted. This requires the 'adoption of a "missiological" orientation ... equated with doing foreign missions' (Bielo 2009a, p. 132). What Baker at Grace is doing is affirming the idea of a changing culture, but reframing what is foreign. This culture is not foreign for those who go to Grace. What is foreign is the way the inherited church worships.

This claim for authenticity, and the way it is framed in relation to faith and culture, raises significant challenges for the Creedal affirmation of the church as one. What happens when the authenticity of one person's faith expression comes into conflict with the authenticity of another? Who defines oneness in the midst of cultural change? Can assertions of individual authenticity deconstruct inherited understandings of cultural identity? This chapter will examine ecclesial questions raised by authenticity – first, in relation to authenticity, second, in relation to innovation and, third, in relation to mission practice, in particular the complicity of mission in the assertion of cultural domination.[2] Lyrical analysis of first expressions songs, along with first expression focus group questions exploring the impact of the arrival of Fresh Expressions as an organization in 2004, provide a source of empirical data. The argument is that authenticity was essential in first expression grassroots ecclesial innovation.

Oneness at Grace

Lyrics of the songs sung by Grace provide a way to examine the interplay between faith, culture and expression. What happens to notions of oneness? Four songs are sung – 'Dancing to a New Expression', 'We believe', 'Counter to the Culture' and 'God be in my head'. Each is original to Grace. I will explore how together they show a dynamic interplay between faith, culture and expression (shown in Figure 7).

The argument is that oneness is located not in faith, culture or expression, but in the body-ing forth of all three. Grace believe they are dancing to a new song, of an ancient rhythm. In other words, oneness is located not in the uniformity of belief, but in the body-ing forth, the interactions between faith and culture by which 'God ... attends to every changing thing – in particular. This is the work of the Spirit, this bodying forth of God in ... our world' (Soskice 2007, p. 33). Let us consider first how oneness might be understood as a result of analysing the lyrics, before considering the implications for the church as one.

The first song was titled 'Dancing to a New Expression'. It involved the multiple repetition of two lines:

> Dancing to a new expression, of an ancient rhythm
> Singing out a new song, in praise to the name of the Lord
> ('Grace' – *God in the House* 1996, 1:00–4:02)

For three minutes, Grace literally dance, arms waving, moving their bodies – body-ing forth – to the rhythm and beats of dance club culture. Faith is en-acted – lyrically in dance, singing and praise; musically with conga drums and electric guitar.

A second song was titled 'I believe' ('Grace', 7:28–11:55). The song is introduced as 'a version of the Creed, updated a little bit'. The phrase, 'I believe' is sung multiple times, supported by a soundscape in which rhythm guitar, synthesizer and conga drums are dominant. The affirmations are orthodox – 'Three are one and united; God made earth and heavens; Jesus [is] born of a woman, Son of God, teacher, healer, who died, betrayed and rejected, bore the power of evil, rose to God's right hand, judge of dead and living. The Spirit is [a] life-giver of healing and forgiveness. Life everlasting and resurrection of the body' – all are affirmed. What is missing is affirmation of belief in the church and the communion of saints. There is no indication that this is an intentional act of theological reflection. A more likely option is a musical pragmatism, given that the song already runs over four minutes, and the repetition of 'I believe', while faith affirming, runs the danger of monotony.

There is a symmetry between these two songs. Grace is literally writing new songs. They are dancing to a new expression of an ancient rhythm, the belief of the Creeds. For Grace, oneness is not located in faith in the Creeds alone, in isolation from culture or expression. Rather is it located in expression, in their body-ing forth of fresh worship, drawing on new technologies and the dance beats of the club culture music they love.

A third song was titled 'Counter to the Culture'.[3] After the emphasis on authenticity and bringing 'your own self', this song complexifies the relationship with culture. The song follows the reading of the story of Zacchaeus and is introduced because 'God's kingdom [is] being subversive'. The chorus calls for the need to be 'Going against the flow' because 'Your kingdom is upside down'. Authenticity is clearly more than self-actualization. To give is better than to receive; cancel debts and love your enemies. Cultural relevance includes the challenge to undermine the idols of technology and science, the need for the latest gadget or appliance. There are political ('justice, peace, and righteousness, the politics of your government') and environmental dimensions ('the earth is inherited by the meek'), all while using video to project images.

Charles Taylor argues that we live in an age of authenticity, an era which prizes the finding of one's life 'against the demands of external conformity' (1992, pp. 67–8). His argument is that, correctly practised, authenticity need not result in individualism or tribalism. Rather as the authentic self is freed from external restraint, it realizes that it can only truly be an authentic self as it lives in authentic relationships with others. Hence Taylor argues for the possibility of an ethical authenticity, a generation of people 'made more self-responsible' (p. 77).

This is clearly what is envisaged at Grace. Living 'counter to the culture' involves an authenticity that includes freedom from restraints of the acquisition of technology and the choice to embrace relationships of equality, giving, justice and care for the earth. This is clearly a community seeking to embody Taylor's self-responsibility. Engagement with culture is an essential dimension of authenticity. Faith cannot be expressed apart from in relationship to politics, environment, technology, gender relationships and economic lifestyles.

The fourth and final song was an up tempo mix of 'God be in my head'.[4] The authentic self is body-ied forth in understanding, seeing, speaking and thinking. The authenticity in relationship to culture expressed in the 'Counter to the culture' will be lived in the 'departing' from worship. The lyrics are sourced from a Book of Hours, dated 1514. Again we see a connection to a faith, one that is 'ancient'. Again, we see a 'new expression' in the use of electric guitar, bass, synthesizer and conga drums. There is also a visible dance culture reference, with the use of a whistle. According to *Electronic Beats* (2017), the 1990s were 'peak whistle era', with the use of the whistle being a sign of 'the dance floor's appreciation of a mix well done'. It thus stands as an appropriate 'dance culture' gesture as this service of worship ended.

Oneness for Grace involves authenticity. It is the integration of faith with culture and in ways that are body-ing forth their faith. Faith is affirmed, yet 'updated'; culture is loved, yet needs to be countered. Faith

Figure 7: Authenticity as the interplay between faith, culture and expression

Faith
('ancient rhythm'; Creed;
Beatitudes; Book of Hours)

Culture
('love the music'; 'love the
visuals'; 'new expression'
'updated a little bit'; electronic
music; dance music, whistle)

Authenticity

Body-ing forth
('new expression'; creating
original music, living 'Counter to
the culture')

is personal, 'I believe', yet lived in relationship with others, systems, organization and earth.

What might this mean for how Grace views other communities of faith? Presumably this involves them being authentic as a community in ways that are body-ing forth their integration of faith with the culture they are part of. Grace does not expect other communities to love the dance music. It would be inauthentic for such communities to blow whistles if participants were not part of dance culture on Saturday nights. But the value of authenticity as expressed in the interplay of faith, culture and body-ing forth provides a commonality. Oneness is possible, through authenticity.

We have examined Grace and analysed the way their assertion of authenticity is reflected in the music they create and the lyrics they sing. A consideration of authenticity more broadly, including as understood within dance culture in the 1990s, provides a way to understand tensions that emerged in the innovation that was Fresh Expressions.

Authenticity-as-originality

Philip Vannini argues that use of the term **authenticity** in the social science literature has been at best eclectic, and at worst unscrupulous (2011, p. 74). He seeks definitional clarity by asking that authenticity be parsed in three ways – factual, original and sincere. A failure to attend to these distinctives, mixed with a 'paucity of systematic empirical research' has resulted in abstract speculation (p. 75). Having already, in the examination of Grace's lyrics, undertaken 'systematic empirical research', it is instructive to apply Vannini's theoretical frame – authenticity as factual, original and sincere – to religious innovation both of first expressions as grassroots communities and Fresh Expressions as an organization.

For first expressions, *authenticity-as-originality* is essential to their identity creation. This has two dimensions: first, to articulate their relationship with culture (as *authentically original* in contemporary cultures) and, second, to define themselves as marginal from mainstream religious expression.

We see both these dimensions at Grace. Their body-ing forth in worship is *authentically original* in contemporary cultures because it is about 'what flies for us'. They are 'into the music. We love all the visuals. It's not like we're putting it on for someone else' ('Grace' – *God in the House* 1996, 18:50–19:13). The second dimension is evident in the comment that Grace is 'different. It is not like a normal boring service' ('Grace', 13:20). In their body-ing forth as *authentically original* in contemporary cultures, they are different from mainstream religious expressions. This authenticity-as-originality gives vibrancy to their life. Indeed, returning to the lyrics, authenticity-as-sincerity is not enough. Faith needs to have a 'new expression' and be lived counter to the culture. The Creed needs to be 'updated' 'by adding dance beats' (*authentically original* in contemporary cultures). As there are more of the 'latest gadget or appliance', so comes more opportunity to live faith authentically, to decide whether this technology might be an idol, or might be part of body-ing forth.

We also see *authenticity-as-originality* as essential more broadly in the identity creation among first expression communities. We have noted already, in Chapter 1, how the worship of The Nine O'Clock Service (NOS) was experienced by one participant:

> We enter a round, darkened room where there are forty-two television sets and twelve large video screens and projections around the walls – projections of dancing DNA, dancing planets and galaxies and atoms … this was a very friendly place for a generation raised on television and images … these people … are doing it themselves *and in the center*

of the city and in the center of their society: at worship itself. (Fox 1996, p. 9–10, italics original)

This description makes a number of appeals to authenticity. The phrase 'a generation raised on television and images' implies another generation not raised in digitally rich environments. A cultural distinction has been created. Two cultures can watch the same television, but one will be the generation 'raised on television and images'. Rogerson described NOS as 'a bold and imaginative attempt at contextual theology ... [P]eople were attracted to it in the first instance for aesthetic and cultural reasons' (2006, p. 51). The priority on the aesthetic and the cultural, in contrast to the doctrinal, suggests a valuing of *authenticity-as-originality*. Like Grace, NOS was 'counter to the culture'. For Rogerson, NOS offered 'an alternative way of living in a materialist and acquisitive world' (p. 50). This resonates with Charles Taylor's argument that authenticity can be practised in ways that make people 'more self-responsible' (1992, p. 77). Creativity, described as 'doing it themselves', allows a generation 'raised on television and images' to connect faith with justice-making in relationships with others, organizations, systems and the environment.

Another example of the appeal to a 'doing it themselves' *authenticity-as-originality* is evident in the following reflection:

People were willing to play around and to say, well who knows what will happen if we run this video clip or commercial next to this sixteenth-century religious painting and if we play, you know, *Black Flag* or some weird band underneath it ... And what will it feel like? Well let's try it and see. (Gay 2001)

The interplay between faith (sixteenth-century religious painting) and culture (*Black Flag*, an American hard core punk band formed in 1976), is central. The word 'weird' is deployed to signify an *authenticity-as-originality* that is 'alternative', musically distinct from the mainstream. Indeed, the very term 'alternative worship' is significant. Sociologist of religion Abby Day argued that 'boundary-marking [creates] an identity' (2011, p. 50). Applying Day, the term 'alternative' is being used to create an identity in contrast to the existing, mainstream church. Ironically, the mainstream is needed in order to define against, to create identity by being *authentically original*.

Authenticity-as-originality and interactions with the mainstream

A helpful conversation partner in teasing out the interactions between 'doing it themselves' grassroots innovation and organizational innovation is Sarah Thornton, who researched dance clubs in Britain during the time period when Grace and other first expression communities emerged. Thornton highlighted the value of authenticity, which she argued was deployed in club cultures to create 'subcultural capital' (1996, pp. 98–105). The whistle used at Grace during 'God be in my head' is a fine example of subcultural capital, marking Grace as distinct in their connection with dance culture and original in incorporating dance culture into their worship. For Thornton,

> authenticity is arguably the most important value ascribed to popular music … Music is perceived as authentic when it *rings true* or *feels real*, when it has *credibility* and comes across as *genuine*. In an age of endless representations and global mediation, the experience of musical authenticity is perceived as a cure both for alienation … and dissimulation. (Thornton 1996, p. 26, italics original)

Thornton is arguing that in this manifestation of youth culture, authenticity is valued. 'Doing it yourself' has value, in contrast to the consumption of production by mass (mainstream) music (pop) cultures. Originality is valued because it has credibility and is deemed genuine. It can be valued not only by those who produce, but also by those who consume (dance) as they assign value, deeming the 'doing it yourself' creativity 'rings true' and 'feels real'.

Thornton understood society as networked. She recognized the complex roles of media and commerce in constructing distinctions. This enabled her to analyse the interplay between mainstream and marginal and explore how authenticity was understood when an alternative innovation created in a club became a mainstream success (p. 119). She argued that in club culture, losing authenticity ('selling out') was perceived to have happened only when the marginal community 'loses its sense of possession, exclusive ownership and familiar belonging' (pp. 124–6). Words like possession and exclusive are not isolationist words, given the way Thornton traces the interconnections between creators, designers, producers and club participants. Rather they are words that seek the ability to maintain authenticity-as-originality. The ability to innovate, to create further 'new expressions', is sustained.

Applying Thornton, first expression innovations can be drawn upon by the wider church. Alternative can be part of the one, holy, catholic and apostolic church. This can be for the benefit of both the grassroots innovation and the wider church. But for durability of the grassroots innovation, they need to maintain their sense of identity over time.

Working from empirical research into dance cultures, Thornton provides a framework that can clarify the interplay between innovation and wider systems. This is valuable as we turn to analyse the arrival of Fresh Expressions as an institutional innovation.

first expressions and Fresh Expressions

As described in Chapter 7, Fresh Expressions emerged as a distinct organization from within the Church of England and the Methodist Church in Britain and Ireland. It was an innovation within an established organization. It has an intriguing relationship with first expressions, first because Fresh Expressions drew on first expressions for legitimation as it developed. At the same time, Fresh Expressions offered a vision that has implications for, and made judgements about, first expressions.

Hence the frameworks provided by Thornton provide clarity. How did the discourse deployed by Fresh Expressions in creating innovation engage 'alternative worship' as an existing innovation? How did these 'alternative worship' groups, who had found generative energy in their location as an alternative – *authentically original* – expression, respond to this move of appropriation by mainstream religious life?

The use by Fresh Expressions of first expressions for legitimation is evident in *Mission-Shaped Church* (2004). As described in Chapter 1, the report researched recent religious innovation in England, grouped under 12 headings (alternative worship communities, base ecclesial communities, cafe church, cell, network and seeker church models, multiple and mid-week congregations, new forms of traditional churches, school and community-based initiatives, traditional church plants, youth congregations). Recognition of authenticity in these 'alternative' innovations was evident in the institutional discourse. When I interviewed Archbishop Rowan Williams, he spoke of his commitment as a bishop:

> [I decided] to spend a certain amount of quality time with people on the edge. Consequently when I was asked initially what are [my] priorities [as archbishop] I said, 'Well, this is what I've been watching [on the edge ...] I really want to see how that could impact on the Church of England as a whole.' (Williams 2013)

Williams used the already existing work of first expressions ('this is what I've been watching') to bring change ('I really want to see how that could impact on the Church of England as a whole'). What had until then been marginal ('on the edge'), what had until then generated identity as being *authentic-in-originality* in contrast to the mainstream, was now being appropriated by the mainstream. *Mission-Shaped Church* was aware of this complexity, describing 'alternative worship' as containing 'a strong desire to be different and is most vocal in its repudiation of existing church' (2004, p. 45). Nevertheless, it was appropriated by the mainstream.

My argument has been that 'alternative worship' drew on a discourse of *authenticity-as-originality*, both in explaining how it body-ied forth faith and culture and in defining an identity in contrast to mainstream religious expression. Both moves – of explanation and definition – were essential. They are tropes which foreground culture in faith, allowing the adoption of a '"missiological" orientation' (Bielo 2009a, p. 132) within the context of a diversifying United Kingdom.

Yet when we turn to analyse the appropriation of first expressions by Fresh Expressions, we find that the definitions of authenticity begin to slide. *Mission-Shaped Church* affirmed *authenticity-as-originality*, applauding the 'ways in which the Church of England has sought to engage with the diverse cultures and networks that are part of contemporary life' (2004, p. 80). It made explicit the connection between originality and authenticity. 'Some pioneers and leaders have yearned for a more authentic way of living, being, doing church' (p. 80). Such statements affirm *authenticity-as-originality*.

Yet *Mission-Shaped Church* also introduced what could be defined as *authenticity-as-sincerity* as a caution to *authenticity-as-originality*. 'Fresh expressions should not be embraced simply because they are popular and new, but because they are a sign of the work of God and of the kingdom' (p. 80). In this statement, evaluative criteria are introduced ('sign of the work of God'). Such *authenticity-as-sincerity* signs, defined in relationship to being from God, are placed as necessary to evaluate *authenticity-as-originality*. The result is a parsing of authenticity, offering sincerity as distinct from originality.

Missiologist John Flett urges a missiology in which being sent orders continuity, rather than continuity orders being sent. He notes the latent power of the inherited church, which results in a primacy given to continuity. For Flett, 'cultivation ... directs and establishes a range of controls over the ... communication of faith' (2016, p. 16). He describes the trajectories:

Cultivation, in other words, is the governing factor beside which all others are asymmetrically ordered. Its priority shapes the nature and purpose of structures and the ends to which sacraments and the accompanying interpretive measures, such as order and liturgy, are directed. It conditions theological formulations of the church's 'visibility,' the nature of its historical continuity and the relationship of the local to the universal. (p. 16)

In other words, the *authenticity-of-originality* as Grace dances to a new expression is becoming directed by definitions of what is 'a sign of the work of God and of the kingdom'. Phrases like 'sign of the work of God' are 'accompanying interpretive measures'. They allow the inherited church to condition the 'theological formulations of the church's "visibility"'. There are far more theological resources aligned to clarify the signs of God in history than in understanding the signs of God in the popular and new.

Using Vannini's call to attend to the differences in the use of the term authenticity, it becomes clear that in *Mission-Shaped Church* the institutional innovation was drawing power from first expressions. Yet the definitional work being done to create Fresh Expressions was conflating innovation, by compressing 12 expressions of church under a new label.[5] It was also critiquing first expressions, making innovation contestable by drawing on two notions of authenticity – *authenticity-as-sincerity* and *authenticity-as-originality* – all without attending to the differences and making possible 'abstract speculation' (Vannini 2011, p. 75). So what was the result of this interplay between first expressions and Fresh Expressions? How did first expressions respond to the conflation and contestability?

Conflation and contestability

First, it is intriguing to ponder why *authenticity-as-sincerity* was introduced into *Mission-Shaped Church*. Why might it need to be stated that first expressions 'should not be embraced simply because they are popular and new, but because they are a sign of the work of God and of the kingdom' (2004, p. 80)?

One possibility is the awareness of the risk in an age of authenticity of a society that is more individualized and tribal (Taylor 1992, pp. 55–6). To put it in distinctly ecclesiological terms, how can the church as one, holy, catholic and apostolic be carried forward if *authenticity-as-originality* is celebrated at, and by, the margins? Will innovation contribute to more atomized, self-absorbed and fragmented expressions of church?

Yet Taylor is adamant that authenticity can be embraced without an inevitable slide in these directions. Taylor argued that humans share a 'horizon of significance' in common (p. 52), in which one's own 'identity crucially depends on [one's] dialogical relations with others' (p. 48). In other words, oneness is located not in authenticity, but in the body-ing forth of relationality. To put it in distinctly ecclesiological terms, catholicity is the carrier of oneness. We will develop this more practically in Chapter 10, when we consider apostolicity, and Chapter 12, when we consider sacrament and governance in the ordering of innovation. This also returns us to the discussion earlier in this chapter of how authenticity can be generative of oneness, not by expecting all communities to share the same expressions. Rather by affirming that authenticity-as-originality can exist as a commonality for all communities, a sharing in the bodying forth of faith in response to the particular cultures in which they are located.

Second, how did first expressions respond to how they were drawn upon, yet critiqued? The value of longitudinal empirical research is that it allows this sort of exploration. Returning in 2012–13, some eight years after the launch of Fresh Expressions, I added an interview question and invited the first expression focus groups to reflect on their perceptions of the impact, if any, of Fresh Expressions. The responses can be grouped into three categories: minimal impact, a sense of affirmation and a contested complexity.

With regard to *minimal impact*, some 'alternative worship' communities perceived that the arrival of Fresh Expressions had minimal impact on their shared expression of faith. The following quote was representative: 'Has had no impact at all actually. Apart from to be slightly puzzled' (Sanctuary 2013a).

Others found the advent of Fresh Expressions provided a *sense of affirmation*. 'Fresh expressions is ... an enabling concept. It was very powerful' (Foundation 2013). Respondents in this category felt that their innovations within alternative worship had contributed to, or been valued by, the innovation of Fresh Expressions. This is a contrast to the experiences described in Chapter 1, of church leaders standing back cautious of 'a few *entrepreneurs* doing their own thing ... "Will they stand the test of time?"' (Vincent 1976, p. 100). Instead, in *Mission-Shaped Church*, those pioneering in first expressions see a validation of their intuitive innovation.

Interestingly, those who expressed a sense of affirmation were more likely to have a vocational role that in some way had become connected to Fresh Expressions. They were speaking on pioneering or involved in leadership development. Drawing on Thornton, they had 'subcultural capital' invested in the organizational and systemic innovation (Thornton 1996, pp. 98–105). Thornton argued that in the complex networks through which culture flows, certain people, for example DJs, have more influence in the ascribing of authenticity. There is a mutuality by which Fresh Expressions was legitimated by the involvement of first expression leaders, as these leaders' pioneering and risk-taking was affirmed by the wider church. This is the value of *authenticity-as-originality*. It nourishes the church as one in innovation.

For others, the arrival of Fresh Expressions had resulted in a *contested complexity*. The following quote was representative: 'It's a crap piece of establishment branding ... [but then] we're just snobs' (Grace 2013). This comment returns us to my initial framing of *authenticity-as-originality*. I would argue that 'we're just snobs' has a similar rhetorical effect as '*Black Flag* or some weird band'. It is an act of marginal self-location essential in the construction of innovation and identity. It is a response to the conflation of 12 expressions of church – alternative worship and base ecclesial communities, cafe, cell, network and seeker church models, multiple and mid-week congregations, new forms of traditional churches, school and community-based initiatives, traditional church plants, youth congregations – under one label. Each of these expressions has a different degree of *authenticity-as-originality*. Each is engaged with a different dimension of the cultural landscape. Conflating them reduces the distinctiveness of identity formation.

Again, Thornton provides a framework to help clarify this interplay of contested complexity between grassroots innovation and organizational appropriation. As part of her longitudinal research, she explored what happened when a song from a club, which had defined itself against the mainstream and as 'hip', suddenly experienced mainstream success (1996, p. 119). What is relevant to this investigation into religious innovation is her argument that in club culture, 'selling out' is perceived to have happened only when the marginal community 'loses its sense of possession, exclusive ownership and familiar belonging' (pp. 124–6).

I would suggest that this is what is happening within 'alternative worship' in response to the arrival of Fresh Expressions. Both 'alternative worship' and Fresh Expressions are religious innovations. But Fresh Expressions defined itself in a way that conflated the space. It meant that the boundary marking so essential to 'alternative worship' was lost. Some gained from this. Others struggled with a loss of imaginative and cultural creativity, a softening of *authenticity-as-originality*.

More importantly, the discourse around Fresh Expressions also introduced *authenticity-as-sincerity* as a value that could be used to contest *authenticity-as-originality*. Whether intended or not, this also challenged the ethic of authenticity already created by these 'alternative worship' communities. Their *authenticity-as-originality* was already a practising of an ethic of authenticity. While 'crap' is a strong word, it reveals a deep sense of investment. As first expressions, these groups were already deeply invested in exploring what it means to be 'counter to the culture', offering a bold, imaginative, aesthetic and cultural attempt at contextual theology (drawing on Rogerson 2006, p. 51).

I have analysed the interplay between first expressions as grassroots innovation and Fresh Expressions as an organizational innovation. I have noted how Fresh Expressions drew legitimation from first expressions, yet also offered critique through the conflating of authenticity-as-sincerity with authenticity-as-originality. I have described how this generated three responses – minimal impact, affirmation and contested complexity.

My data set is limited, and the gift of hindsight is a beautiful thing. However, it does invite reflection. Thornton demonstrates that it is possible for grassroots innovation to be legitimated by mainstream innovation. If the church seeks to be not only one, but also apostolic and catholic, then the interplay between centre and edge, grassroots and institutional, is an essential part of ecclesiological vitality. In a context of decline, and with the perceived success of Fresh Expressions, it is likely that organizational attempts at ecclesial innovation will be attempted in other denominations and in other countries. If innovation is to be sustained, then the interplay between grassroots innovation and organizations needs to be generative, for the sake of both.

Authenticity-as-originality applied to organizational innovation

We discussed in the previous chapter ('Moves in mission') how the ecclesial body takes different organizational shape in different environments.

One lens by which to consider other options for how an organization might interact with first expressions is offered by Paas, who writes of the importance of innovation as the only way to resolve 'long-term challenges for which solutions are still unknown' (2016, p. 225). Given that innovation is impossible to plan, Paas argues for a concentration on processes rather than results. This comes as the church 'succeeds in creating its own critical margin' (p. 225). Three different types of environments make this possible: free havens, laboratories and incubators (pp. 226–39).

A *free haven* is an unregulated, countercultural place of mild anarchy (pp. 226–9). An example would be a group of artists coming together in a historic building. Within Christian history, festivals can function as free havens, providing a context in which creativity can flourish. A free haven is more likely to flourish when it is located on the edge and at some distance from the centre of an organization. It seeks solutions considered important but too radical for the majority. This requires a two-track understanding, in which free haven innovation functions as a complementary system within the church. Those in the free haven offer an environment of radical commitment, which lives in complementary difference as a church within a church.

A *laboratory* is a community of difference, in which 'creative people from different backgrounds work together to solve shared problems' (p. 229). They work best by drawing on processes in which cross-fertilization results in unexpected encounters and generates new questions. An example is a research laboratory in a university, in which very different individuals work with others on a shared quest. Within Christian history, Paas points to early Pietist societies initiated by leaders like Count Zinzendorf. They did not seek to create an 'alternative self-sufficient structure' that pushed 'certain answers to their limit' (p. 230). Rather, they facilitated unexpected encounters between people from different worlds, disturbed their routines and offered them enough challenges to send them out in adventurous mission (p. 233).

An *incubator* draws on elements of both free haven and laboratory but is considered separately given an incubator is more dependent on external support, including finance. Hence, they offer the greatest possibility for programmed innovation (p. 233). Within Christian history, Paas points to Fresh Expressions as an incubator, with the institution of the church reforming to provide supportive structures like Ordained Pioneer Ministry and Bishops' Mission Orders. '[T]he great challenge for innovation through incubators is to have enough autonomy to allow genuine renewal to happen' (p. 238). The area of greatest vulnerability is 'the invisible networks of communication between the power center and the pioneers' (p. 239).

These three types provide options for organizations considering ecclesial innovation. All three have been present in Christian history, offer different possibilities, and present different trajectories and challenges. Describing all three types allows us to appreciate the contested complexity tensions described above. First expressions fit well the description of a free haven. They offered a countercultural space in which their authenticity-as-originality was a form of mild anarchy. If allowed to maintain a radical distance, they could, as Thornton observed in DJ club cultures, maintain a creative edge while generating resources that benefit the mainstream.

With the gift of hindsight, Fresh Expressions needed to find ways to encourage first expressions to keep pushing certain answers to their limits. This is possible with a two-track model, in which environments of radical commitment live in complementary difference as a church within a church. This would have involved nurturing the existing grassroots innovations in a number of spaces – some as free havens, others as laboratories – while at the same time offering incubators. These would work on the invisible networks of communication, celebrating grassroots learning, locating it in contexts of research and training, in which those from the wider church can be encouraged in the establishing of their own free havens and laboratories. To put it simply, to establish within

Fresh Expressions a number of clearly defined spaces, free havens that encourage radical commitment and push radical answers to their limits, laboratories to generate new questions and incubators in which the learnings are clarified and communicated.

Conclusion

The Creed affirms the church as one, holy, catholic and apostolic. In this chapter, I have examined how the trope of authenticity might contribute to the church as one. In acts of empirical research, the lyrics of a first expression community and focus group data have been analysed. Oneness for Grace involves authenticity. It is the integration of faith with culture and in ways that are body-ing forth their faith. The result is a faith creatively engaged in new forms of expression.

I have then examined how the church more widely responded to this authenticity. *Mission-Shaped Church* (2004) drew on what was authentic for Grace in justifying ecclesial innovation.

At the same time, *Mission-Shaped Church* introduced complexity. The definitional work being done to create Fresh Expressions compressed under one brand what was the diversity of multiple expressions of *authenticity-as-originality*. *Mission-Shaped Church* also introduced *authenticity-as-sincerity* as a contested value. Unless significant extra theological resource was to flow towards discerning the signs of God in *authenticity-as-originality*, it was likely that 'historical continuity, stability, order and office' would maintain a 'governing factor' (Flett 2016, p. 16).

Thornton describes how *authenticity-as-originality* was maintained among creative communities, even when their creative resources were drawn into the mainstream. However, interviews with first expression communities suggest this has not been the case. Some individuals felt affirmed. However, other first expression participants articulated a contested complexity.

An essential argument in this book is that early innovation provides significant learnings, as a way of awakening the body of Christ. This can be applied not only to first expressions, but equally to Fresh Expressions, which as a first organizational expression was pioneering organizational innovation. Hence, I turned to the work of Stephan Paas, and the three different types of environments – free havens, laboratories, incubators – by which an organization might encourage innovation. This was applied to Fresh Expressions.

Authenticity-as-originality might be better resourced through establishing a number of clearly defined spaces. Fresh Expressions could have remained an overarching brand, which championed free havens to push radical answers to their limits, laboratories to generate new questions and incubators in which the learnings are clarified and communicated.

This chapter has demonstrated the importance of authenticity in innovation. However, authenticity as a trope is never neutral. How does the assertion of faith being about 'what's authentic and flies for us' experience meaningful engagement with the other? In order to address these questions, we need to consider apostolicity, holiness and catholicity more deeply.

Notes

1 The use of video footage, both in this chapter and in Chapter 11, is a way of drawing on empirical research that is available in the public domain.

2 This chapter develops earlier published work, see Taylor 2015.

3 Chorus – 'Counter to the Culture, Going against the flow; finding new directions, Your kingdom is upside down (×3). Verse 1 – 'Justice, peace, and righteousness, the politics of your government; the poor are blessed and the strong are weak, the earth is inherited by the meek.' Verse 2 – 'Resistance to the Spirit of the age, Live a lifestyle that can be sustained; Undermine the idols of technology and science, the need for the latest gadget or appliance.' Verse 3 – 'Women and men have equal worth, lay down power and learn to serve; To give is better than to receive, cancel debts and love your enemies'. Lyrics transcribed from 'Grace' – *God in the House* 1996, 16:01–18:50.

4 'God be in my head, And in my understanding; God be in my eyes, And in my looking; God be in my mouth, And in my speaking; God be in my heart, And in my thinking (×3); God be at my end (×2), And in my departing'. Lyrics transcribed from 'Grace' – *God in the House* 1996, 22:16– 25:15.

5 Hence in *Mission-Shaped Church* (2004, pp. 43–84), alternative worship is named as one innovation alongside eleven others (alternative worship and base ecclesial communities, cafe, cell, network and seeker church models, multiple and mid-week congregations, new forms of traditional churches, school and community-based initiatives, traditional church plants, youth congregations).

Becoming apostolic in ambient witness

You will be my witnesses in Jerusalem, in all Judea and Samaria, and to the ends of the earth. (Acts 1.8)

The church is formed by witness. This chapter examines the witness of first expressions.

In order to understand what it means to witness – not in Jerusalem but in central London, not in Samaria but in Swindon, not at the ends of the earth but among the historic buildings of York – the work of Charles Taylor is utilized. His outline of the shape of contemporary conversion clarifies the nature of Christian witness in today's secular world.

Three case studies of contemporary witness will be described: buildings that breathe in York, angels that hover in Swindon and spirituality as humanization in central London. Two of the case studies are drawn from my first expression empirical research, the third provides an independent account for the purposes of benchmarking. Each of the case studies of contemporary witness is analysed in relation to Taylor's portrayal of the nature of conversion in a secular age.

A bearing of ambient witness is proposed, acts of apostolicity that invite conversion in a secular age. First expressions have found ways to offer witness that disrupt the public/private dualisms of secularity, provoke questions, maintain en-culture-ated freshness and promote human agency. In order to begin this task, definitions of witness, apostolicity and ambience are necessary.

Defining witness, apostolic, ambient

Our images carry theology. The missionary in a pith helmet or a crusader wielding a lance on a charging horse depict a set of assumptions about God, witness and mission. Missiologist Stanley Skreslet argues that the images that portray Christian witness 'speak volumes about the fundamental sense of vocation that guides and defines missionary praxis' (2006, p. 2).

Witness

Witness is the term for mission in Acts (Gaventa 1982, p. 416). The noun witness occurs once in Luke and thirteen times in Acts. 'For Luke, witnessing is the primary activity of mission ... to tell the truth to the world' about the actions of God (p. 417). Witness begins with God, the One who establishes the 'times or periods' (Acts 1.7) in which 'you will be my witnesses' (Acts 1.8). Witness comes from God as a promise not a command – the verb is indicative not imperative (Gaventa 1982, p. 416).

The nature of witness in Acts is shaped by particularity. They 'arise out of and speak first to people living in specific times and places' (Skreslet 2006, p. 3). Speaking to 'devout Jews from every nation' (Acts 2.5), the Old Testament is a key resource,[1] along with respect for the 'ancestor David' (Acts 2.29). In Acts 14, 'proclaiming the good news' in the 'surrounding country' (Acts 14.6–7), the 'witness' comes from 'rains from heaven and fruitful seasons' (Acts 14.17) rather than from Old Testament Scriptures. Among the 'extremely religious' in Athens (Acts 17.22), the witness draws on existing religious mystery (the altar to an unknown God, Acts 17.23), 'some of your own poets' (Acts 17.28). The respected ancestor is not David as in Acts 2, but the one who made 'all nations to inhabit the earth' (Acts 17.26). Witness in Jerusalem takes a different shape as it moves toward the ends of the earth. Acts 'portrays a mission that is adaptable to culture, and the mission takes on different forms in different contexts' (Gaventa 1982, p. 422). Hence this chapter will consider the bearing of Christian witness not in Jerusalem and Samaria, but in central London, Swindon and among the historic buildings of York. Charles Taylor's work will be essential in framing the nature of Christian witness today, in particular his analysis of the shape of contemporary conversion.

Apostolicity

Apostolicity is defined as continuity of mission, in which the development of a world Christianity emerges in faithfulness to the origins of the gospel (Flett 2016, p. 16). A theology of apostolicity, Flett argues, understands the gospel expressed in vernacular word, deed and structure as essential to the continuity of that faith (p. 19). The church is understood as a 'visible society in the event of cross-cultural transmission' (p. 53). Hence witness, as local, embodied and contextual, through different cultural contexts, from Samaria to the ends of the earth, is understood as essential to the apostolicity of the church. The interplay between witness and apostolicity is striking in the launching of Fresh Expressions. *Mission-Shaped*

Church located fresh expressions in relation to the Declaration of Assent, which Church of England ministers make at their licensing, which affirms belief in

> the faith the Church is called upon to proclaim afresh in each generation ... The term 'fresh expressions' echoes these words. It suggests something new and enlivening is happening, but also suggests connection to history and the developing story of God's work in the church. (2004, p. 34)

Hence fresh expressions are an expression of apostolicity, as the church witnesses ('proclaims') afresh faith in changing contexts ('each generation').

Ambient

Ambient is defined in *The Oxford Living Dictionary* as 'relating to the immediate surroundings of something'.[2] This definition prioritizes the particular, cultural and contextual. It makes sense of Christian witness as apostolic, as linked to proclaiming faith afresh in changing contexts. The *Oxford Living Dictionary* provides a second definition, which relates ambient to 'advertising that makes use of sites or objects other than the established media'. This definition suggests a cultural engagement of experimentation that is distinct from the mainstream. It shares obvious similarities with the definitions of first expressions as alternative in the previous chapter ('One in authenticity'). If Christian witness is to be ambient, it will need to be located both in relation to advertising, yet in distinction from mainstream advertising. Alongside these dictionary definitions, ambient has in recent decades been defined in relation to music, as a genre in which tone and atmosphere are more important than traditional musical structure or rhythm. Features of ambient music include, first, close linkages with new musical instruments, particularly the synthesizer, and, second, drawing on other music genres.

A key influence in defining and developing ambient was Brian Eno, who named and popularized ambient music with his 1978 album *Ambient 1: Music for Airports*. For Eno (1978), ambient music offered a number of approaches to being human. First, it provided 'a space to think'. Second, it offered a way to engage and integrate. 'Ambient Music must be able to accommodate many levels of listening attention without enforcing one in particular; it must be as ignorable as it is interesting' (1978). Third, Eno understood ambient music as countercultural, a way of responding to mass production and commodification. The irony, which will be important for our analysis, is that the album *Ambient 1: Music for Airports* was produced by a commercial record company. It was countercultural within the circulation of consumer culture. This will be essential when we examine the expressions of witness of these first expression communities.

In the late 1980s, ambient music developed further. It was linked with house and techno music, including chillout rooms. These were located outside of the main dance floor and provided a down tempo space. Then with the advent of the internet, ambient music became further woven with lifestyle. Uploaded pieces of ambient music and video gained millions of hits, as a background that shaped practices of sleep, study, meditation and peace.

Missiologist Stanley Skreslet describes how 'image-language often permeates and subtly shapes what we think about evangelization and witness' (2006, p. ix). This chapter considers 'ambient witness' and how it might shape a contemporary image of mission. The notion of ambient witness is consistent with the life of many of the first expressions I researched, who created ambient forms of dance music and sought to provide worship environments similar to chillout spaces. The image-language invites consideration of Christian witness as the good news about being human and attentive to well-being, spirituality as a space to think and formation as an engaging with culture that is alternative and resistant to mainstream dominant cultures.

Witness in a secular age

In Acts, witness is detached from conversion. For Gaventa, witness in Acts is marked by adversity rather than numbers increasing daily. '[T]he "Word of the Lord" grew and multiplied, but that is not always true of the witness or the church' (1982, p. 417). Instead of arguing for a correlation between witness and conversion in relation to numerical growth, Gaventa argues that the conversion narratives in Acts are theological accounts. Conversion narratives are to be studied as 'an aspect of God's action in the world' (p. 422). This approach by Gaventa is congruent with the first expressions methodology introduced in Chapter 1, in which in every 'little thing', in paying attention to the small and the singular, we find ourselves contemplating God: as Maker, Lover, Keeper. Similarly, singular conversion narratives, whether in Acts or in empirical research in relation to first expressions, invite us to study a contemporary 'aspect of God's action' in the secular world (rephrasing Gaventa, p. 422)

The work of Charles Taylor is essential in examining contemporary conversion narratives. His analysis of the shape of conversion in the modern world in *A Secular Age* (2007) is a prerequisite in contemplating the nature of Christian witness today. Writing from the United States, philosopher James Smith considers *A Secular Age* to offer 'a philosophical ethnography of the world you inhabit, and in which you minister' (2014, p. viii). Writing from Europe, missiologist Stefan Paas describes Taylor as a 'leading thinker' (2016, p. 189) who needs to be read in order to understand the post-Christian character of Western Europe (p. 188). The witness in Jerusalem looks different from the witness to the ends of the earth, and it is the work of Taylor that helps clarify the differences between Jerusalem, Samaria and the ends of the world in Acts, and central London, Swindon and York today.

After over 700 pages of social analysis in *A Secular Age*, Taylor concludes with a chapter titled 'Conversions' (2014, pp. 728–72). His argument is that individual conversion narratives 'enlarge our palette' in relation to the points of contact by which divine life is experienced, then communicated in a secular age. Both are important: in a culture in which belief is 'unbelievable', how might one process a 'believing' experience? Having processed – how might one communicate a 'believing' to a culture in which belief is 'unbelievable' (p. 729). He turns to individual conversion accounts, examining the lives of those who have broken out of a secularizing frame. In the chapter, he briefly mentions individuals 'who went through some kind of "conversion"' (p. 728), including Vaclav Havel, Ivan Illich, Charles de Foucauld, John Maine, Jean Vanier, Mother Teresa and Thérèse de Lisieux. However, he gives considerable space to the conversions of two individuals (both men), Charles Peguy (pp. 745–55) and Gerard Manley Hopkins (pp. 755–65). The descriptions provided by Taylor include not only their moment of conversion (their birthing) but also their ongoing attempts (their becoming) as they seek to communicate their 'believing' experience to a culture in which belief is considered 'unbelievable'. Taylor draws on biographical details and individual writings: the prose of Charles Peguy and the poetry of Gerard Manley Hopkins.

Taylor's descriptions help us consider the nature of Christian witness. In what follows, the accounts are used to clarify what it might mean to bear Christian witness 'afresh' in the secularized contexts of Britain today. *Mission-Shaped Church* called for 'a new inculturation of the gospel within our society' (2004, p. xii). Key features of giving witness to conversion in a secular world, as located in the accounts of Charles Peguy (Taylor 2007, pp. 745–55) and Gerard Manley Hopkins (pp. 755–66), are identified and illustrated in Table 8. These features can then be used to examine the witness of first expressions. How does the witness of these communities compare and contrast with the conversion narratives as identified by Taylor? Is there evidence of an enlarged palette? In this way, the bearing witness – as described by Taylor and provided in the empirical data from the first expression interviews – is treated not as the basis of straight correlations between witness and conversion ('Witness like this and people will be saved and your church will grow') but as an aspect of God's action in the world.

Table 8: Witness to conversion in A Secular Age

Conversions in *A Secular Age*	Disruptive paradigm shift	Subtler language within, yet pointing beyond immanent frame	Affirmations of enfleshment	Critique of 'flatness of modern civilization'	'Complete, direct and powerful' experience of fullness

For Taylor, conversion in a secular world involves five features. First, a *disruptive paradigm shift* in existing thoughts, actions and piety (2007, p. 731). 'The convert's insights break beyond the limits of the regnant versions of immanent order, either in terms of accepted theories, or of the moral and political practice' (p. 732). This disruption can be conceptual ('accepted theories') or in habituated practice. Second, the realization of the need for 'a new "subtler language"'. Such language is grounded in immanence, yet points 'beyond ordinary, "immanent" realities' (p. 732). Third, affirmations of *enfleshment*, the belief that God is on the side of creation, blessing materiality (pp. 743–4). 'Resurrection only makes sense when we take enfleshment seriously' (p. 741). Taylor develops this by drawing on the New Testament Greek work *splangnizesthai*, a love that responds from the bowels. The result is conversions into moments of shared bonding, as individuals are invited to act with compassion and form new relationships (p. 730). Hence the disruptive paradigm shift must both realize the flawed self-understandings of the present immanent orders of self-understanding (p. 744), yet be experienced and articulated within those immanent realities. Fourth, a critique of existing political, cultural and intellectual orders ('the *flatness of modern civilization'*, p. 734) and fifth, a more 'complete, direct and powerful' *experience of fullness* as a way of being in the world (p. 729). This experience is a heart-transforming and life-changing understanding of participation in divine love (pp. 729–30).

The last two features – the *flatness of modern civilization* and the *experience of fullness* – require a redrawing of the relationship between Christian faith and history. For Taylor, this is a challenge that needs to be experienced uniquely by those who inhabit Western culture.

> I want to remark that ... the Western convert (one might say, 'recon-vert' to Christianity) is in a unique situation. It is hard to conceive of

Table 9: Witness to conversion in A Secular Age *illustrated*

Conversions in *A Secular Age*	Disruptive paradigm shift	Subtler language within, yet pointing beyond immanent frame	Affirmations of enfleshment	Critique of 'flatness of modern civilization'	'Complete, direct and powerful' experience of fullness
Illustrations from the life of Charles Peguy	Authentic action is freedom; '[i]t is the highest freedom to be moved by one's mystique' (p. 749)	*Fidelité* as a creative reapplication of the spirit of the tradition; drawing from the past while excluding the habituated (pp. 747–8)	Creative actions of making, sowing, reaping, praying are handing down; 'the spiritual is always incarnate' (p. 751)	Mystique in the present disrupts a mechanistic view of time as linear, mechanical and habitual.	Creative actions that link different periods point toward Christian idea of eternity as a 'redeemed or gathered time, in which all moments are reconnected in the same moment' (p. 750)
Illustrations from the life of Gerard Manley Hopkins	'But vastness blurs and time I beats level. Enough! the Resurrection';[3] poetry unsettles existing ontological commitments.	'Glory be to God for dappled things';[4] poetry uses human language to articulate 'constitutive, revelatory power' (p. 758) in the particularity of immanent life.	'The world is charged with the glory of God';[5] poetry articulates human experience in human language, using language that can 'make once more experientially real' the actions of God (p. 757)	'All is seared with trade; bleared, seared with toil';[6] ('God's Grandeur'); modernity has flattened language.	'The world is charged with the glory of God';[7] poetry is potentially world-making (p. 756)

a new Christian in Africa or Asia thinking in these terms. The hold of the former Christendom on our imagination is immense. (2007, p. 734)

While every age has to achieve a distance from its own embedding (p. 745), again we are reminded that bearing witness in central London, Swindon and York is different from bearing witness in Jerusalem and Samaria. Christian witness in a secular age, as part of fullness within immanent realities, must engage the overhang of Christendom. This is a challenge unique to Western cultures.

These are complicated concepts and Taylor is a complicated writer. In order to demonstrate how these five features are grounded in lived reality, I have provided illustrations from the lives of Charles Peguy and Gerard Manley Hopkins in Table 9.

My focus is Christian witness. I have drawn on the cultural analysis of Charles Taylor and clarified five features significant to the nature of Christian witness in a secular age. This provides a conversion frame for those engaged in secular witness.

These features have been illustrated in the lives of Charles Peguy and Gerard Manley Hopkins as a way of studying the missiology of God's contemporary action in the secular world. This conversion frame can then be used to examine the empirical data from first expressions. How have they given witness? How have they engaged with the overhang that is Christendom? These questions will now be asked in relation to three empirical studies: buildings that breathe in York, angels that hover in Swindon and spirituality as humanization in central London.

Illuminating at Visions

A fascinating experience of witness and conversion emerged in the interviews with Visions, as they described their work in York to illuminate historic buildings. I offer an extended quote, which I then analyse in relation to Taylor's frame of conversions in a secular age.

> Now York has lots of old churches. It makes sense to use old churches partly because we can live and breathe them well. We can create atmospheres within them well. But also because within the city of York they seem to have a prominent place. And the people relate to them in a different way than you may do in the centre of Leeds. The closest equivalent to some of that club stuff has been providing visuals in a church, but rather than for a club scene, for a Vespers in Latin. And having hundreds of people turn up and the church full till the point their queueing outside. But which is not something that we would

have expected ten years ago ... The visuals side of things is something where always we've been strong and had quite a distinct contribution. (Visions 2013)

Through illumination, Visions enable what is stone to 'live and breathe well'. They 'convert' buildings, creating atmospheres in which what is inanimate and historic can now 'live and breathe'.

Using Taylor, Visions offer 'enfleshed' immanence. The buildings that they light are immanent in the sense of existing already, having a 'prominent place' within the public consciousness. The use of lighting is another enfleshing of immanence, as modern lighting technologies enable this inert building to 'live and breathe'. A further dimension of immanence is the use of darkness, the naturalness of night, central to the creation of 'atmospheres'. Amid all the immanence, in the dark of night and the wash of colour that which has been and always will be becomes an epiphany, a revelation of beauty.

This is a double conversion, for in the 'converting' of buildings, Visions are offering a witness that is 'converting' moments. This is evident in the feedback: 'Wow, that's amazing' as a comment as one particular church was illuminated by Visions ('Time & Space' 2014). That which is known, a 'prominent' place in the city, the stones of history, has been witnessed afresh. There is nothing explicitly Christian about 'Wow, that's amazing.' At the same time, using Taylor's frame, wonder is being expressed within the ordinary. A moment of something bigger is being made visible. The existing is revelatory. This is an invitation to convert, to see the immanent 'afresh'.

These 'converting' moments are public. They involve prominent buildings and occur in publicly visible spaces. Hundreds of people turn up to share in these epiphanic experiences of conversion. The power of social media allows a sharing of their 'wonder' at enfleshed immanence. As Visions illuminate within the framework of the Illuminating York Festivals, they are bearing witness in the context of public partnerships. There is a sense of serving the greater good of the community as Visions participate in illuminating their city.

These moments of 'enfleshed' immanence are, for Visions, part of an ongoing embodiment. The invitation to convert is being offered by a community, who continue to offer witness. The illuminations occur within the framework of the Illuminating York Festivals, a programme within which Visions are promoted as artists. 'So we're in a position where in York there is an Illuminating York Festival ... We'll still be doing it after they've gone' (Visions 2013). By participating in public witness, Visions are made visible. The result is connections, routes by which people might continue to explore transcendence, either by returning to the church (in this case St Helens) or by attending other events (church services) offered by Visions.

The work of Taylor as it applies to Visions can be summarized in Table 10. The dimensions of converting buildings and converting experiences are both considered.

Table 10: Witness to conversion in a secular age embodied by Visions

Conversions in *A Secular Age*	Disruptive paradigm shift	Subtler language within, yet pointing beyond immanent frame	Affirmations of enfleshment	Critique of 'flatness of modern civilization'	'Complete, direct and powerful' experience of fullness
Visions: converting buildings	'old churches can live and breathe'	Existing, everyday, historic buildings are illuminated by lighting and video technologies	Existing stone, historic buildings; 'people relate' to buildings in York in a different way, lighting technologies	Historic buildings can be re-fashioned, converted, to something of beauty	The possibility of experiencing transcendence in a church building
Visions: converting experiences	Embodiment by Visions of ongoing 'providing visuals in a church'	'create atmospheres'	Seen with the eyes, experienced in the darkness	'Wow, that's amazing'	The possibility of transcendence

To draw from Matthew 5.14–15, the light/ing gifts and skills of Visions are not being put under a bushel. Nor are they being hidden within the existing walls in the act of regular worship. Rather, Visions are acting so that their 'city built on a hill' will not be hidden. These public acts are congruent with Visions' sense of identity. They articulate an identity as participatory creatives – 'the ability to do creative worship acts together and participate' (Visions 2013). To return to the themes of Chapter 9, Visions are being authentic to their place, the city in which they are planted, willing to serve the greater good of the community. They are also being authentic to their unique identity – 'live and breathe … create atmospheres … well'. Their visible witness is totally congruent with their visible worship. They are also being authentic with a sense of catholicity as they illuminate the value of history, the gift of the buildings that people in York walk beside every day. For Visions, 'One of the things about alt. worship is going back to the roots of the past' (Visions 2013). In illuminating York, Visions are bearing witness to that history. The 'flatness of modern civilization' is being critiqued, disrupted by the possibility that inside and outside historic church buildings, moments of wonder and amazement are possible. Through the enfleshment of lighting 'complete, direct and powerful' experiences of fullness are offered.

As Visions illuminate buildings, they are expressing transcendence 'afresh'. Such is the witness of Visions, an embodiment of all five of Taylor's features significant to the nature of Christian witness in a secular age.

Angels over Swindon

To date, the empirical research in this book has emerged from my own research. A helpful comparison emerges when the witness by Visions is placed alongside empirical research conducted by others into organizations in contemporary Britain seeking to bear witness in public places.

Over three years, between 2006 and 2009, Matthew Engelke (2013) conducted empirical research, mixing participant observation and interviews, into the British and Foreign Bible Society. As part of that research, Engelke describes Angels in Swindon. This was a project undertaken by Luke Walton, a newly appointed arts officer for the Bible Society, which placed 12 angels in an outdoor shopping centre in Swindon. The outdoor shopping centre is a 'good example of the modernist architecture that dominated so much postwar building in Britain' (Engelke 2013, p. 37). The angels, at four metres in length, were professionally designed for this particular event by a London-based company, Kite Related Designs. The local council press release described Swindon's Angelic Christmas as 'a large piece of public art' and noted the partnership between Swindon Borough Council, Town Centre Management and the Bible Society (for a picture, see 'Swindon's Angels' n.d.). From a Bible Society perspective, the project was communicated as angels 'making a come back in an attempt to get the Christmas message going again' (David 2006). Alongside the 12 showcase angels, the Bible Society produced smaller versions that people could purchase and fly as kites, along with posters 'The Angel Said Unto Them: Don't Worry, Be Happy!' (Engelke 2013, pp. 42–50).

The aim, for Luke Walton and the Bible Society, was to 'build bridges' with 'the person who hasn't considered a spiritual dimension to life' (interview with Luke Walton in Engelke 2013, p. 48). Walton was challenged by what it might mean to bear witness in a secular world: to 'earth it, make it very real, very tangible' (p. 48). In the words of Charles Taylor, to find within the particularity of immanent life – Christmas shopping in Swindon – language to articulate 'constitutive, revelatory power' (Taylor 2007, p. 758). The year prior, the Christmas celebrations had been themed around Harry Potter. What might it mean to bear witness in this secular, public space?

The angels were intended to have a material impact. In the physicality of their immanence, they conveyed a 'paradoxical mix of movement and groundedness' (Engelke 2013, p. 45). 'What was at work here? Kite? Wind? *Maybe* something more? Maybe the spirit of Christmas; maybe an angel? These were the kinds of questions and associations Luke hoped to provoke' (p. 45).

This materiality drew comment. On the BBC Wiltshire website, one person wrote of how the angels were 'swaying in the wind beautifully – what a clever idea' (Engelke 2013, p. 49). This was an affirmation of the affective nature of the angels' physicality and sensuality.

The work of Taylor as it applies to the angels in Swindon is summarized in Table 11.

Table 11: Witness to conversion in a secular age embodied by Angels in Swindon

Conversions in *A Secular Age*	Disruptive paradigm shift	Subtler language within, yet pointing beyond immanent frame	Affirmations of enfleshment	Critique of 'flatness of modern civilization'	'Complete, direct and powerful' experience of fullness
Angels in Swindon		an affirmation of the affective nature of the angels' physicality and sensuality	'earth it, make it very real, very tangible' 'swaying in the wind beautifully – what a clever idea'	'there was something deeply spiritual' (Engelke 2013, p. 48)	'the recognition that there are spiritual beings' (Engelke 2013, p. 48)

Placed side by side, the angels in Swindon and the illuminating of buildings in York shed light on the nature of Christian witness in secular Britain. Both are first expressions, in different ways seeking for the first time (lighting buildings, angels in main street) to offer Christian witness. Both occur during a similar time period – the angels in Swindon in 2006, Illuminating York between 2009 and 2016. Both emerge in outdoor and public spaces – the outdoor shopping centre in Swindon, the Illuminating York Festival. Both are entwined with consumer culture – Christmas shoppers in Swindon, tourists attracted to York. Both attract large crowds – in Swindon over 1,000 people attended the launch event (Engelke 2013, p. 49). Both were seeking to use creativity and the arts in bearing witness in these secular, consumer spaces.

Engelke concludes that the angels in Swindon are an example of 'ambient witness'. They are a way for the Bible Society to resist the public/private dualisms of secularity. They allow a witness that affirms a material Christian spirituality, providing a 'sensory presence that ... served as an important sign of faith and act of public engagement' (p. 58). This is, argues Engelke, a way of being unashamed in public contexts of their faith. It lowers barriers, seeking contemporary, cultural ways to be accessible. Importantly, it does not megaphone a Christian faith. '[I]t is up to the other, pedestrian and patron, to engage ... Bible Society does not do megaphoned messages' (p. 59). This promotes human agency, providing a way to witness that moves beyond historic traditions of an imposed faith. We will develop the trajectories of 'ambient witness' further in the final section. For now, we have established that Visions and Angels in Swindon are bearing witness in secular spaces, converting public places into sites of material spirituality. However, both the illuminating of buildings and the erecting of four-metre angels work at a distance. It is a witness detached in the moment from a fullness that is possible in enfleshed relationships. Hence, we need to consider a third empirical case study, of a first expression bearing witness in a secular age in ways that are relationally enfleshed. We turn to Moot, a first expression community in central London.

Moot as a leisure centre of spirituality

Moot describe themselves as 'a London-based community of spiritual travellers that seek to live in a way that is honest to God and honest to now'.[8] Members of Moot annually commit to live by a rhythm of life, as part of living within a new monastic tradition. This involves spiritual practices including prayer, meditation and presence.

In 2010, Moot were invited by the Bishop of London 'into the mixed economy of the different churches of the centre of London, because they recognized they weren't doing well with the spiritual seekers or the dechurched or the unchurched who are not interested in traditional forms of church' (A leader of Moot 2013). This involved locating themselves at St Mary Aldermary, a 900-year-old church in the centre of London, near Mansion House Station, where Moot began to offer daily prayer, regular worship services and a range of meditation and discussion groups, along with courses on conflict resolution and mindfulness.

St Mary Aldermary is a Guild church, designated and established under the City of London (Guild Churches) Act 1952 and 1960. Guild churches are distinct from ordinary parish churches. They are located in a parish where there is already a parish church. They exist, as defined in the Preamble to the London (Guild Churches) Act 1952 and 1960, to 'minister to the non-resident population of the city' providing leadership that is 'suitable to offer specialized ministrations or services'.[9] Amended in 1960, at the time it was described as an 'important and imaginative scheme' that had resulted in 'an interesting assortment of specialist centres'.[10] Examples in 1960 included paying special attention to the ministry of healing, marriage guidance, concern with relations with churches worldwide, along with the approach of the church to all sections of industrialized society.

This is significant missiologically. Moot offer a witness that is place-based, inhabiting St Mary Aldermary, where '30,000 people walk outside here from the tube station every day' (A leader of Moot 2013). During the interview, as an act of active listening, I summarized what I was hearing regarding the impact of place on the life of Moot. My summary is in normal type, with my interview participant's repeated affirmations in italics.

So even in the space of *Yes*
six months, *Yes Yes*
the simple rootedness *Yes*
in a place *Yes. Yes*
has changed your community *Yes*
and your spirituality, *Yes. Yes.* (Moot 2013)

Place has been essential in the becoming of the first expression that is Moot. At the same time, Moot is a Guild church, set aside to offer specialized ministry to the non-resident. The 30,000 people who walk by outside are not from the geographic parish.

One way to understand a Guild church is ministering to social networks. Manuel Castells (2000) suggested that the world is reconfiguring around networks which are changing every aspect of society. Interactive skills in communication-rich networks become the dominant form of organization. A Guild church, while set up in the 1950s, provides an organizational structure to engage a network society, offering ministry to the non-resident through specialized services. (Indeed, this makes Guild churches a first expression.) Moot was described as offering 'a mixture between a cafe and a leisure centre for mission'. The concept of leisure centre is church as a specialized service that offers prayer and meditation, along with along with art, discussion and dialogue events in the neighbouring pub, all intended to 'open up Christian spirituality to people' (Moot 2013).

As with Visions and the angels of Swindon, this is no megaphone approach to Christian witness. There is, in offering mediation and mindfulness, the same 'semiotic bundles of determined undeterminedness' (Engelke 2013, p. 45). The inhabiting of spaces in practices of prayer, creativity and hospitality 'really does engage with the consumptive society who are seeking to shop for spirituality and therefore open to experience then, because it's very experiential' (Moot 2013). This includes drawing attention, through leisure centre spirituality offerings, to the 'flatness' of contemporary culture, in ways that are embedded within, while pointing beyond, the immanent frame.

> It's not a linear pathway. I think there are cycles and circles ... The cultural context is that everybody is formed into a consumer society. So everybody is basically addicted to consumption as a way of life. Particularly in London, and United Kingdom, which is now a market society. So actually what we tend to do is find people that come here who are deeply unfulfilled by a society defined by materialism and commodification of life. (Moot 2013)

The result is a 'complete, direct and powerful' experience of fullness. 'Get beyond our full self. Get beyond our own self-obsessions and narcissism, to something much more integrated (making a lovely round arm gesture at this point in the interview)' (Moot 2013). So the clarification of fullness ('something more integrated'/lovely round arm gesture) results in a disruptive paradigm shift (beyond 'self-obsessions and narcissism').

The work of Taylor as it applies to the Moot as a leisure centre of spirituality is summarized in Table 12.

Unlike Visions and the angels of Swindon, there is a fullness that is possible in enfleshed relationships. Moot see themselves as 'spiritual directors to a non-Christian, consumptive society' (Moot 2013). This requires a relational approach to bearing witness. The inspiration is Christ: 'Christ who did that through relational engagement and relationships of challenge and integrity' (Moot 2013). As part of this relational approach to bearing witness, Moot offered a clarity about the human person in mission.

Table 12: Witness to conversion in a secular age embodied by Moot

Conversions in *A Secular Age*	Disruptive paradigm shift	Subtler language within, yet pointing beyond immanent frame	Affirmations of enfleshment	Critique of 'flatness of modern civilization'	'Complete, direct and powerful' experience of fullness
Moot	beyond 'self-obsessions and narcissism'	'engage with the consumptive society who ... shop for spirituality and therefore open to experience then, because it's very experiential'	'help people become more self-aware of the depth of the God who is already there in their lives'	'people that come here who are deeply unfulfilled by a society defined by materialism and commodification of life'	'Get beyond our full self'

the assumption ... isn't that God is absent from the world, or that God is absent from people's lives. They are just not aware that God is in the details of their lives. So it's ... about trying to help people become more self-aware of the depth of the God who is already there in their lives and they haven't noticed it. So it's much more generous. (Moot 2013)

This promotes human agency as people are invited to pay attention to what only they can discern – 'the depth of the God who is already there in their lives' (Moot 2013). These discoveries are made through relational engagement, as Moot facilitate discussions, groups and meditative experiences.

Conversion 'afresh'

The argument is that first expressions are offering witness 'afresh' in a secular age. This has been demonstrated by using the work of Taylor to analyse the public witness of three first expressions. Visions allow public buildings to live and breathe well. In so doing, by creatively offering immanence (lighting technologies), they create public moments of wonder as 'complete, direct and powerful' experience of fullness, which critique a 'flattened' reading of church buildings and inherited religious traditions. Angels in Swindon creatively offered angels as a sensory presence in the midst of the consumerism of Christmas. This was a contemporary, cultural way to introduce glad tidings – Don't Worry, Be Happy! – in ways that invited passers-by to consider the possibility of a subtle beauty amid the secularity of Christmas. Moot reinhabit the Guild church charism of specialized ministry to non-residents by offering a spiritual leisure centre spirituality. They inhabit the ambiguity of the spiritual search in consumer culture, offering mediation and dialogue in order that individuals might, in an experiential way, become more self-aware of the depth of the God who is already there in their lives. All three resist megaphone messaging. Instead they use subtle language, affirm the senses and the experiential in keeping alive wonder, mystery and beauty in the immanence of daily life. As such, all three bear witness in ways congruent with the 'conversions' documented by Charles Taylor.

Ambient witness as apostolic witness in a secular age

Engelke applies the term of ambient witness to the approach of the Bible Society in Swindon, and I have traced the similarities across three case studies. Hence empirical data demonstrates the nature of Christian witness in first expressions. These communities profess in public in a 'new and enlivening' way the 'faith the Church is called upon to proclaim afresh in each generation' (*Mission-Shaped Church* 2004, p. 34).

This invites the possibility that first expressions might provide 'hermeneutic discoveries' (Paas 2016, p. 239), including fresh understandings of bearing witness. To examine the implications, I will draw together the empirical data from the three case studies and argue for ambient witness as offering a particularized 'afreshness' for a secular age as it disrupts the public/private dualisms of secularity, provokes questions, maintains en-culture-ated afreshness and promotes human agency.

Ambient witness disrupts private/public dualisms

In Luke 19.28–44, Jesus enters Jerusalem. He walks a public road into a capital city. As he walks, Jesus declares that if the disciples fell silent (in this public space), the stones would shout out (Luke 19.40).

Metaphorically, a silencing of the voices of the church in public spaces is one way to understand the claims of a secular age. The insistence that faith should be privatized in order that the public square be neutral is a worldview unique to modernity. Susan Gal argues that private/public distinctions are cultural categories (2002, p. 78). Because they are cultural, there are subtle ways that actors can disrupt the distinction.

Ambient witness disrupts the private/public distinction. Projecting light on public buildings and hanging angels in outdoor shopping areas disrupts the dualism. Stones cry out. Not literally, but as churches 'live and breathe well' the public function of religion and religious buildings is reconceived. Angels move in the wind. Is this literal? Or could it be that a subtle spirituality is possible amid the secular of modern shopping? Gal argues that in the disrupting, there are possibilities for 'change, creativity, and argument' (p. 85). Could it be that churches could be part of creating wonder and evoking beauty, not just during an installation or at Christmas, but permanently in public spaces? Could there be a witness that is not megaphoned, but is subtle, that suggests approach without coercion, that is content to be one message among a plurality of voices? Ambient witness locates the spiritual search in the midst of the public.

Ambient witness provokes questions

But is ambient witness a pandering to consumerism? Alongside the private/public dualism, a key feature of the contemporary context of late capitalism is the shift from an industrial economy to a consumer society. This is the context in which churches are called to witness 'afresh'. By participating in public events, are individual acts being subsumed by this consumer culture?

One response is to consider Engelke's description of the angels as 'semiotic bundles of determined undeterminedness' (2013, p. 45). He observes that despite the contexts in which the angels fly, as symbols they remain determinedly designed to provoke questions. This provocation continues no matter what consumer narratives operate around them.

The power to provoke questions becomes an enduring way to resist consumerism. It is consistent with the recent analysis of the emerging church by sociologists Josh Packard and George Sanders. They argue that the emerging church resists institutionalizing systems through tropes of 'messiness' and 'conversation'. By adopting a posture of open-ended conversation, the emerging church 'embraces indeterminacy, openness, unpredictability, and contingency' (Packard and Sanders 2013, p. 438). It makes them inclusive and malleable and able to avoid institutionalization. For Packard and Sanders, 'while corporatization may be a powerful force within religion, it is by no means totalizing or inexorable' (p. 438). The argument is significant, given that it emerges in the context of the United States, in which the forces of consumerism in relation to religion are particularly acute.

Can the argument regarding the power of questions to avoid corporatization in religious contexts be applied to corporatization in culture more generally? What interests me is the approach to culture. Engelke's observation of the angels of Swindon as semiotic bundles of determined undeterminedness seems equivalent to Packard and Sanders's observation of the emerging church as indeterminate, open, unpredictable and contingent. Is the power of corporatization in religious cultures of the United States of a different order of magnitude than the powers of consumer cultures in general? Can ambient witness – the cultivation of life, beauty and experience – escape the colonizing power of consumer culture?

James Bielo argues yes. Drawing on five empirical studies of emerging churches – including in England, Ireland and the United States – he notes the imperative among emerging churches to create: 'Create a riff on something recognizable. Create an alternative to something deemed spiritually or institutionally problematic. Create something new. Just create' (Bielo 2017, p. 24). He locates these instincts – so evident in the approaches of the three case studies – in relation to anthropological models of culture change and concludes that the creative instincts are essential in ensuring vitality. The maintenance of creativity subverts the colonizing power of consumer culture.

Engelke (2013, pp. 60–3) also argues yes. He notes that ambience occurs not only in music, but also in media. In music, he notes the irony of Eno using a record label to sell a record critiquing consumerism. In media, he notes the vitality of ambient advertising. 'Ambience is a useful mediating concept in these various projects, a way of challenging the sufficiency or aptness' (p. 63). What is essential is differentiation. The provocative question – in the form of stone buildings that breathe well, the angels that raise the clever question, the experiential spirituality of Moot's leisure centre approach – maintains differentiation. The willingness to create maintains the provocative question, invites the open-ended conversation and ensures the vitality of first expressions.

Ambient witness is maintained by en-culture-ated afreshness

Can first expressions maintain this vitality? It can as it remains engaged with cultural movement. Ambience was defined at the beginning of this chapter in relation to the particular, cultural and contextual, especially as developed in music. Analysing ambient music, Daniel Warner notes the essential role of new technologies. Technologies including the tape recorder, transistor circuitry, the turntable, the microphone and the computer have resulted in 'one of the most significant cultural shifts of the last century' (Warner 2017, p. 7). These technologies have made music more portable, affordable and hackable. As a result, new types of artist emerge (p. 170). In turn, they create a distinct identity, a culture capable of provoking unexpected results. As Julian of Norwich reminds us, as she paid attention to the one small thing that was the hazel-nut in her hand: God made it, God loves it, God preserves it. It is through these commitments, to making and being loved, that preservation of vitality is possible.

Witness that promotes human agency

God is at work. God is Maker, Lover, Keeper. People are given choice as they respond. If they don't respond immediately or as expected, God remains Maker, Lover, Keeper. These theological affirmations result in a respect for human agency.

Ambience is by definition 'part of the background noise of daily life' (Engelke 2013, p. 52). Musically, ambience is created to be in the background. It accommodates many levels of listening attention. It does not enforce one level of listening, 'it must be as ignorable as it is interesting' (Eno 1978). Music can be created, yet it does not force itself on the hearer. This is a fascinating approach to understanding the action of God. The Maker is a gentleperson, a respecter of agency.

Engelke (2013, p. 59) observes of the Angels at Swindon how important it was that space was given for those who were outside and other to engage. (As quoted above, 'it is up to the other, pedestrian and patron, to engage … Bible Society does not do megaphoned messages.') Similarly, for those at Moot, God is not absent from the world or from people's lives. God is already there in their lives (and they haven't noticed it). Equally, ambient witness seeks to be in the background. It expects to remain asking proactive questions and be part of open-ended conversations. Ambient witness respects human agency.

This respect for human agency frees ambient witness and is generativity of creativity. It allows a 'production' that has a range of performance possibilities (Engelke 2013, p. 50). Ambient witness can be impromptu, virtual, epiphenomenal, and as playful as 'Don't Worry, Be Happy!'

In preceding pages, I have drawn together the empirical data from the three case studies. The argument is that ambient witness offers a particularized 'afreshness' for a secular age as it disrupts the public/private dualisms of secularity, provokes questions, maintains en-culture-ated afreshness and promotes human agency.

The theology of Julian of Norwich, introduced as a methodology in Chapter 1 and developed in Chapter 2, has provided particular insight in relation to en-culture-ated afreshness and human agency. In singularity, God is Maker, Lover and Keeper.

Conclusion

The Apostles' Creed affirms the church as one, holy, catholic and apostolic. This chapter has examined apostolicity, paying particular attention to the nature of Christian witness.

Witness has been argued to be particularized and conversion accounts theorized as sites for God's action. Understandings of conversion in a secular age, drawn from Charles Taylor, have provided a theoretical sensitivity and enabled the development of an apostolicity of Christian witness from the empirical research of first expressions. Three case studies have been examined, the illumination of public buildings in York by Visions, the creation of angels as public art in Swindon and Moot as a leisure centre of spirituality. Each has been analysed in relation to Taylor's five features. Each bears witness in a secular age. This suggests a hermeneutical discovery: of ambient witness as it disrupts the public/private dualisms of secularity, provokes questions, maintains en-culture-ated afreshness and promotes human agency. This offers possibilities for any community seeking to bear witness 'afreshness' for a secular age.

Ambient witness was not a theoretical construct by which these first expressions sought to enact mission. Rather it emerged from their life, a birthing that became a becoming. In other words, authenticity generated apostolicity. This returns us to the work of the previous chapter and suggests a relationship, perhaps one of birthing and becoming, between first expressions as one and first expressions as apostolic. One can imagine Visions, not Grace, exclaiming to a *God in the House* camera: 'We [too] love all the visuals'; lighting buildings is 'what's authentic and flies for us'.

However, this assertion threatens to leave a gap between the authenticity of first expressions and the apostolicity of ambient witness. How does authenticity become apostolicity? More disconcertingly, in an age of self-fulfilment, is there a danger that authenticity serves as an excuse to maintain cultural tastes? How might 'what flies for us' be challenged by encounter with a genuine other, across generations and cultures? To address these questions, we need to consider in the next chapter the church as holy and first expressions as constructive formation.

Notes

1 Joel 3.1–5a in Acts 2.17–21; Psalm 16.8–11 in Acts 2.25–28; Psalm 101.1 in Acts 2.34–35.

2 https://en.oxforddictionaries.com/definition/ambient.

3 Gerard Manley Hopkins, 'That Nature is a Heraclitean Fire and of the comfort of the Resurrection', see Philips (1995, p. 163).

4 Gerard Manley Hopkins, 'Windhover', see Philips (1995, p. 117).

5 Gerard Manley Hopkins, 'God's Grandeur', see Philips (p. 114).

6 Gerard Manley Hopkins, 'God's Grandeur', see Philips (p. 114).

7 Gerard Manley Hopkins, 'God's Grandeur', see Philips (p. 114).

8 www.moot.uk.net.

9 City of London (Guild Churches) Bill, 25 February 1960 vol 618 cc670-84. Available at https://api.parliament.uk/historic-hansard/commons/1960/feb/25/city-of-london-guild-churches-bill-by [viewed 24 May 2019].

10 Sir Hubert Ashton, followed by Mr Tom Driberg, during the Second Reading of the Bill. City of London (Guild Churches) Bill, 25 February 1960 vol 618 cc670-84. Available at https://api.parliament.uk/historic-hansard/commons/1960/feb/25/city-of-london-guild-churches-bill-by [viewed 24 May 2019].

11

Becoming holy in making

It was the power of making that drew me to first expressions. On an alt.worship website, around 1996, I found a photo of a worship event offered by Visions in York.[1] It included eye-popping visuals, a large projected display with words, an image of Jesus, stars and lights, in rich reds, gentle yellows and vibrant greens. This was worship that expected you to pray with your eyes open, not shut.

This visual approach to worship being offered at Visions was an invitation not only to look, but also to make. This was a world pre-digital camera.[2] For Visions to make this projected wall of colour required taking slides (reversal film) of every word and image needed in worship. It required locating, then positioning, multiple slide projectors. A far greater range of skills was being required for the making of worship. As Jonny Baker wrote:

> In many church circles the only gifts that are valued for worship are musical ones or the ability to speak well. This attitude needs shattering, and opening up so that poets, photographers, ideas people, geeks, theologians, liturgists, designers, writers, cooks, politicians, architects, movie-makers, storytellers, parents, campaigners, children, bloggers, DJs, VJs, craft-makers ... can get involved. It's so exciting to be part of *making* and producing in this way. (2010, p. 12, emphasis mine)

This making approach to worship is more than technical. It invites questions which are in fact formational. To address the technical question of what images should be projected requires exploring content and making ethical judgements. What images might interpret a biblical theme? From which culture could these images be sought? What are the ethics of sourcing and displaying images? At this juncture, worship as making has become formational.

Theology meets ethics. Attempts to understand God and God's activity in the world become interwoven with consideration of how to act in that world.

God is encountered in the stuff of everyday life, not outside it. So worship makes two moves: It brings the real world into church, and it
enables God to be encountered back in the real world. This is a direct
challenge to an experience of the church as a world apart, unrelated
to the rest of life. (Jonny Baker interviewed in Gibbs and Bolger 2005,
p. 75)

Making was, in the incarnation, an embodiment of the 'central burning
conviction that God's rule is now actively present' in all of life (Hurst
1992, p. 221). In Jesus, God has 'tabernacled' (John 1.14) in creation.
There is a 'deliberate overriding of purity concerns' (Westerholm 1992,
p. 131) in search of a making of God's kingdom come on earth (Matt.
6.10).

Making was a repeated experience in my research with first expressions. I learnt to make bracelets out of wool, weaving three colours into
one (Grace 2001). I heard in interviews that worship involved people
being willing to 'play around ... [to] run this video clip or commercial
next to this sixteenth-century religious painting ... let's try it and see'
(Gay 2001). I heard how the making of stations showed the formation
of faith across generations (Sanctuary 2013a). I read that alternative
worship was 'faithful improvisation'. It required 'knowing the scales',
of being 'located in the Christian story' in ways similar to a musician
making music, an architect designing a project or an actor performing
(Baker, Gay and Brown 2003, p. 101). I saw the joy in the eyes of a focus
group as the activity of making buildings 'live and breathe well' (Visions
2013) was described and faith was understood as integrated into all of
life (Moot 2013).

This chapter will consider making as a formational practice of the
church as holy. It will define making, paying particular attention to how
making is a way of becoming holy through engaging culture, by drawing
on the work of Jesuit scholar Michel de Certeau and theologian Kathryn Tanner. This theoretical work will be enriched by empirical research
on spiritual growth, which grounds making in the interplay between
spiritual formation and becoming holy. This will include a detailed
examination of making at Late Late Service, using the concept of social
drama as a tool to explore the interplay between formation and culture.
Finally, it will examine making and the ethics of the other, detailing ways
that 'what's authentic and flies for us' includes a decentring caused by
meaningful engagement with the other and destabilizes the potential for
instrumentalization of mission.

Making in theory: Certeau

How is making a becoming holy? One place to start is the work of French intellectual Michel de Certeau, who argued that making is a formational practice through engaging culture.

Michel de Certeau was born in 1925, in French Algiers. He entered the Jesuits in the 1950s, 'on the basis of an adult decision that he never called into question' (Certeau and Giard 1997, p. vii). As a scholar, his early research focused on sixteenth- and seventeenth-century mysticism. A key event in Certeau's life was the student and worker riots in France during May 1968. He described this as a 'founding rupture' (p. viii). It turned him from the study of mysticism to the study of contemporary popular culture.

In 1974 Certeau was employed by the French government to direct a research project on the interaction between culture and society. For Ahearne, this marked 'a watershed in [Certeau's] intellectual itinerary' (1995, p. 2). From this research arose the articulation of 'making do', which is most clearly explored in *The Practice of Everyday Life* (1984).[3] It was this research of everyday contemporary cultural practices that has led to Certeau being extensively utilized by 'English-speaking theorists of popular culture' (Frow 1999, p. 52).

Certeau researched everyday practices. He was essentially optimistic about the human ability to subvert authority and order by choosing their style of everyday life. 'The central thrust of *The Practice of Everyday Life* is thus to affirm the resilience and inventiveness of "ordinary men and women" against the analyses which present them as entirely informed or crushed by the economic and cultural apparatuses which set the terms of social life' (Ahearne 1995, p. 185). Certeau (1984, p. 32) felt that too much attention had been paid to a perceived colonization by Western mass media when, in reality, people are invariably resistant to external sociocultural production. His research involved collecting examples of how people's '"stories" [can] provide the decorative container of a narrativity for everyday practices' (p. 70). He researched acts of window shopping, the meaning of street names, the use of rail, the way people dress, the practices of graffiti, advertising, purchasing and cooking. These everyday practices were for Certeau a poetics of play in which culture was dismantled and reused in transformative ways (p. 33). This was done to resist the controlling influences of mass media and consumer culture. Individuals 'make (*bricolent*) innumerable and infinitesimal transformations of and within the dominant cultural economy in order to adapt it to their own interests and their own rules' (pp. xiii–xiv).

Hence, innovation and creativity belong to all. Individuals are 'making do', creatively subverting in countless ways the influence of popular culture (p. xi). The focus was not on production, but on the use of popular cultural resources.

> [H]ousing, clothing, housework, cooking, and an infinite number of rural, urban, family or amical activities, the multiple forms of professional work, are also the ground on which creation everywhere blossoms. Daily life is scattered with marvels, a froth on the long rhythms of language and history that is as dazzling as that of writers and artists. (Certeau 1984, p. 142)

This has echoes of God being encountered in the stuff of everyday life and the valuing of making in worship by poets and parents, cooks and craft-makers (Baker 2010, p. 12). Using the theoretical work of Certeau, making is a creative practice by which meaning is articulated and dominant culture is resisted. This is holiness, the assertion of God's rule in all of life. The making of worship is a praying of 'your kingdom come on earth', emerging from the everyday cultures which are the bread of human existence.

Hence Certeau provides a way to understand making as a formational practice. The way individuals engage culture is an assertion of their identity, a demonstration of their creativity and a way of resisting dominant cultural narratives. In what follows, I will consider this, first, in relation to theology and, second, in relation to empirical studies of new forms of church, including first expressions.

However, while utilizing Certeau, I will use 'making' rather than 'making do'. Making do as an idiom is defined as a way of coping without all the resources that one would ideally like to have (thefreedictionary. com). While a lack of resources is often a reality in first expressions and can often be a catalyst for innovation, it suggests a utilitarian dimension which is at odds with the playful creativity I encountered in my research. In addition, it is inconsistent with the grace and generosity of God as Maker, as understood by Julian of Norwich, evident even in one, small thing held in the palm of one's hand.

Making in theory: Tanner

Another place to engage theologically in making as formational through engaging culture is in the work of Kathryn Tanner. She has been described as engaging 'an extraordinary range of theological and ethical concerns' in ways that make her 'the most accomplished theologian of her generation' (Thiel 2015, p. xxi).

In *Theories of Culture*, Kathryn Tanner argues that Christianity works piecemeal, block by block (1997, p. 117). The engagement with culture is the work of 'the *enculturated individual*' (p. 112). This involves processes of consumption, as the enculturated, indwelling Christian consumes artefacts both of the ecclesial tradition and contemporary culture. Theological creativity is the

> creativity of a postmodern 'bricoleur' – the creativity, that is, of someone who works with an always potentially disordered heap of already existing materials, pulling them apart and putting them back together again, tinkering with their shapes, twisting them this way and that. It is a creativity expressed through the modification and extension of materials already on the ground. (Tanner 1997, p. 166)

This provides a theological account of 'poets, photographers, ideas people, geeks, theologians, liturgists, designers, writers, cooks, politicians, architects, movie-makers, storytellers, parents, campaigners, children, bloggers, DJs, VJs, craft-makers' (Baker 2010, p. 12), who 'play around ... run this video clip or commercial next to this sixteenth-century religious painting ... let's try it and see' (Gay 2001).

In ways similar to Certeau, Tanner argues that cultures are not best understood by a search for shared values. Instead, there is the need to examine 'local manifestations of intersections and exchanges' (Tanner 1997, p. 54). This involves paying attention not to universality but to resistance, appropriation, subversion and compromise, seeking to understand how common elements are handled and transformed. Hence research is needed that focuses on the use of Scripture, ritual practices, elements of culture and the interactions of Christians (p. 87).

The sites of interaction, the places where culture is engaged, are the essential places in which to search for identity (in this case the church as becoming holy). 'What is important for cultural identity is the novel way cultural elements from elsewhere are now put to work, by means of such complex and ad hoc relational processes as resistance, appropriation, subversion, and compromise' (p. 58). This encourages a focus on the life of the church as lived, the church as becoming holy in which people in the life of the church have an 'artisan like inventiveness' (p. 87).

What Certeau suggests by examining popular culture in Europe through the 1970s, Tanner frames theologically in the 1990s. She argues that by examining making – 'artisan like inventiveness' – in local ecclesial communities, we find the practice of distinct Christian identities.

Making grounded

To date, the argument has been theoretical, outlining the work of Michel de Certeau and Kathryn Tanner. However, a number of empirical studies point to the value of making in the interplay between spiritual formation and becoming holy.

Sociologists of religion Sally Gallagher and Chelsea Newton (2009) researched spiritual growth by studying four congregations in the North West of the United States. One of the communities they studied identified as an emerging church. This provided a comparative study, as the growth patterns could be contrasted with mainstream communities (in this study, the other three congregations were conservative Protestant, mainline Protestant and Eastern Orthodox). Gallagher and Newton interviewed ordinary people in the congregations. In seeking to understand how they experience spiritual growth, they found unique understandings of formation in the emerging church, shaped by three tropes: relationships, piecemeal approach to culture and authenticity.

First, Gallagher and Newton concluded the emerging church was based on relationships of dialogue and community: 'At the Urban Village emerging church, a consensus around spiritual growth centred on relationships with God, family, and friends within the church and broader community' (2009, p. 258).

Second, participants pointed to the use of diverse elements as being important for their growth. These included arts, science, nature, a range of service opportunities and adult education offering theology and film, medieval spirituality, Hebrew and spiritual formation outdoors. 'Individuals in this group placed somewhat less emphasis on what happens Sunday morning as a source of spiritual growth than people in other congregations' (p. 253). These diverse range of elements required a making. The elements provided a 'piecemeal bricolage' to use the theory of Certeau and Tanner. This generated a search for connections. This is a form of making. In 'the deconstruction ... we heard the echo and rephrasing of historically traditional themes that find expression within well-established Christian traditions' (p. 260). The individual work of making connections, facilitated by offering a wide range of elements, was significant in generating spiritual formation. This making was enhanced by activities that happened outside the Sunday gathering (in contrast to other groups). 'One other facet of spiritual growth that was central ... was the place of the physical world in facilitating spiritual growth ... part of its broader mission to include teaching and activities that focus both on global as well as local social concerns' (p. 254).

Third, this search for authenticity 'resonates with a generation that deeply values diversity and authenticity' (p. 257). Authenticity was as third trope, working as a generator of energy in the task of formation, affirming the value of a faith that was culturally connected.

A second empirical study was conducted by Packard and Sanders. They researched six communities in the United States who identified as a new form of church. They argued that tropes of 'messiness' and 'conversation' are used to embrace a radical contingency, which avoids adopting rigid, rationalized systems of meaning. They locate this as a deliberate way of practising (making) a resistance to the corporatization of American culture. Packard and Sanders identify a making, in that participants were 'expected to contribute cultural artifacts through zines, books, web sites, blogs, sermons, presentations, colloquia, and other media' (2013, p. 452). This again is seen as a contrast to a corporate culture. In other words, making is a way of becoming holy when seen as a practising of resistance to contemporary consumer culture.

These two empirical studies point to the value of making in the interplay between spiritual formation and becoming holy. We now turn to a detailed examination of making at one particular first expression communion I researched, Late Late Service.

Making and first expressions: making at Late Late Service

Late Late Service described themselves as a Christian community based in Glasgow. An 'ecumenical missionary congregation', they worked to develop 'creative ritual, physical spirituality and radical community' (God in the Flesh 1994). Andy Thornton (n.d.), who moved from involvement with Late Late Service to leadership of Greenbelt, described 'a committed attempt at reinventing Christian worship for the post-modern era'. Reinventing is another way of describing making. In this case, the making is possible because of the juxtaposing of 'post-modern' culture and 'Christian worship'. I examine the essential formational role of making through engaging culture, first, through interviews and, second, by analysing an act of making, a 'radical alternative Christian service'. This demonstrates the value of the intentional cultivation of space for making, along with the power inherent in a bricolage approach to engaging culture.

The essential role of making was a feature in each of the four interviews I did with members of Late Late Service.

> We could all contribute, we could all do something. We produced a lot of original music for services at that point ... We would get our theme a month in advance. And we would say what do we need to put on a good bit of worship for this. Well we need photos shot, we need art made up,

we need new tracks. We would write 3 or 4 new pieces of music sometimes for a service. (Group 8*, 2001)

The making is shaped by a theme and requires a diverse range of skills,
including songwriting, photography, art and sound recording. The Late
Late Service developed a structure. A high point was a monthly worship
service, in which the making was performed. In between, the making was
planned. For one participant in a focus group:

> what happened in a group became part of the service. We would go
> away on retreat and at the end we would design worship. And invari-
> ably what happened in the retreat became part of the service. There is
> no gap between day-to-day living and church. (Late Late Service 2001)

The allocation of space for making (going away on retreat) was experienced as integrative, as eliminating a gap between 'day-to-day living and
church'. For another participant in a focus group, 'we're just reinventing
the wheel but we learnt so much from doing that' (2001). For this participant the making produces learning. 'It was a chance to be involved in
creating worship. The planning was almost as good as the service itself.
It made it all seem more real, more valuable ... LLS was about the fact
that I was actively involved. I grew to understand so much more about
the function of liturgy than before' (2001). Making leads to integration,
of daily life and life, and to formation, of understanding more about the
function of liturgy.

Making was formative because of the way culture was understood, in
particular an approach of bricolage, of making from a diverse range of
elements.

> we saw postmodernism ... as a liberating force in the sense it was no
> respecter of the origins of things and therefore allowed pick and mix
> approach. I think we never knew what we were doing but we liked that.
> You could take a little bit of Greek Orthodox stuff here and a little bit
> of traditional Anglican liturgy and mix it up with Presbyterian Scottish
> Calvinism. We saw that as postmodern ... We felt like we were borrow-
> ing from a treasure chest of tradition. (Group 8*, 2001)

In French, the word *bricolage* means 'DIY' or 'do-it-yourself projects'.
It captures the making that happens at Late Late Service as a creation
from a diverse range of available elements. Rather than take worship
from another source, they seek to 're-invent'. They approach the Christian tradition as a 'treasure chest' of diverse elements. This is ecumenical,
an opening to what is other, from across cultures and times. This pick

and mix approach is experienced as liberating. It is facilitated by a playful approach, in which intuition, experimentation and risk are valued. This playfulness was important for formation of faith not only for those making, but also across generations: 'Playfulness in worship was great. Some of the best times were being playful. Playing board games, breaking a pinata at Christmas services. Under 15s loved the worship more than anyone, even the 20s clubbers. So alt.worship was great for the kids' (Late Late Service 2001). It generates learning, including 'about the function of liturgy' in other communities of faith, including Greek Orthodox, Anglican and Presbyterian Scottish Calvinism.

I have established the essential role of making in this first expression. Interviews among four different groups of participants make clear that the way the Late Late Service was structured and the approach to culture facilitated a making. This making was experienced as formational. But how does making through engaging culture facilitate a church becoming?

The question is clarified when we turn from interviews about making to an analysing of making-as-performing. As introduced in Chapter 9, *God in the House* was a series of six TV programmes featuring a 'radical alternative Christian service'. Late Late Service was profiled, with their Christmas service, titled 'World of Wonder' (1995), televised.[4] Given the focus of this chapter on engaging with culture, my analysis focuses on three moves: the opening, the offering and the closing. I use the tropes provided by Tanner – the use of Scripture, ritual practices, elements of culture and the interactions of the gathered community – to clarify how Late Late Service are making: becoming holy through engaging culture.

Engaging culture is essential to the making of Late Late Service. The call to worship is located within the remaking of a world of dance culture. There are no pews, chairs or service sheets. Instead there are synthesizer, flashing lights and projected visuals. This is an act of 'seeking and being sought' in which people participate by dancing.

The 'world of wonder' is one in which God will be seeking to come and dwell among the dance cultures of Glasgow. Becoming holy begins with inculturation.

An act of offering involves a sequence of three liturgical acts. First, children bring in large candles (*God in the House* 1995, 7:13). The invitation is then made to 'come forward and put your candle in the sand, so that our light burns together as one light'. The candles are passed among the dancing participants, then placed in a tray of sand. Second, an invitation is made to empty pockets: 'let's empty our pockets and leave our possessions, remembering that we come to God as God came to us, in simple humanity'. Third, the request is made: 'we'll join our hands to show our need to overcome our fear of each other' (1995, 8:52).

Table 13: Elements of worship in 'World of Wonder' Christmas service

	Scripture	Christian ritual	Elements culture	Interactions of gathered community
Call to worship	'In an act of seeking, and being sought by God,' 'we will use images, music, ritual and chants to mark a journey and stimulate this worship experience, we hope you can make them your own'	Ancient Advent hymn, 'O Come, O Come Emmanuel'	Synthesizer, pulsing disco lights, multiple TVs with changing images, people dance	Hands raised in dance modes
Offering	Theology of God self-emptying: 'we come to God as God came to us, in simple humanity'	Bells rung	Ambient synthesizer music	Three moves: bringing candles, holding hands, emptying pockets
Benediction	Luke 2.13–14	'God loves; God longs; God yearns; God holds; God forgives You don't have to change to be loved by God. Go in peace.'	Original music; 'I saw Heaven Opened' (Gay/ Thornton)	People participate by dancing

Formation requires community ('join our hands') and invites a willing-ness to give of what is in 'our pockets'. All the time, synthesizer music is playing. The music is ambient, a wash of synthesizer chords. The ambient witness described in the previous chapter begins here, in a for-mation which has an ethic of community and sacrifice. This sequence of liturgical actions – bringing candles, holding hands, emptying pockets – begins with the sound of bells being rung. In some church traditions, bells are rung during the Eucharist: in the Roman Catholic tradition, while the Spirit is being invoked over the host (Smolarski 2003, pp. 20–1). In some Anglican traditions, the bell is rung three times, to signify the real presence of Christ. In this Late Late Christmas service, the transformed body is not the elements of the Eucharist but these gathered people, joined in community, across generations, participating with Christ incarnate through acts of self-emptying.

The conclusion involves a further making, an original song titled 'I saw heaven opened'. Indeed, all the music in this service has original elements, composed (made) by different members of the community.[5] The lyrics of 'I saw heaven opened' are drawn from Luke 2.13–14: 'And suddenly there was with the angel a multitude of the heavenly host, praising God and saying, "Glory to God in the highest heaven, and on earth peace!"' Hence as this Christmas service closes, the world indeed has wonder because the 'sky is alive with angels' and these 'angels dance'. Dance culture is not something to flee. Rather, participation in dance culture is a sharing with the angels. This dancing comes with the promise of revelation, of seeing 'heaven open' and of hearing 'songs of joy at Jesus' birth'. God can be seen and heard in dance. This is the engaging with culture that is forming Late Late Service.

In terms of the question of how engaging culture facilitates a becoming holy, the conclusion offers music and words that together articulate a dance floor ethic of participation. The angels sing 'songs of peace on earth'. God's kingdom come on earth is a dance party, joining with the ecstatic praise of angels. The words of sending clarify the ethic further: 'God loves; God longs; God yearns; God holds; God forgives. You don't have to change to be loved by God. Go in peace.' The world might – like you – need to be changed. Nevertheless, love. This is how holiness for Late Late Service is embodied, a dance of peace in response to God's seeking and being sought.

This act of worship as a participation in a 'world of wonder' opens and closes as a dance party. What would 'songs of joy at Jesus' birth' look like? It would involve dance, in which participants embody a Christian ethic of peace. One behaves on the dance floor in ways that bring peace on earth. This is a challenge to alcohol consumption and relationships that form on the dance floor. Theology ('God is seeking and being sought') and ethics ('The angels dance') are interwoven. Making by engaging culture offers a formation in ways of acting in the world.

I have used an extended analysis of one first expression, drawing on interview data and worship analysis, to show a making that is formative as it engages culture. Making can happen through different processes and in different spaces: in planning, in performance and in participation. Making weaves theology and ethics, offering a becoming holy that is inculturated within, and integrative of, daily life. Hence the theory of Michel de Certeau and Kathryn Tanner, including the potential of 'making' as a way to creatively subvert popular culture and the way that Christianity can work piecemeal through the enculturated individual, is embodied in this first expressions community.

Equally the tropes identified in the empirical studies of Gallagher and Newton, Packard and Sanders are also evident. The tropes of relationships ('we could all contribute'), the piecemeal approach to culture and authenticity, defined as 'no gap between day-to-day living and church' are all evident at the Late Late Service. This leave us with two challenges to consider, one in regard to transience, the other in regard to the other.

Making and the challenge of transience

Making as an act of formation at Late Late Service ultimately was transient. One of the interviews I conducted in 2001 was after an Annual General Meeting at which the future of the Late Late Service was an agenda item. Within a year, the community would end. Hence the challenge of transience needs to be considered empirically in relation to Late Late Service as they tried and died.

For the Late Late Service, sociology was a significant factor.

> Age and stage. Twenty somethings becoming thirty somethings and having kids and moving to the suburbs and changing. And other forces. Mobility. You get an urban student population. Five years on its too late unless you get the next lot of students in. (Group 8*, 2001)

Indeed, each of these sociological factors mentioned in Chapter 5 is, with hindsight, in evidence in the televised Christmas service.

The call to worship acknowledged the building in which they met for worship: Woodlands Methodist Church. It is near the centre of Glasgow, close to the University of Glasgow. Glasgow, a city of creativity and culture, attracts creative people, those likely to be attracted to the making and engaging with culture evident in the Late Late Service. Equally, a city of creativity and culture also farewells creatives.

The service met in the evening. While televised footage included young children and babies, evenings are difficult for families. As the Late Late Service community aged, so the pressure would fall on an evening event as a formative mode of making for all ages in the community, in particular primary school-aged children. Indeed, one of the ironies of the interviews in 2001 was pausing in order for the person being interviewed to bathe a primary school-aged child.

One response to transience is to seek stability. The interviews in 2001 wrestled with this tension. The sustainability equation was clearly at work.

sustainability = sociological stability × evolving group identities × flexibility

Could a different expression of 'making', with a less demanding setup and pack down routine, be offered? Would a 'sheltering' denomination provide sustainable support? Could a different approach to ecclesiology, membership and thus participation produce a different experience of making? Could a less intense approach to 'making' have conserved energy? All of these assume the value of permanence.

Another approach is to focus not on maintaining the gathering, but valuing the layers of ecclesiology. These, as outlined in Chapter 5, include not only gathering, but leadership incubators, faith formers, artefact creators and gifters of ecclesial interconnectedness.

The *God in the House* televised worship included original songs by Andy Thornton, Doug Gay and Rachel Morley. These creative people would soon move to London to pursue other forms of Christian ministry. Should they have stayed? Or was the body of Christ enhanced as Late Late Service acted as leadership incubator and gifter of ecclesial inter-connectedness?

The challenge of transience can also be considered theoretically. Gerald Arbuckle, in *Culture, Inculturation and Theologians* (2010), seeks to understand how cultures change and the consequences for mission and ministry. Arbuckle is blunt: 'if we continue to accept the modern definitions of culture we are trying to dialogue with something that does not exist' (p. xxii).

First, Arbuckle draws on recent insights from anthropology to clarify the church's dialogue with contemporary culture. Cultures are not static, but change over time, 'constantly interacting, mixing, and changing' (p. xxi). This provides important insights in examining ecclesial innovation. It would accept that in a city attracting creatives, the embodiments of church will be as constantly changing as the culture.

Second, theologically, Arbuckle argues that Jesus uses social dramas to foster the process of inculturation (pp. 152–65). He demonstrates this in relation to the Gospel narratives including the healing of Bartimaeus (Mark 10.46–52), the encounter with the Syro-Phoenician woman (Mark 7.24–30) and the Samaritan woman (John 4.1–42). What is interesting is that for each of these people the social drama is transient. Jesus moves on. In a sense, each of these people are left to make. For Arbuckle, 'Inculturation is ... above all a journey of faith, a journey of listening and letting go' (p. 165). Hence making as a formative practice of becoming holy is not defined by the longevity of the first expression but by the transformative impact as individuals participate in social drama. This provides a theological way to respond to transience.

Third, for Arbuckle, social drama outlines four stages – breach, crisis, redressive action and reintegration – by which transformation happens (pp. 90–7). This becomes a frame by which to understand the making that was the Late Late Service. The *breach* happens because culture changes. According to Charlie Irvine, the Late Late Service began with a group of friends 'who felt alienated from mainstream church' (*God in the House* 1995, 2:49). While this is outside the control of the church, it produced a *crisis*. For Irvine, 'we have no option but to try to use our own culture. In a sense it's a form of survival. It's a form of saying we have a faith, we want to worship together, we don't really know how to do it, so let's try something' (1995). What results is a *redressive action*: 'let's try something that uses the music that we grew up with and forms of learning that we're comfortable with' (1995). This leaves *reintegration*. Again, the layered approach to ecclesiology becomes essential in framing reintegration.

A gathered ecclesiology provides too narrow an understanding of *reintegration*. As described above, integration is evident through the making-as-planning. Integration is also evident as creative people move to London, taking with them their experiences of social drama as making at Late Late Service to enhance their ongoing ministry. Finally, integration is evident in those who simply participate in the event. *God in the House* is available on YouTube. On the website is a comment from a Jim McManus: 'that was brilliant! I used to bring a bunch of youth with no church background over to the LLS – it made sense to them (and me!), inspired us all.' That the worship 'made sense' expresses social drama and the formational value of this making. What happened at Late Late Service needs to be located not in continuity of a first expression community, but as an inculturation 'above all [as] a journey of faith, a journey of listening and letting go' (Arbuckle 2010, p. 165).

Fourth, social drama provides a transformative lens on deconstruction. It affirms an unfolding social ritual which involves all four stages – breach, crisis, redressive action and reintegration. A number of books examine new forms of church using the lens of deconstruction. Marti and Ganiel in *The Deconstructed Church* offer a transnational assessment of 'a creative, entrepreneurial religious movement that strives to achieve social legitimacy and spiritual vitality by actively disassociating from its roots' (2014, p. ix). *Mission-Shaped Church* affirms alternative worship as 'one of the most thoughtful attempts to relate worship and culture ... they have a profoundly mission-based instinct' (2004, p. 45). They also note they 'tend to act more as a safety net for those falling out of existing church ... People in recovery from an institution are not the most obvious apologists to invite others to join' (p. 45). Both of these assessments use a lens of deconstruction. What is helpful is how social drama provides another way to understand deconstruction. Breach and crisis are essential stages in a drama. As stages, they are meant to be transient, places to move from, not settle in. The social drama ends with reintegration. As argued already, this reintegration has layers. It is more than the *Mission-Shaped*

Church conceptualization of an invite to join the institution. Rather the reintegration is a becoming (to return to Soskice), which has layers that include leadership incubators, faith formers, artefact creators and gifters of ecclesial interconnectedness. Reintegration comes by way of a birthing, the redressive actions by which first expressions make through engaging with culture.

When making is understood as social drama, it provides a way to appreciate transience. This is threefold: in movement through each stage of the drama, in valuing each drama for its value in making, and in seeing reintegration as possible not only by sustaining of a gathered community, but equally in leadership incubators, faith formers, artefact creators and gifters of ecclesial interconnectedness. The social drama that was Late Late Service was a 'transforming ritual' for that moment. It stands as a wonderful inculturation. If it had sought to retain young adult leaders, it would have stifled other forms of creativity in other cities and contexts. Such is the challenge of transience, reframed in conversation with Arbuckle's social drama and as a making in contemporary culture.

Making and the challenge of the other

Empirical research – both interview data and worship analysis – of the Late Late Service has shown a making that is formative as it engages culture. Making can happen through different processes and in different spaces: in planning, in performance and in participation. I have examined the challenge that results in regard to transience, locating the tried and died that was Late Late Service in relation to social drama.

A second challenge is with regard to the other. How does the assertion of faith being about 'what's authentic and flies for us' experience meaningful engagement with the other? At the heart of the church as apostolic is sending. Traditionally, missiology sees a movement across a culture. Mission is the 'effort to effect passage over the boundary between faith in Jesus Christ and its absence' (Bonk, Dries and Sunquist 2012, p. ix). The standard communication model has a sender, a message and a receiver. A sender is willing to effect passage over a boundary in order that a receiving culture might experience faith in Christ embodied. Applied to mission in Western culture, the church as sender needs to find ways to effect passage across a boundary to a receiving culture. What is fascinating about first expressions is the claim that faith is already being experienced 'over the boundary'. This is the challenge inherent in the articulation of first expressions being about 'what's authentic and flies for us'. In their commitment to an authentic faith, how will first expressions experience a cultural other? Is authenticity in first expressions enculturated mission?

Or is it actually an assertion of monocultural imperialism, albeit dressed in the hipness of dance culture? As with the challenge of transience, the challenge of how to encounter the other can also be considered both theoretically and empirically.

Theoretically, Jan Pranger reads the work of Kathryn Tanner, introduced earlier in this chapter, from an intercultural perspective. Pranger notes that while Tanner has provided 'one of the most probing theological discussions of culture', her work has gained little attention from intercultural theology and missiology (2015, p. 175).

> Yet most theologians with whom Tanner is in discussion focus implicitly or explicitly on the particular relationship between Christianity and Western culture ... These theologians are usually not directly concerned with the interaction between cultures, relationships with postcolonial or non-Western cultures, or with questions of power and inequality. (pp. 183–4)

So, can Tanner's claims that Christianity can work piecemeal through the enculturated individual, who offers an 'artisan like' making in local ecclesial communities, be understood in relation to a postcolonial missiology? Pranger works with Tanner, and two of the lines of thought have particular relevance to the challenge of the other as it relates to first expressions and the claim to authenticity.

First, the valuing of local theology in the processes of inculturation. Pranger (pp. 193–5) develops the distinction between a postcolonial inculturation and a universal inculturation. A postcolonial inculturation is a critical, continuous yet indigenous conversation located in the particularity of a local culture. A universal inculturation is the abstract commitment in dominant cultures to inculturation. Applied to first expressions, the claim of 'what's authentic and flies for us' is attending to this particularity. It is articulating a distinct identity as a postcolonial inculturation. In doing so, it is declaring that the existing church culture that surrounds it in the United Kingdom is not universal and that inculturation is not something that happens over there in an overseas mission field. The affirmation of 'what's authentic and flies for us' is locating as contextual other forms of faith, for example Anglicanism as practised in charismatic evangelical or inherited Anglo-Catholic communities.

Using this analysis from Pranger makes the development of *Mission-Shaped Church* in response to the presence of first expressions quite remarkable. A colonial Christianity has accepted distinct particularity within itself. It has accepted the claim of another and, in doing so, opened itself as an established church to critique.

Second, Pranger argues that Tanner helps reconceive the complicated relationship between colonial Christianity and indigenous cultural forms. This speaks to power:

> In colonial Christianity, theology was usually constructed relational to the colonial culture rather than to the culture of colonized. This outside Christian culture was considered superior ... Moreover, the power to reject or accept such cultural elements was, at least in the mission churches, in the hands of cultural outsiders, that is, missionaries and missionary organisations. (Pranger 2015, p. 191)

This speaks to the danger that lurks in *Mission-Shaped Church* (2004, p. 80), which was introduced in Chapter 9. In the claims that fresh expressions should not be 'embraced simply because they are popular and new', who gets to discern the signs 'of the work of God'? Is it in the hands of the culture of the inherited Christian culture? If so, they are outsiders to the experiences of 'what's authentic and flies for us'. Pranger argues that Tanner provides the necessary resources with her argument that the test is not whether what is authentic and flies 'seem to threaten the established character of Christianity' but rather if the 'use distorts that to which Christians are trying to witness' (Tanner 1997, p. 150). Tanner acknowledges that there is no simple test for this. But it does invite, expect even, that first expressions will judge their own ambient witness. To illustrate, the appropriate use of a dance club visual in an act of Christian worship is best judged ethical by those who inhabit dance clubs. They are most aware of the nuances and authenticities in regard to appropriation of symbols from their cultural world. Tanner's approach thus helpfully serves to destabilize any unintended power in the claim to 'what's authentic and flies for us'. Any and all in a first expressions community may offer a judgement on what 'flies'.

Hence one way to respond to the challenge of the other is to hold first expressions to the trajectory of their claims. As they assert that they are a postcolonial inculturation, they are inviting themselves to a critical, continuous yet indigenous conversation located in the particularity of a local culture. They are expecting their culture not to be stable, but to be globalized, shifting, piecemeal and changing. God's Word enfleshed afresh for every generation is a timeless truth for contextual missiology. Hence 'what is authentic and flies' is continuously shifting and is continuously open to critical conversation from those within the culture.

To put it another way, if 'what's authentic and flies for us' asserts the universalism and continuous stability of its expression of authenticity, then it is neglecting its own birthright, the very transience of culture that it deployed as a trope to establish an identity distinct from 'the established character of Christianity'. As it ceases to be open to the cultural change and the ethic of the other, it loses the authenticity of its very authenticity as it ceases to fly.

This is a theoretical argument. I have considered the challenge of the other by turning the insights of postcolonial Christianity back on the assertions of first expressions.

There is a more empirical, more grounded way to respond to the challenge of the other. Doug Gay, introduced earlier in relation to the Late Late Service, points to the vital role of ecumenism in first expressions. He notes that new forms of church have a 'generalized respect for and interest in a wide range of Christians traditions' (Gay 2011, p. 73). He argues that 'retrieval' is a key value (p. 23) and points to the use of the church year, set prayers, ritual actions, images and icons (pp. 39–43). Each of these opens existing and inherited expressions of worship to the other. He points to a world faith through the influences of the World Council of Churches and 'post-colonial theologies, in particular Latin American liberation theology' (p. 80). All of these are ways of hearing the other. They are more likely to be experienced by first expressions, given their constant search for what is new. Thus the very trajectories within the movement allow them to hear the challenge of the other, often mediated through worship.

This returns us to making. Making is by definition active. Making involves a working with the piecemeal fragments of culture. Making enables first expressions to respond to the challenge of the other. As first expressions remain attentive to voices that are not their own, their processes of formation ensure these are woven in as challenges to their inherited presumptions. This is an empirical response to the challenge of other.

Conclusion

This chapter has examined how grassroots innovative communities form people. I have argued that making is essential to first expressions. Making has been defined theoretically, using Certeau as a way to creatively subvert popular culture. Making has been clarified theologically, using Tanner to argue for an approach to engaging culture as 'artisan like inventiveness' in local ecclesial communities which are body-ing forth distinct Christian identities.

Making as essential to formation has been detailed empirically with an extended analysis of one first expression. Using interview data and analysis of worship, the significance of making as planned has been demonstrated, while making as performed, in the Christmas worship of the Late Late Service, has been shown to integrate theology and ethics and offer a becoming holy that is inculturated within, and integrative of, daily life.

Two challenges to making have been considered, one in regard to transience, the other in regard to the other. This has affirmed again the value of making as essential to formation. First, the potential of social drama to appreciate transience; second, the active nature of making, which is therefore constantly de-centring any claims to universalizing inculturation.

I have considered the church as one (Chapter 9), apostolic (Chapter 10) and now holy (Chapter 11). The locating of holiness after mission follows Williams (1994) who argues that communicating the faith (apostolicity through ambient witness) comes before cultivating the faith (holy through constructive formation). However, Williams laments the fact that so often in the life of the church apostolic and holy end up pointing in different directions (p. 253). This brings us to catholicity.

For Williams: 'If God's action is single and coherent, there must be a coherence to the shape of Christian holiness, a coherence we can look for in the pattern of Christ's action and passion' (p. 265). What does this mean for becoming the church as catholic? Can God's eucharistic actions of take, thank, break and give order the interplay and tensions between first expressions and Fresh Expressions?

Notes

1 Originally at www.alternativeworship.org/. For a collection of later images, from 2000 to 2008, see www.smallfire.org/visionspage1.html.

2 1995, the first digital camera was being tested and cost $20,000 (Zhang 2015).

3 See also Certeau, Giard and Mayol 1998; Certeau and Giard 1997.

4 The Late Late Service featured in a one-off *God in the House* Boxing Day special in December 1995. Then during the summer of 1996 a *God in the House* series featured six different alternative worship communities, as outlined in Cummings (1996).

5 The album cover lists 19 different individuals (*God in the House* 1995).

12

Becoming catholic in sacrament and structure

I watched the removal of Rowan Williams. It was Sunday evening in Bath and members of Sanctuary were setting up for worship. St Thomas à Becket is the oldest city church in Bath, yet this evening the liturgy was being shaped by punk music. As with much alternative worship, making this critique of consumer culture would require a data projector. However, Rowan Williams was in the way. To be precise, a picture of the archbishop was centred in the middle of the best available projection space in the building.

I pondered the various layers of irony. Practically, Rowan Williams was in the process of being removed, having concluded as archbishop to become the Master of Magdalene College. Organizationally, in the months ahead, a photo of a new archbishop would need to replace Rowan on the wall of St Thomas à Becket. Symbolically, as described in Chapter 6, here was a person central to ecclesial innovation – who had written the foreword endorsing *Mission-Shaped Church* and declared Fresh Expressions the 'biggest most positive focus' in the Church of England (2007) – being removed by a first expression to make way for video projection.

No disrespect was intended. My impressions of Rowan Williams, whom I would meet a few days later, was that no disrespect would be taken. Yet here was a visible demonstration of the dynamic interplay that exists between innovation and order.

The theological word is polity. It is the study of theology as it relates to the operational and governance structures of the church. The church is one, holy, catholic and apostolic, and this is embodied in the way it organizes itself.

In the real world, ecclesial innovation requires ordering. The mission of God has a church and the ideal church funds mission. In reality, the church has multiple priorities and limited funds. The building that is St Thomas à Becket requires maintenance and Sanctuary requires a data projector. Both are important in a world with finite resources. How does a church order itself in relation to mission? Are people safe – when the key leader is accused of misconduct or the missional experiment in a local cafe is running at a loss?

Governance is an embodiment of polity. So are the sacraments. How might the sacramental order of the church be birthed and body forth in first expressions? The claims of authenticity, as outlined in Chapters 9 and 11, result in an increasing diversity of Christian practice. What might a postcolonial inculturation (Pranger 2015, pp. 193–5), with diverse sacramental practices, mean for becoming the church as catholic? For Tanner: 'Far from threatening the stability of a Christian way of life, the fact that Christians do not agree in their interpretation of matters of common concern is the very thing that enables social solidarity among them' (1997, p. 122).What does this mean in the empirical life of a first expression? In this chapter, the church as catholic is examined. Amid the diversity that results from first expressions, what are the implications for governance and sacraments?

Sacraments

A few days after the photo of Rowan was removed (and returned after the service, complete with a careful dusting), I was in Cambridge to interview Rowan Williams. What was striking was the way his thinking about fresh expressions emerged from a theology of the sacraments. In response to an initial question about the discernment by which fresh expressions was tested, I was immersed in a theology of baptism.

> Baptism brings you into the proximity of Jesus ... when you are in the proximity of Jesus you are in the proximity of the people [Jesus] is in proximity to. And who are those people? Well they're the ones who get left out. So the baptized charism, the baptized grace, the being where Jesus is, involves that. Just as much as baptism brings you, as the fourth gospel puts it [to] the bosom of the father, next to the heart of the father, so it brings you next to the heart of ... [the ones who get left out]. (Williams 2013)

In this account, fresh expressions are located in relation to a theology of sacraments. Apostolicity is sacramental as baptism brings us into proximity with 'the ones who get left out'. This proximal ordering in mission is for all the baptized: the whole people of God 'equally as applicable for a lay person, a vicar, a bishop, an archbishop' (2013).

A second sacrament, that of the Eucharist, was also described. A metaphor of ripples was used in considering how sacraments order the church in mission:

the eucharistic life of the church is much more like a concentric set of circles. In the heart of it is the offering of the church's prayer, in the name and Spirit of Jesus Christ, over bread and wine, which you share, as a means of deepening your affiliation to God, your status as a daughter or son of the eternal. That's the heart of it all. Now flowing out from that in ripples are a number of different kind of associational gathering that allow some of that to happen. And the agape meal, the ordinary social meeting. (Williams 2013)

The image of ripples offers a distinctive approach. Ripples offer an ordering in mission based not on inclusion and exclusion, but of being immersed in the love of God and in so doing, finding oneself being 'rippled over' by the sacramental life.

Significantly, it is the 'the name and Spirit of Jesus Christ' which lie at the centre and cause the ripples. As Flett argues, apostolicity is located not in the church, but in the sentness of Christ (2016). Hence, the church as catholic is ordered by an immersion in the ripples of God.

This invites making: intentional formation in the becoming of sacramental life. Williams (2013) argues that 'sacramental communities don't just happen'. In the interview, this was underlined with a gesture, a click of his fingers. This is certainly the case for communities birthed in new contexts of mission. In Chapter 2, we used Soskice to frame ecclesiology as a birthing and becoming. So if sacramental life does not just happen, and if sacramental life is not an in or out, then how do first expressions experience the baptismal proximity with Christ and the eucharistic being 'rippled over' by 'the name and Spirit of Jesus Christ'? If church is a birthing and becoming in which reality is theology, then how does sacramental life 'become' in the empirical reality that might be a network of seaside surfers? Or spiritual seekers in a city centre? Or a community garden in a suburban allotment?

One way is to explore making with specific attention to the pattern of the eucharistic actions of take, thank, break and give. Williams understood Anglicanism as 'not being a structural pattern but a patterning of Word and sacrament' (2013). This integrates sacrament and order. A patterning is provided in the eucharistic actions mapped by Jesus in the Gospels. At the Last Supper, in Luke 19.22, Jesus 'took a loaf of bread, and when he had given thanks, he broke it and gave it to them, saying, "This is my body, which is given for you. Do this in remembrance of me".' Four verbs are present: take, thank, break and give.

Patterning of sacrament and the life of Christ

Our focus is patterning. We are looking, as Rowan Williams reminds us, for ripples. So let us take these four verbs and consider the patterning in Scripture.

First, we consider the acts of Jesus during his life and ministry:

- **Take** – a feature of Jesus' ministry was his taking of meals and fellowship in the houses of tax collectors and sinners (for example Luke 15.1–2). Sacramentally, as Williams notes, it defines baptismal proximity – 'when you are in the proximity of Jesus you are in the proximity of the people [Jesus] is in proximity to ... the ones who get left out' (2013). Hence 'Table fellowship' as taking hospitality is an important patterning of the eucharistic table.
- **Thank** – in the three parables of Luke 15, finding what was lost – one sheep, one coin, one son – is followed by rejoicing (15.7, 9, 32). A practising of gratitude is a participation in sacramental patterning.
- **Break** – Jesus not only takes and thanks. In the patterning of the New Testament Jesus also receives, as an alabaster jar is 'broken open' over his head (Mark 14.3). This patterning is significant: wherever the good news (a patterning of word) is proclaimed, this action of breaking (a patterning of sacrament), will be told (Mark 14.9). Just as Jesus experiences the ripples of this pattern, so do all those who experience costly love.
- **Give** – the four eucharistic actions are all present in the feeding of the crowds in Matthew 15.36–37: 'Jesus took the seven loaves ... giving thanks, he broke them and gave them ... and all of them ate and were filled.' This patterning occurs in the context of pilgrimage and mission. Jesus is in Gentile territory, out of his ethnic comfort zone, between Tyre and Sidon (Matt. 15.21), where understanding of the ripples of God's love are challenged by a Canaanite woman. To continue the metaphor, the patterning of table fellowship expands. It ripples ethnically across cultures, geographically beyond Israel and physically to the crumbs that lie on the floor (Matt. 15.27). This narrative is only one of two places in Matthew where Jesus affirms great faith (15.28). The other time is when Jesus encounters the Centurion and describes him as having a great faith (Matt. 8.10). Both the Canaanite woman and the Centurion are Gentiles, seeking to be given an experience of God's shalom.

These are the ripples as 'the eucharistic life' spreads 'like a concentric set of circles' (Williams 2013). These four actions, patterned in the life of Christ, can help a first expression grow their participation in the eucharistic story. The Gospels are a prelude. As these stories are shared, so a community is becoming into the patterning of word and sacrament.

Patterning of sacrament and the Old Testament

But ripples, like a stone dropped in a lake, spread. The four actions of the Eucharist are not only patterned in the life of Christ. They also ripple through the history of the Old Testament. As Williams comments, 'When the church gathers to offer Eucharist, it gathers with a history' (2013). Old Testament narratives thus serve to deepen participation in the patterning of word and sacrament. Again, the four actions provide a focus, a way of growing the eucharistic story.

- Take – At first glance, the story in 1 Kings 17 fits oddly in a patterning of word and sacrament. Yes, a loaf of bread is present (1 Kings 17.13). But how might this narrative of drought and desperation help in a sacramental ordering? However, when 1 Kings is read in light of Luke 4.18–30, a rich eucharistic theology emerges. First, the telling in Luke 4.25–26 of the Old Testament story of 1 Kings 17 generates enough anger that the very life of Jesus might soon be taken. Second, as a proximity story, the mission of Jesus is located not with Israel, but with the widow of Sidon and Naaman the Syrian (4.27). It is a Gentile (the widow of Sidon) who provides bread for the prophet of God (Elijah) and a Gentile (Naaman the Syrian) who receives healing. The Spirit of the Lord (Luke 4.18) is thus located in proximity with the poor, captive, blind and oppressed of any culture. Third, both Jesus and Elijah are 'sent'. The action of taking as it unfolds in 1 Kings 17.8–17 patterns apostolicity as sacramental, located in God's mission. The taking of bread requires one to be, like Elijah and Jesus, sent into proximity with 'the ones who get left out' (Williams 2013).[1]
- Thank – The people of God in the Old Testament lived with a pattern of making altars. At multiple times, altars mark encounter with God. In their physicality, they invite future generations into moments of thankfulness, recalling the work of God in human history.
- Break – The Exodus narrative involves the dividing of the waters of the Sea of Reeds (14.21–26). The result of this breaking is salvation of a people. It is this deliverance that is echoed as Jesus eats the Passover with his disciples (Matt. 26.17), breaking a loaf of bread as he becomes the Passover lamb (1 Cor. 5.7).
- Give – The provision of manna from heaven in Exodus 16.4–35, as God provides daily bread from heaven, is gift. Manna 'awakens sensuous images, a heaven-sent food whose literal and symbolic references

enrich the Bible from Exodus to Psalms, from John to Revelation' (Ryken, Wilhoit and Longman 1998, p. 534). Jesus becomes the true manna from heaven, sustaining life in this world and the one to come (John 6.58).

My intention here is not to be exhaustive. There are other Old Testament narratives. Rather, my intention is to provide a taster in order to demonstrate the patterning.

The events of the Last Supper are soaked in these wider biblical narratives. These narratives give meaning to the four actions of take, thank, break and give. As these narratives are shared as story in communities of faith, they are part of a making of the sacramental life of the community. A sacramental ordering becomes a finding of oneself being 'rippled over' by the sacramental life. Every narrative shared, as it is related to the actions of take, thank, break and give, enables the becoming of a first expression.

Patterning of sacrament and the risen Christ

The ripples are evident in the history of the past. They are also evident in the present. We see this in the narrative of the Emmaus road. The risen Christ repeats the four eucharistic actions. 'When he was at the table with them, he took bread, blessed and broke it, and gave it to them' (Luke 24.30). These actions occur before Jesus is recognized, and it is in these actions that Jesus is recognized. 'Then their eyes were opened, and they recognized him; and he vanished from their sight' (Luke 24.33). This is significant in the making of a sacramental ordering. The four actions of take, thank, break and give can be performed before a community is aware of the risen Christ. Equally, the four actions can be revelatory, allowing the risen Christ to be seen.

This provides another dimension in the becoming of a first expression. We look for the actions of take, thank, break and give. We reflect on our week, scan the newspapers, consider the life of those gathered around the table with us.

- What are the ordinary things we can **take** in our hands?
- What does it mean to give **thanks** for these things?
- As we hold these things, what is **breaking** our heart?
- What needs to be **given** up sacrificially, that this community might experience life?

In these questions, lived experience is being woven into the eucharistic verbs. In the sharing of the stories of these actions, we look to recognize the presence of the risen Christ.[2] The presence of the risen Christ today becomes recognized.

Patterning of sacrament and ecclesiology

In the Foreword to *Mission-Shaped Church* Rowan Williams defines church as:

> what happens when people encounter the Risen Jesus and commit themselves to sustaining and deepening that encounter in their encounter with each other, there is plenty of theological room for diversity of rhythm and style, so long as we have ways of identifying the same living Christ at the heart of every expression of Christian life in common. (Williams 2004, p. vii)

This is an ecclesiology tied to the encounter of people with a Christ that is living. In this definition, while sacraments are not named, they are implicit in the context of the role they play in 'sustaining and deepening that encounter'. This sustaining and deepening occurs through the patterning I have outlined. Sustaining and deepening occurs in paying attention to our world and to Scripture, seeking to discern the actions of take, thank, break and give in the world around us, all the while informed by the biblical narratives that enrich the patterning.

In this way, a sacramental life is made in a first expression. There is no 'weird' holy moment when the sacraments suddenly appear. Rather there is an emerging sacramentality, a becoming into order, which has coherence with the discerning of a living reality and a dwelling in biblical narratives. Sacramental capacity is built over time.

This ecclesiology is coherent with the recent work of Latino scholar Ruben Rosario Rodriguez. Rodriguez argues that Karl Barth and Paul Tillich offer theologies of revelation 'within the framework of a Kantian epistemological perspective' (2018, p. 39). In light of global Christianities, Rodriguez develops a doctrine of revelation sourced in the work of the Spirit. The indwelling of the Spirit makes human experience of God possible, providing a doctrine of revelation 'grounded on the presumption that God not only speaks but also that humanity can hear and understand this divine self-communication' (p. 140). The work of the Spirit makes possible a 'very thick and complex understanding of divinity' (p. 141). First, by preserving Christ's unique saving role; second, valuing contributions from other cultures; third, providing a phenomenological vocabulary for describing divine agency in human history. My argument is that the four actions of take, thank, break and give provide this phenomenological vocabulary and hence a way of becoming a sacramental community, one that is grounded in the history of sacrament, and revealed in emancipatory movements in the First and New Testaments and in contemporary culture.

Paying attention to these four eucharistic actions allows a catholicity. They provide a way to become an apostolic sacramentality. For Williams,

> catholicity and mission are dimensions of the Church's form of life, a life endlessly sensitive, contemplatively alert to human personal and cultural diversity, tirelessly seeking new horizons in its own experience and understanding by engaging with this diversity, searching to see how the gospel is to be lived and confessed in new and unfamiliar situations; and doing this because of its conviction that each fresh situation is already within the ambience of Jesus' cross and resurrection, open to his agency, under his kingship. (Williams 1982, pp. 63–4)

Catholicity is visible in the conversations around the diversities in which take, thank, break and give are discerned. Tanner argues that what enables catholicity is not agreements regarding Christian identity. Rather it is the shared commitment to investigate how to live ethically in sites of struggle (Tanner 1997, p. 125). In other words, not to seek to define a universal inculturation, even if that includes diversity. Rather, the shared (catholic) commitment is to enact take, thank, break and give in whatever unique postcolonial inculturation (Pranger 2015, pp. 193–5) one is 'sent' to authentically inhabit. The catholicity that unites is 'a concern for true discipleship' (Tanner 1997, p. 152), as people commit themselves to a becoming of the four actions that will sustain and deepen the encounter with the Risen Jesus.

So what, empirically, might this look like? How might the inherited church encourage the possibility of bread for the missional journey in ways that are coherent with each unique postcolonial inculturation?

How might the sacraments nourish communities in mission?

Let me explore this by reflecting on an empirical moment. During participation in one first expressions worship experience, I observed increased whispering among those leading the service. Eventually they announced that a promised vicar had not arrived. Out of respect for the polity of the church, the Eucharist would now not occur, as advertised, in this particular worship experience.

This provides an insight into catholicity. An inherited church has systems in place, which locate sacraments within the ordered polity of the church. This is one way to order the church, including in relation to sacramental life. The interplay between being one church and being the church catholic, across diverse contexts, results in the setting aside of a licensed ministry agent, who is then able to offer the sacraments, including the catholicity of the church, as body-ing forth in this first expression.

In this empirical narrative, there are two approaches to sacramental life. First is an approach of abstinence. The first expression chooses not to participate. This is stated to be out of respect for the polity of inherited church. While a gracious response by those leading the service, the result is a denial of sacramental life to this part of the ecclesial body of Christ. Williams might note in an interview that baptism brings you into the proximity of Jesus, who is located with 'the ones who get left out'. But as eucharistic sacramental polity is enacted at a more local level in this particular empirical moment, 'the ones left out' are participants in this first expression at this particular moment.

A second approach evident in this empirical narrative is the stated supply approach to sacraments. A person from the inherited church is made available. They drop in as part of a rostered life. There is little sense of connection with the ongoing life of the community. Sacramental life is enacted but in ways that seem to suggest a privileging of the inherited church. It does feel like the first expression is receiving the 'crumbs that fall from their masters' table' (Matt. 15.27).

What other options are available? Let me offer some potential solutions. They are imaginative and will not work with the polity of every church.

A third approach is intentional rehearsal of sacramental patterning. Imagine a process in which over a number of years, biblical narratives have been shared as part of the formational making of this community. These are shared intentionally, with attention to the eucharistic actions of take, thank, break and give. For example, particular attention was paid over one year to the action of thanks. A range of passages that express thanksgiving is explored in the life of the first expression. As an acting of making, a prayer of great thanksgiving for that community is developed. This attends to the church as becoming holy within their particularized context. Such prayers can be prayed regularly as part of the patterning of sacramentality, with or without a licensed agent from the inherited church. Williams points to this approach when he describes the ripples that 'are a number of different kinds of associational gathering … the agape meal, the ordinary social meeting' (Williams 2013). This is building a sacramental patterning in relation to Eucharist.

A fourth approach could involve a reframing of the reserved sacrament as 'bread-to-go'. In some parts of the church, elements of the Communion are reserved for the sick. In the life of the early church, Justin Martyr noted that the Eucharist ended with the distribution 'and to those who are absent, [the deacons] carry away a portion' (First Apology 65). The United Methodist Church has a tradition called 'Extending the Table for those unable to be present'. This involves training lay people to take the communion elements to the sick. This is not 'celebrating the sacrament again, but ... recalling it and extending it to those who are otherwise forced to be absent from the Holy Meal' (Benedict 2013). This relies on a particular sacramental theology, but it does invite some apostolic sacramental thinking. An inherited church could 'reserve the sacrament' not only for the sick but also for 'the ones who get left out' (Williams 2013). This would enable eucharistic participation by a first expression. It would also make catholicity more visible for the inherited church, a reminder of the breadth of the ecclesial body.

A fifth approach could involve missional licensing. The feeding of the multitudes is intriguing, for it locates the eucharistic actions in the context of mission and pilgrimage. On the journey between Tyre and Sidon (Matt. 15.21) and Caesarea Philippi (Matt. 16.13), the multitude are fed. Geographically Jesus is on mission, beyond Israel, and in the actions of take, thank, break and give (Matt. 15.36) all the hungry are filled. There is the provision, bread, on a journey that itself is provisional. A missional licensing would draw from the sacramental patterning of this text, along with Rowan Williams's proximity argument: 'baptism brings you into the proximity of Jesus ... when you are in the proximity of Jesus you are in the proximity of the people [Jesus] is in proximity to ... the ones who get left out' (2013). The sacraments can be practised for the duration of a missional pilgrimage. If the community ceases, or becomes established, or gains a recognized minister, the license would cease. In turn, this would enhance the catholicity of church, for all those who hold a missional licensing are in rich contexts of learning. What they are experiencing offers much to the wider church, both inherited and other first expressions. Those offering the missional licensing, whether bishops or courts of the church, would seek regular conversations with those who hold missional licences. In this approach, sacramentality not only orders the church, but also brings the church together. These are conversations that might clarify 'hermeneutic discoveries' (Paas 2016). At the least, they would affirm unity, apostolicity, becoming holy and sacramentality.

As is clear from the empirical experience I observed, a polity in which one part of the church holds sacramental life in ways that those involved in apostolic encounters are deprived is a distortion of catholicity. In response, in this imaginative exercise, I have extended Williams's notion of patterning. By focusing on the four actions of take, thank, break and give, I have offered eucharistic insights that might be practical to first expressions. Each action is in fact a potential worship event. The four questions discerning the risen Christ today could be woven into a small group. At the same time, I have sought to enhance the catholicity of the church, providing ways for 'catholicity and mission to interplay together as dimensions of the Church's form of life' (Williams 1982, p. 63).

Governance

Sacramentality is one way in which church orders itself, revealing particular tensions in the interplay between apostolicity and catholicity. Another way in which the church orders itself is through governance. Can innovation occur at the same time as the church ensures that 'all things should be done *decently and in order*' (1 Cor. 14.20)?

Governance seems a particularly modern word. Yet long before boardrooms, strategic planning and matters arising from minutes, there was governance. The word comes from the Latin word *gubernator* and was used to describe the person wielding the rudder at the back of a galley full of rowers. Hence governance involves the actions of providing direction and ensuring the craft and crew are fit for purpose. For Eraković and McMorland, a modern board is a steersperson (2014, p. 202).

Governance is the capacity to focus on strategic issues in contrast to the operational day-to-day running of the organization. When governance is working well, vision is clarified. There is accountability around decision-making. Risk is managed. Evaluation of what is working and what is not is rigorous.

Governance and related terms like polity, order and structure are not often heard in first expressions conversations. In 445 pages of creative and theological reflection on innovation, mission and ecclesiology, Michael Moynagh (2017) makes no mention of governance or structure. The *'Defining Issues for Today's Church'* raised by *Mission-Shaped Questions* begin by introducing 'a principled and careful loosening of structures'.[3] Governance changes included the Bishops' Mission Order, the designation of ordained pioneer ministry and guidelines for the recognition, training and support of lay pioneers (Croft 2008, pp. 6–7).

Indeed, first expressions provide all sorts of 'steerage' questions. A key leader is accused of misconduct, named on social media. The missional experiment in a local cafe is running at a loss. A creative experiment is instructed to cease innovation while a review is conducted. How should the church respond to these situations? How can innovation be fit for purpose? Questions regarding governance appear sharply in relation to the first expression that was Nine O'Clock Service (NOS), as introduced in Chapter 1. Positively, there is the 'steerage' involved in moving to

Ponds Forge leisure complex in the city centre in 1992, along with the ordination of Chris Brain.[4] Negatively, there was the 'steerage' required in the crisis generated by the misconduct charges made against Chris Brain. However, 'steerage' involves ensuring the craft and crew are fit for purpose, and thus raises governance questions in relation to the regular life of NOS in the months and years before the crisis.[5]

The impact of governance on catholicity as it applied to first expressions was strewn through my interview data. Positively, there was the impact of Bishops' Mission Orders in Foundation. Negatively, there was the impact of Fresh Expressions. Some of this is described in Chapter 9. Other examples from the interview data included the first expression being asked to find a new church home because a new youth church wanted to start at the same time as the first expression held worship. Another first expression in confidence noted constant tensions with their sponsoring parish. My aim is not to relitigate conflict but to consider governance. In each of these interactions, whether positive or negative, a feature is the location of 'steerage' with the inherited church. The systems of governance exclude first expressions from decision-making processes. Can ecclesial innovation be ordered across the body of the church?

Ecclesiology and governance

Denominational structures, including their governance structures, are embodiments of culture. Roxburgh (2015) describes denominations as built on a genetic code that sought to maximize productivity and efficiency. Denominations embody a hub and spoke structure. This is based on four assumptions. First, that centralizing is the most efficient way to handle resources. Second, that spokes are an efficient way to carry resources from the centre to the regional and the local. Third, that managing geography requires intermediary structures (presbyteries or dioceses). Fourth, that governance structures are best located at the centre of the hub.

Roxburgh is concerned that one-way movements and centralized governance offer a malformed ecclesiology. A hub and spoke model is not agile and responsive in contexts of either rapid change or ecclesial innovation. 'Culture change in adaptive environments is *about cultivating among people at the local level the capacities to reimagine and experiment*' (Roxburgh 2015, p. 126; italics in original). The danger is that governance finds itself detached from this reimagination. At the spokes there is experimentation, while at the centre there is a commitment to maintain the genetic codes of productivity and efficiency. This result is a two-speed understanding of innovation. Governance moves at a different speed, distorting the ordering of the church as one dimension of catholicity.

Roxburgh contrasts the hub and spoke model that once served denominations so well with a model of a grid. A grid model redraws the connections. A decentralization occurs through the development of centres for distributive learning communities. These centres begin to connect directly with each other, rather than through a centralized hub. The result is a distributive and networked grid, based on local nodes.

In this approach, denominations remain significant. They cultivate the spaces in which distributive learning communities form. They resource the necessary practices of discernment through experimentation. They enable the communicating of learnings across localities.

Such a model still requires governance. Roxburgh (2015) argues that governance that is agile and responsive will

- attend to the technical work of goals, roles, resources
- hold open the unknown by keeping alive the questions about the challenges the system currently does not have the answers for
- learn with and among local experiments
- encourage adaptivity rather than efficiency.

Roxburgh points to agile and responsive organizations within our current rapidly changing world. He argues that they have KPIs based not on efficiencies but on two-way interactions between local communities (rather than on communication out from a hub). This approach is based on inter-relationality. It is a way to think theologically about structures, as nurturing catholicity through a grid model.

Fresh expressions of governance

Fresh expressions of governance are possible. Bradshaw, Hayday, Armstrong, Levesque and Rykert (1998) argue that governance in stable conditions is different from governance in conditions of innovation. The separation of roles and responsibilities, outlined in the Carver model (1980), at times can limit 'the ability of nonprofits to innovate and change' (Bradshaw et al. 1998, p. 6). A similar argument is made by Eraković and McMorland who argue that there are approaches to governance that are viable and challenge the traditional Carver separations between governance and management. This is possible when the focus is generative and on creative activity and direction finding (Eraković and McMorland 2014, p. 216).

A typology of governance is proposed by Bradshaw et al. (1998):

- Policy governance model – board and CEO of a unitary organization working in a stable context with conditions that are familiar and comfortable.
- Constituency representation model – larger and more broadly representational board in a pluralistic organization working in conditions of stability.
- Entrepreneurial model – board and CEO of a unitary organization working in a context that is adaptive with a focus on effectiveness.
- Emergent cellular model – a small, yet flexible core board, able to draw in others as needed in a pluralistic organization working in conditions of innovation.

Governance of an emergent cellular model involves an ordering that combines independence and interdependence (Bradshaw et al. 1998). Organizationally, this is ordered not through a central board but through self-managing teams. These function as cells that can operate alone, yet through technology, including email and teleconferencing, can interact with other cells. Governance is structured through annual face-to-face meetings, one an AGM, the other a retreat for strategic planning and visioning. In addition, there are two meetings a year by teleconference. Finally, there are opportunistic meetings. These occur when a quorum of board members find themselves in the same geographic locality. Governance processes include protocols in which decisions are minuted and shared for information with those not in attendance.

Bradshaw et al. (1998) focus on the function of governance, rather than the form of governance. The functions include

- stewardship of the vision and values of the organization
- allocation of resources and planning for the future
- accountability and fiduciary responsibilities
- ambassadorial and legitimating
- obtaining the optimum amount of relevant information about how the organization is performing
- self-reflection and learning.

They argue that all the functions of good governance can be embodied in an emergent cellular model. In other words, while centralized governance is one way to structure organizational life, it is not the only way. Denominations need not be shaped by the social conditioning of history.

Fresh expressions of governance are not only possible. More importantly, fresh expressions of governance are consistent with the missio-ecclesiology of Rowan Williams, in which the church is renewed by mission. For Williams, 'a theological reading of church history might suggest that the church always gets renewed from the edges rather than the middle' (2013). It is tempting to imagine renewal as individual and local and communal. Yet as Paul reminds us (1 Cor. 12.12–26), the body has many parts. Churches are more than individuals and individual congregations. The church is visible, ordered and structured, with polity outworked locally, regionally and globally. The internal organisms of heart and kidney, the structures of bone and sinew equally need renewal. First expressions invite a reformation of the entire body, in order that the gifts of innovation and experimentation might be shared, not only at the edges, but in the functioning of governance. Fresh expressions of governance are a logical outflow of mission.

Order in the body of Christ is not detached from the body that is the church. 'But all things should be done *decently and in order*.' So ends an extended meditation on the dynamic relationship between innovation and order in 1 Corinthians 14.40. Corinth is one of a number of first expressions planted in Greece. In this community, creative expression, in particular the use of charismatic gifts, is being encouraged. It is needed as part of apostolicity, in order that this first expression might 'bear witness to the character of God' (Witherington 1995, p. 289).[6] There is no separation in which order floats free in detached authority from the work of God in the church at Corinth. The structured body of 1 Corinthians 12, defined by love in 1 Corinthians 13, is renewed decently and in order by innovation in 1 Corinthians 14. Innovation across the ecclesial body includes fresh expressions of governance and the body-ing forth of structures that order 'the ability of nonprofits to innovate and change' (Bradshaw et al. 1998, p. 6). A church that does things decently and in order will, in the way of Christ, be open to reformations of structure.

'Steerage' for the journey

So practically, how might this occur? Most inherited church systems of governance have been formed in stable state contexts. With the advent of first expressions, they find themselves connected with groups working in shifting, innovating contexts. How might governance developed for the stable conditions of the nineteenth century transition in response to innovations at the edges like first expressions?

Eraković and McMorland helpfully point out that governance is a journey (2014). They researched 40 not-for-profit organizations, with budgets of between $500,000 and $5 million, in Aotearoa New Zealand and charted the transitions in governance over time. They note that invariably the governance required is never static. Governance in these not-for-profit organizations has constantly changed as the organizations have grown and developed. This invites us to consider steerage as a journey, not only of the organization, but of the governance structures and functions. Governance is a becoming.

Based on their empirical research, they offer wisdom for the journey of developing fresh expressions of governance. In what follows, I will place their wisdom in conversation with the Nine O'Clock Service. This allows us to end where we began, considering the empirical realities, even if uncomfortable, of first expressions.

First, **trusted advisors**. Eraković and McMorland helpfully observe that governance in the initial stages of innovation begins not with boards but with trusted advisors (2014). An individual comes alongside, meets regularly and in an informal capacity provides governance functions including strategic decision-making, managing risk and sharing in accountable evaluation.

Trusted advisors can also be used by governance boards seeking to go on a journey away from stable state governance to adaptive governance. This involves appointing an agreed trusted advisor as *ex officio* on governance boards. She is expected to speak on behalf of innovation, in this case of first expressions. This ensures two-way, rather than one-way communication. It clarifies the differences between governance and management and ensures continuity as management changes.

Second, **cardboard cut-outs**. A colleague in ministry was working with an elderly church. In a somewhat playful manner, he made life-sized cardboard cut-outs from photos of two young people from his community. The cardboard cut-outs were brought along to every church governance meeting. Before a crucial 'steerage' decision, the governance group were invited to consider what a young person from the community would say about the decision. Biblically, *cardboard cut-outs* are perhaps a man from Macedonia (Acts 16.9) pleading for decisions that will enhance the unfolding mission of God.

Third, **engagement**. Eraković and McMorland note the importance of sector knowledge in order to inform steerage decisions (2014). In a context of change and innovation, those in governance have a responsibility to engage in their own lifelong learning. Each individual needs to find ways to be connected, not only with the specific decisions of the governance group, but with the wider issues facing the sector. Governance in adaptive contexts needs to include the systemic questions generated by the particular temptations and risks present in every sector.

Fourth, **nurture connectivities**. Governance groups have a collective capacity that is grown through nourishing threads of connection. Nurture of connectivities is needed both during and between meetings. While a board chair is key in this, Eraković and McMorland note the responsibility of board members to stay connected not only to the agency's work but also to the work of governance as a shared task (2014, p. 211). Decision-making is enhanced and future-facing difficult decisions more likely to be made in governance groups in which connectivity is nurtured.

These four insights emerged from researching 40 not-for-profit organizations and seeking to understand the factors that enhanced governance in groups experiencing transition.

What happens when this wisdom is stress-tested by being placed in conversation with the Nine O'Clock Service? NOS is used as an example, given it was a first expression in which governance was called into question. From the early days of NOS, a trusted advisor would have been appointed. They would not have been in a line management role but would instead have met regularly with Chris Brain in a steerage role, reflecting on direction and ensuring the craft and crew were fit for purpose. As NOS grew, the trusted advisor would have been added to the council, providing continuity in steerage over time. A trusted advisor would have provided relational accountability links that were two-directional and continuous over time. A cardboard cut-out of two Sheffield youth, present at every governance group, would have provided a visual reminder of the proximal youth community whom Jesus desired to be present among. This would be enhanced by sector engagement, including reflection on the particular temptations and risks that might be present for those engaged in mission. The ability to ask probing questions and make difficult decisions would be enhanced by the nurture of connectivities. A connected governance group also has more sources of data and relations of connection, which increases the possibility of earlier discerning of warning signs.

Conclusion

As with my reflection on how the sacraments might nourish communities in mission, the reflection on NOS is an imaginative attempt to ground a theology of governance in adaptive contexts in an empirical reality. It is easy to be wise in hindsight and at distance (upside down and 12 hours ahead in time zones).

What is clear is that a dynamic relationship exists between innovation and order. Governance is a becoming. If we place innovation at the edge and governance at the centre, the result are power imbalances in which innovation is placed at the mercy of governance. If that governance is poor, then the consequences resonate with far greater impact on those located at the edges than those at the centre.

More important is what the grounded case studies both say theologically about catholicity. Governance, along with sacraments, are ways that the church orders itself. If we affirm church as catholic and as reforming, we need ways to involve centre and edge in reformation.

I have examined centre and edge in relation to sacraments. I have noted the importance of sacraments in Rowan Williams's theologic of first expressions. I have developed his notion of patterning by immersing the four eucharistic actions of take, break, thank and give in Scripture and in light of the risen Christ. I have argued that while this provides a becoming of ecclesial life, sacramental practices that locate sacraments within the ordered polity of the church can misshape the life of first expressions.

I have examined centre and edge in relation to governance, first, by placing an inherited hub and spoke model of governance in contrast to a grid model and, second, by drawing on research into governance in not-for-profits. This demonstrates an emerging cellular approach to governance and points to governance as a journey. Four practical actions have grounded this research in an ecclesial becoming, showing how governance, whether in a local, regional or national context, can provide 'steerage' for the journey.

The call is radical. Innovation in mission invites a becoming of catholicity. Mission is a converting ordinance that invites reformation at individual, communal and structural levels. The eucharistic actions of take, thank, break and give can be applied not only sacramentally, but structurally. Existing governance structures are invited to break themselves, to remake their existing patterns, in order to ensure ecclesial life is shared among the entirety of the body of Christ. Such is the vision of catholicity possible when first expressions are considered ecclesiologically.

Notes

1 While outside the argument being developed in this chapter, the narrative of 1 Kings 17.8–17 also provides wisdom in relation to community development in a time of climate change.

2 For Rodriguez, '*wherever* the work of establishing justice, extending compassion, and facilitating human liberation occurs, *there* is the true Spirit of God' (2018, p. 176).

3 A phrase used by the Archbishop of Canterbury in the General Synod debates in February 2004, according to Croft 2008, p. 200.

4 Lyon (2012, p. 243, footnote 3) argues that the ordination of Chris Brain was intentional design as part of NOS's expansion strategy.

5 Hence Anglican church leaders found themselves 'soundly castigated for failing to provide sufficient controls' (Lyon 2012, p. 238).

6 Witherington calls this an 'extraordinary note' upon which to conclude the discussion. It endorses innovation, in the form of prophecy, despite the problems it has generated within the community (1995, p. 289).

13

Coda:
A theologic of first expressions

This is a book about ecclesial innovation, about how innovation emerges, the theologies of why innovation emerges and the implications for becoming the body of Christ. It began with empirical research of ten communities. The terminology of first expression was used in relation to time, to define experimental forms of worship that occurred first and to convey the vulnerability and fragility of those who take the risks of being first to journey. A return, 11 years later, provided a longitudinal lens. Two trajectories were traced, first, the sustainability of these ten communities (first expressions), second, the denominational responses to grassroots innovation (Fresh Expressions). Eleven years on, the trying and dying of first expressions was read in light of Philippians, while a twelve strengths model and mission history in Great Britain helped understand Fresh Expressions. What has resulted is a three-way dialogue between the empirical realities of grassroots innovation, organizational innovation and theologies of birth and becoming.

Birthing a body

The theologies of Julian of Norwich and Janet Soskice helped interpret the initial empirical data (from Chapter 2). A first expressions research methodology emerges from Julian's valuing of a hazel-nut and seeing in the contemplation of one small thing the activity of God as Maker, Lover and Keeper. Listening to the individual birth narratives of individual first expressions revealed God as active in the motivations to **create as a gifted body,** explore **relational community** and develop **a spirituality authentic to contemporary culture.** Theologically, Soskice notes the priority of birth images in Scripture and argues that birthing is a becoming through time and space. Her articulations of Julian of Norwich's anthropology provide a theology of culture, interpreting the interplay in first expressions between faith and culture. Humans are becoming in the image of God. Our becoming begins with God who dwells in all of our bodily nature, working with us in body-ing forth God's image. Such body-ing forth can ever and only ever be embodied in the particularities of the culture and contexts we inhabit. This provides a theologic of first expressions, first, in the attentiveness to the empirical, second, in the affirmation of birth, growth and change and, third, in appreciation of a body-ing forth of generativity as God is attentive to every changing thing.

Becoming a body: organizationally

In order to give body-ing forth as a theological concept a more coherent shape, four different understandings of innovation – from commerce, ecology, indigenous (Maori) and craft – were examined (Chapter 3). This offered a way to connect lived experience of ecclesial innovation with theology.

Each frame is present in Scripture. Importantly, each understanding was reframed in Scripture. This gives an ecclesial theology of innovation.

- We value growth, and from Scripture we pay attention to the smallness of the mustard seed and the generosity of the farmer scattering seed.
- We value composting, and from Scripture we remember to celebrate death for life.
- We value the spiral of knowledge across generations, and from Scripture we remember to include diversity from across cultures.
- We value mending, and from Scripture we remember to applaud communities that empower the marginalized.

Essential to Soskice's becoming and body-ing forth is a theology of kinship. 'The bonds of love and friendship we have with one another' are constitutive of God's desire to be with humankind (Soskice 2007, p. 187). Much talk of innovation is underpinned by mindsets that value growth. These easily absorb the competitive notions of *Dragon's Den* and reduce the body-ing forth of innovation to numerical gains. The four frames provide a way to develop kinship, offering theologically formed insights into how organizations can respond to ecclesial grassroots innovation.

The four understandings of innovation are instructive, providing a map of how an organization might support grassroots innovation. A wise organization will seek to resource in every frame. They will especially resist the culture that pushes toward a valuing only of growth. It is hard to imagine a grandparent leaning back at the news of their first grandchild and going, to borrow from Vincent in Chapter 1 – 'Just a few *entrepreneurs* doing their own thing ... "Will they stand the test of time?"' (1976, p. 100). Instead, there is love and attention (using Soskice 2007,

Table 14: Organizational ways to nurture kinship with grassroots innovation

Grow	*Compost*
Sow with generosity	Conduct place-based research
Scaffold what grows	Work with rhythm of the seasons
Key resource is energy emerging with progress	Affirm death with services of closure
Pay attention at every stage of the S curve	Key resource is sacrifice, in patterns of death and resurrection
Spiral	*Mend*
Key resource is stories	Value recycling
Use appreciative enquiry to discern ancestor stories of life	Prioritize contributions of those on the edges
Weave connections with new technologies through storytelling	Key resource is mentoring from someone further down the road
Create space for future generations	

pp. 7–34) paid to their development. The fridge becomes plastered with art, based not on performance but on kinship. These integrate the four understandings of innovation in a becoming formed by a theology of kinship. They can guide other organizations seeking to support innovation.

Becoming a body: each one small thing

In one small thing, declares Julian of Norwich, God is active. Julian's theology was applied not only in birthing, but in becoming. A return to the grassroots communities 11 years later revealed that 50 per cent were no longer in existence (Chapters 4 and 5).

A sustainability equation was developed:

Sustainability = sociological stability × evolving group identities × flexibility

This equation describes the impact of mobility, leadership transitions, event management and wider connections on ecclesial vitality. Sustainability is enhanced by intentional actions that include

- maintaining active connection, particularly through participative technologies
- articulation of the founding story and community values
- annual values audit conversations

- structural shifts to ensure a rotation of leadership
- external support during leadership transitions
- flexible Christian practices.

These intentional actions need to be read theologically as a becoming in which ecclesial life is sustained by human participation in the ongoing economy of God.

An ecclesiology of 'regard as valuable' was identified in the book of Philippians. A woven ecclesiology that appreciates the richness of ecclesial life as gatherings, leadership incubators, faith formers, artefact creators and gifters of ecclesial interconnectedness was argued to offer a richer ecclesiology of becoming than a singular focus on the sustainability of gathered worship events.

Becoming a body: hermeneutic discoveries

Becoming offers insights for mission. Paas calls these 'hermeneutic dis-coveries' and argues that they provide a theologic for innovation. Each one small thing is unique. Each one small thing potentially provides an 'incredible amount of theological, ecclesiological, missiological, and organizational experience' (Paas 2016, p. 235) and offers learnings for the church, inherited and other first expressions.

This provides another way to understand 'regard as valuable'. Kathleen Blee argues persuasively for the value of all stories, particularly birth stories and especially birth stories in times of significant change. Blee studied a failed Christian social movement in a suburb in Chicago. She was present at the birth, writing of the first meeting in a church basement in Pittsburgh. She was present a year later, writing of how this Christian social movement had drifted from their founding dreams and was about to close. Blee argues that we live in a culture that views success in numerical gains. A countercultural move in research is to pay attention to the tried and died. For Blee, 'crucial information about how social movements emerge (or fail to do so) is lost by bypassing such groups and by considering only those successful ones that survive over time. It is difficult to understand how and why people mobilise to change society if we study only groups that are established' (2008, p. 43). First expressions contain crucial information. They yield insight into why people innovate. If we only study innovations deemed sustainable and successful, we lose sight of the initiating generativity, which is a window into God's redeeming possibilities. The actions and choices that shape structure, self-understanding, tactics and outcomes are lost. Blee argues that we need a more 'robust social scientific understanding' of the singular and emergent that does not abstract away from the particular and obscure the shifting complexities of trajectories by which individuals grow (p. 41). In order to capture these rich insights, the church as one, apostolic, holy and catholic was used as a frame.

Authenticity is essential to postcolonial inculturation (Chapter 11). However, a theology of kinship sees any inculturation in relational terms. The whole of the body that is the church is becoming. What flies (Chapter 9) is never for an individual or a single community. What flies is a fuller realization of relationships, including with the whole body of Christ and the world. Authenticity is a fuller realizing of these relationships. This is consistent with visions of authenticity, including as understood by Charles Taylor. In *The Ethics of Authenticity* he argues that authenticity involves a people 'made more self-responsible' (1992, p. 77). Again, we find a making (Chapter 11).

Taylor is adamant that authenticity can be embraced without an inevitable slide into either a greater individualism or a depersonalizing tribalism (pp. 55–6). Humans share a 'horizon of significance' in common (p. 52), in which one's own 'identity crucially depends on [one's] dialogical relations with others' (p. 48). To put this empirically, the turn to an ecumenical and world Christianity (Chapter 11) invites a becoming.

This hermeneutical discovery includes the quest for authenticity in the interplay between faith and culture. It expects a people, as individuals, as postcolonial inculturations and as the becoming body of Christ to be 'made more self-responsible' (p. 77).

This ethical understanding of authenticity works against the possibility that ecclesial innovation in general, and first expressions in particular, will result in an instrumentalization of the church. The church is instrumentalized when it is conformed to another good. For example, when ecclesial innovation is valued because it provides a growth in numbers, or an opportunity to impact a community or develop leaders, then the purpose of the church has been instrumentalized (Paas 2016, pp. 258–64). In contrast, ecclesial innovation that is understood as a making (Chapter 11) in response to the apostolic desire to bear witness (Chapter 10) understands the relationship between church and mission in relation to God as Maker, Lover and Keeper. Ecclesial innovation bodies these theological commitments. Just as a healthy body needs exercise, so mission structures – monasteries, bands, voluntary societies in Chapter 8; free havens, laboratories and incubators in Chapter 9 – body forth a becoming.

Another way to understand this hermeneutical discovery of the church as becoming is to draw on Stephen Bevans's understanding of the church as 'the community of the converted' (2018, p. 142), a school of conversion, 'a place where conversion is developed and fostered' (p. 143). This understanding of becoming offers hope, opportunity and also challenge. Donald Gelpi insists that Jesus' vision of the kingdom results not only in the hope of individual or moral conversion but the challenge of 'sociopolitical conversion'. A person is moved 'beyond the concern of interpersonal relationships into the realm of institutional reform' (1989, p. 26). If the way of Jesus is reformation, then our institutions, including their structures of governance, can be converted. This is mission *ad intra*, an inward mission which involves 'rethinking things and rereading the Bible and tradition to cultivate coherence between speaking and doing' (Tamez 2017, p. 87). This is the gift of first expressions. They invite a reformation. Through birthing, the body of God is invited to become. These are some of the 'hermeneutic discoveries' present in first expressions, those who try and those who die.

The roadmap and 'I'

This research was undertaken because of my own participation in one small thing, an experimental mission community. I had been challenged by the question of metrics. Were there ways, beyond the metrics of numbers and survival, to understand ecclesial innovation?

These questions helped motivate my first research visit in 2001.

The questions became more pointed, more introspective, when the ecclesial innovation I was part of birthing closed in 2008. Should 'try, yet die' change how I understand the value of that community? As a final thank-you gift, the church sent me the handcrafted pottery jar that had been the offering container. As I held that jar, I pondered all the time, talents and tithe that had been invested in that ecclesial innovation. In a world of finite resources, how does the church understand missional investment?

These questions helped motivate my second research visit in 2012–13.

In light of this three-way dialogue between the empirical realities of grassroots innovation, organizational innovation and theologies of birth and becoming, I have fresh convictions about ecclesial innovation.

First, my *respect* for first expression leaders and communities has deepened. In faith, they body-ied forth. At the same time, my caution regarding first expression leaders and communities has also increased. Everyone is human. Humans need kinship as part of an ethic of authenticity. This includes an experience of governance that expects to be mutually converted in the steerage on a journey (Chapter 12).

Second, my understanding of *church* has been enlarged. Innovation is for the entire body, not only the grassroots. To return to the biblical work on Luke 1.39–45 (Chapter 7), Elizabeth has much to learn from Mary, and equally Mary has much to learn from Elizabeth. The Spirit is at work in the bodies of both women. The interplay between first expression and Fresh Expressions, grassroots and organizations, invites mutual, yet supportive, transformation.

Third, the value of *faith exploring spaces*. This includes developing leaders, both lay and ordained (the 'vicar factories' of Chapter 5). It happens through the apostolicity of ambient witness (Chapter 10) and because of becoming holy in constructive making with culture (Chapter 11). We live in a secular age. People need offers of transcendence that can be experienced by incarnational making that emerges from within the culture.

Fourth, the vitality of *gender*. The kin theology of Soskice and her understanding of an eschatological anthropology; the work of theologians of gender like Slee, Hess and Phillips is a challenge. We need to get beyond 'mansplaining' in mission. We need to body forth in ways that encourage play, relationity and express solidarity with suffering.

Fifth, the importance of engaging *culture in growing people*. According to Julian and Soskice, Christ travails in all of a human being, including the intellect and our bodily senses. As seen in the empirical data (particularly Chapters 9 and 11), in the search for an authentic engagement with culture, God as Maker, Lover, Keeper is revealed.

Sixth, first expressions *grow cultural resistance*. While engagement with culture results in growth, there is a complex engagement with culture. The use of punk music at Sanctuary was a complex move, in which culture – in the form of a musical genre – was being deployed to encourage resistance to consumerism. The encouragement at Visions and Grace to dance to a new expression equally includes 'Going against the flow' because God's 'kingdom is upside down'.

Seventh, first expressions *value tradition*. In the midst of innovation, a recurring theme was the valuing of tradition. The ambient witness in which Visions find ways to let buildings 'live and breathe well' and the ecumenical seeking described by Doug Gay show a complex relationship with tradition.

Eighth, ecclesial innovation will *continue in every generation*. The first expressions researched here are now becoming adult. I see them on social media advertising the twenty-first birthdays of their communities. Like me, the leaders whom I met in 2001 and 2013 now have hair beginning to grey and children as old as we were when we began first expression planting. Marys are ageing and, in that process, invited to become Elizabeths.

Ninth, first expressions are *sustained by flexible spiritual practices*. Essential in these communities were 'ember' practices, in which the creativity of their lives was held by patterns of prayer. This invites a focus on practices that consciously celebrate the unique life of each community. It encourages a focus on ways to clarify and communicate the unique story that has birthed the community and the values they are wishing to body forth.

Birth stories must be treasured. In the birth stories that surround Jesus, we see the Spirit embodied as an older woman (Elizabeth) blessing a younger woman (Mary). As a result, fresh insights, including the poetic justice-making of the Magnificat, emerge. Through history, God's Spirit has continued to move, brooding over the bodies of God's faithful servants, giving fresh insight to those who take risks in faithful obedience. This book has drawn on empirical research into grassroots and institutional innovation to tell birth stories – of life and into death.

First expressions and the mission of God

First expressions yield insight into the becoming of the church in the West. They offer unique, empirical insight into the embodiment of Christian life in porous, hybrid spaces. They challenge us to a more radical understanding of being church and a more particularized embodiment of Christian practices. Sustainable innovation is optimized, first, when innovation is simultaneously both bottom-up and top-down, second, when it includes the voice of the other, particularly female voice and, third, when formation is focused on the interplay between faith and culture. Sustainability in first expressions invites a shift from church as stable state to church as an evolving participant in take, thank, break and give. This is an ecclesial becoming which focuses not on church as uniform, gathered and parish, but church as particular, layered and interconnected as incubators of leadership in mission.

Ecclesial structures can nourish first expressions. Fresh Expressions is in continuity with the rich history of mission in Great Britain, which resulted in new structures – first expressions – serving their unique context. As a first expression, Fresh Expressions provides rich insight, including the need for diverse strengths and the vital role that leaders of structures must play in championing innovation. When one part of the body seeks to innovate, another part should never say 'We've seen it all before' ... 'Just a few *entrepreneurs* doing their own thing ... "Will they stand the test of time?"'

Rather, ecclesial innovation is the ants in the pants of the body of Christ. Ecclesial innovation enables a becoming as one, apostolic, holy and catholic church. It makes visible the reality that is the conversion of the Spirit in individuals, communities and organizational structures. Hence innovation has value as it makes the church be the church, awakening the essentiality of becoming as one, apostolic, holy and catholic church. Such is the mission of God through first expressions.

Bibliography

Individual interviews

Cottrell, Stephen, *About the Development of Fresh Expressions*, Margaretting, Ingatestone, Essex, 2013.

Croft, Steven, *About the Development of Fresh Expressions*, Sheffield, 2013.

Gay, Doug, *About the Development of Host and Late Late Service*, London, 2001.

Roberts, Andrew, *About the Development of Fresh Expressions*, London, 2013.

Roberts, Paul, *About the Development of Third Sunday and Resonance*, Bristol, 2001.

Roberts, Paul, *About the Development of Resonance and Foundation*, Bristol, 2013.

Williams, Rowan, *About the Development of Fresh Expressions*, Cambridge, 2013.

Focus group interviews

Foundation, *About the Development of Foundation*, Bristol, 2013.

Grace, *About the Development of Grace*, London, 2001.

Grace, *About the Development of Grace*, London, 2013.

Group 1*, *About the Development of 1**, United Kingdom, 2013.

Group 2*, *About the Development of 2**, United Kingdom, 2013.

Group 3*, *About the Development of 3**, United Kingdom, 2013.

Group 4*, *About the Development of 4**, United Kingdom, 2013.

Group 5*, *About the Development of 5**, United Kingdom, 2013.

Group 6*, *About the Development of 6**, United Kingdom, 2013.

Group 7*, *About the Development of 7**, United Kingdom, 2013.

Group 8*, *About the Development of 8**, United Kingdom, 2001.

Group 9*, *About the Development of 9**, United Kingdom, 2001.

Group 10*, *About the Development of 10**, United Kingdom, 2001.

Group Moot*, *About the Development of Moot**, United Kingdom, 2013.

Late Late Service, *About the Development of Late Late Service*, Glasgow, 2001.

Sanctuary, *About the Development of Sanctuary*, Bath, 2001.

Sanctuary, *About the Development of Sanctuary*, Bath, 2013a.

Sanctuary, *About the Development of Sanctuary*, Bath, 2013b.

Visions, *About the Development of Visions*, York, 2001.

Visions, *About the Development of Visions*, York, 2013a.

Visions, *About the Development of Visions*, York, 2013b.

Secondary literature

'A history of Grace', *Grace: Fresh, Vital Worship since 1993*. Available at www.freshworship.org/node/424 [viewed 23 December 2013].

Ahearne, Jeremy, *Michel De Certeau: Interpretation and Its Other*, Cambridge: Polity Press, 1995.

Allen, R. Michael, 'The Kindness of God: Metaphor, Gender, and Religious Language – By Janet Martin Soskice', *International Journal of Systematic Theology* 12 (1), 2010, pp. 97–9.

Allen, Tom, 'Transcendence @ York Minster', 11 October 2007. Available at http://bigbulkyanglican.typepad.com/bigbulkyanglican/2007/10/transcendence-y.html [viewed 25 February 2013].

Anderson, Athol, Judith Binney and Aroha Harris, *Tangata Whenua: A History*, Wellington: Bridget Williams Books, 2015.

Anderson, Ray S. *The Shape of Practical Theology: Empowering Ministry with Theological Praxis*, Downers Grove, IL: InterVarsity Press, 2001.

Arbuckle, Gerald, *Culture, Inculturation, and Theologians: A Postmodern Critique*, Collegeville, MN: Liturgical Press, 2010.

Baker, Jonny, *Curating Worship*, London: SPCK, 2010.

Baker, Jonny and Doug Gay with Jenny Brown, *Alternative Worship*, London: SPCK, 2003.

Bardsley, Warren, *Against the Tide: The Story of Adomnan of Iona*, Glasgow: Wild Goose Publications, 2006.

Barge, Marian, 'The story of Whyllie – Mission in Action'. Anglican Renewal Ministries. Available at www.anglicanrenewalministries-wales.org.uk/main/magazine/issue28/MBarge.htm [viewed 13 March 2013].

Batt, Linda, 'A Journey through a Labyrinth', *Monmouth Diocesan Newsletter*, Pentecost 2012. Available at www.churchinwales.org.uk/monmouth/news/newsletter/News198Pentecost2012.pdf [viewed 13 March 2013].

BBC, 'Villagers get a prayer with pint', 2006. Available at http://news.bbc.co.uk/2/hi/uk_news/wales/south_east/5147222.stm [viewed 13 March 2013].

Beaudoin, Tom, *Virtual Faith: The Irreverent Spiritual Quest of Generation X*, San Francisco: Jossey-Bass, 1998.

Bede's Ecclesiastical History of England, ed. A. M. Sellar. Available at www.sacred-texts.com/chr/bede/histo61.htm [viewed 20 May 2019].

Benedict, Daniel, *Extending Your Congregation's Communion Table to Those Unable to Be Present*, 2013. Available at www.umcdiscipleship.org/resources/extending-your-congregations-communion-table-to-those-unable-to-be-present [viewed 29 May 2019].

Bevans, Stephen, 'Seeing Mission through Images', *Missiology: An International Review* 19 (1), 1991, pp. 45–57.

Bevans, Stephen, *Essays in Contextual Theology*, Leiden, Netherlands: Brill, 2018.

Bielo, James, *Words upon the Word: An Ethnography of Evangelical Group Bible Study*, New York: New York University Press, 2009a.

Bielo, James, 'The Emerging Church in America: Notes on the Interaction of Christianities', *Religion* 39 (3), 2009b, pp. 219–32.

Bielo, James, *Emerging Evangelicals: Faith, Modernity and the desire for Authenticity*, New York: New York University Press, 2011.

Bielo, James, 'The Question of Cultural Change in the Social Scientific Study of Religion: Notes from the Emerging Church', *Journal for the Scientific Study of Religion* 56 (1), 2017, pp. 19–25.

Blee, Kathleen, 'The Hidden Weight of the Past: A Microhistory of a Failed Social Movement Group', in James Brooks, Christopher R. DeCorse and John Walton (eds), *Small Worlds: Method, Meaning, and Narrative in Microhistory*, Santa Fe, NM: School for Advanced Research Press, 2008, pp. 37–52.

Bockmuehl, Markus, *The Epistle to the Philippians*, New York: Bloomsbury, 2006.

Bonk, Jonathan, Angelyn Dries and Scott Sunquist, 'Preface to the American Society of Missiology Series', in Stanley Skreslet, *Comprehending Mission: The Questions, Methods, Themes, Problems, and Prospects of Missiology*, Maryknoll, NY: Orbis, 2012, p. ix.

Bradshaw, Pat, Bryan Hayday, Ruth Armstrong, Johanne Levesque and Liz Rykert, 'Nonprofit Governance Models: Problems and Prospects'. Paper originally presented at the ARNOVA Conference, Seattle Washington, 1998. Available at www.buildingmovement.org/artman/uploads/nonprofit_governance_models.pdf [viewed 5 March 2019].

Brueggemann, Walter, 'The Bible and Mission: Some Interdisciplinary Implications for Teaching', *Missiology* 10, 1989, pp. 397–412.

Bynum, Caroline W., 'The Female Body and Religious Practice in the Later Middle Ages', in *Fragmentation and Redemption: Essays on Gender and the Human Body in Medieval Religion*, New York: Zone Books, 1991, pp. 181–238.

Cammock, Peter, *The Dance of Leadership: The Call for Soul in 21st Century Leadership*, Auckland: Prentice Hall, 2003.

Carey, William, *An Enquiry into the Obligations of Christians to Use Means for the Conversion of the Heathens*, 1792. Available at http://books.google.com/books?isbn=1419106333 [viewed 13 March 2013].

Carver, John, *Boards That Make a Difference*, San Francisco: Jossey-Bass, 1990.

Castells, Manuel, *The Rise of the Network Society: The Information Age: Economy, Society and Culture*, Volume 1, Oxford: Blackwell, 2000.

Certeau, Michel de, *The Practice of Everyday Life*, trans. Steven F. Rendall, Berkeley: University of California Press, 1984.

Certeau, Michel de and Luce Giard, *The Capture of Speech and Other Political Writings*, Minneapolis: University of Minnesota Press, 1997.

Certeau, Michel de, Luce Giard and Pierre Mayol, *The Practice of Everyday Life. Volume 2. Living and Cooking*, Minneapolis: University of Minnesota Press, 1998.

Church Army's Research Unit, 'Church Growth Research Project Report on Strand 3b: An Analysis of Fresh Expressions of Church and Church Plants Begun in the Period 1992–2012', 2013. Available at www.churchgrowthresearch.org.uk/UserFiles/File/Reports/churchgrowthresearch_freshexpressions.pdf [viewed 14 May 2019].

Clark, J. P. H., 'Nature, Grace and the Trinity in Julian of Norwich', *The Downside Review* 100 (340), 1982, pp. 203–20.

Clawson, Michael and April Stace, *Crossing Boundaries, Redefining Faith: Interdisciplinary Perspectives on the Emerging Church Movement*, Eugene, OR: Wipf and Stock, 2017.

Coakley, Sarah, 'Living into the Mystery of the Holy Trinity: Trinity, Prayer, and Sexuality', *Anglican Theological Review* 80, 1998, pp. 223–32. All citations in this book from the reprinted article in Eugene Rogers (ed.), *The Holy Spirit: Classic and Contemporary Readings*, Chichester: Wiley-Blackwell, 2009.

Coley, Steve, 'Enduring Ideas: The Three Horizons of growth', *McKinsey Quarterly*, December 2009. Available at www.mckinsey.com/business-functions/

strategy-and-corporate-finances/our-insights/enduring-ideas-the-three-horizons-of-growth [viewed 4 August 2019].

Collins, Steve, 'Sanctuary | Stations of the Cross | Easter 2003'. Available at www.smallfire.org/sanctuary_stations.html [viewed 21 April 2019].

Costa, Arthur L. and Bena Kallick, 'Through the Lens of a Critical Friend', *Educational Leadership* 51 (2), 1993, pp. 49–51. Available at www.ascd.org/publications/educational-leadership/oct93/vol51/num02/Through-the-Lens-of-a-Critical-Friend.aspx [viewed 8 March 2013].

Croft, Steven (ed.), *Mission-Shaped Questions: Defining Issues for Today's Church*, London: Church House Publishing, 2008.

Cummings, Tony, 'God In The House: A six part TV series on the alternative worship scene', *Cross Rhythms Magazine* 34, August 1996. Available at www.crossrhythms.co.uk/articles/music/God_In_The_House_A_six_part_TV_series_on_the_alternative_worship_scene/40559/p1/ [viewed 29 April 2019].

Curran, Maris, 'The Master Quilters of Gee's Bend, Ala.' *The New York Times* (2018). Available at www.nytimes.com/2018/11/13/opinion/quilts-while-i-yet-live.html [viewed 11 April 2019].

Day, Abby, *Believing in Belonging: Belief and Social Identity in the Modern World*, Oxford: Oxford University Press, 2011.

Drane, John, 'What Does Maturity in the Emerging Church Look Like?' in Steven Croft (ed.), *Mission-Shaped Questions: Defining Issues for Today's Church*, London: Church House Publishing, 2008, pp. 90–101.

Drane, John and Olive Fleming Drane, *Reformed, Reforming, Emerging and Experimenting: A Study in Contextual Theology Reflecting the Experiences of Initiatives in Emerging Ministry Being Funded by the Church of Scotland*, Edinburgh: Emerging Church Joint Working Party, 2010.

Driver, John, *Images of the Church in Mission*, Scottdale, PA: Herald Press, 1997.

Dunn, J. D. G., *The Christ and the Spirit: Collected Essays Vol. 2: Pneumatology*, Edinburgh: T&T Clark, 1998.

Electronic Beats, 'A Techno Veteran Explains Why People Whistle at Parties', *Electronic Beats*, 10 October 2017. Available at www.electronicbeats.net/the-feed/heres-people-whistle-techno-parties/ [viewed 29 April 2019].

Engelke, Matthew, *God's Agents: Biblical Publicity in Contemporary England*, Berkeley: University of California Press, 2013.

Eno, Brian, *Music for Airports* liner notes, London: Polydor Records, 1978.

Eraković, Ljiljana and Judith McMorland, 'The Major Challenges in Designing Capable Nonprofit Boards', in Jens Mueller and Philippa Katherine Wells (eds), *Governance in Action Globally: Strategy, Process and Reality*, Oxford: Rossi-Smith Academic Publishing, 2014, pp. 201–20.

Everett, Laura, 'REPAIR & RENEW: Mending & Quilting as Models for Christian Institutional Innovation', *Louisville Institute*, 2018. Available at https://louisville-institute.org/awards/pastoral-study-project/13694/ [viewed 11 April 2019].

Everett, Laura, 'The spirituality of mending', *Religion News Service*, 2019. Available at https://religionnews.com/2019/04/10/the-spirituality-of-mending/ [viewed 11 April 2019].

Ferreira, M. Jamie, 'Janet Martin Soskice, The Kindness of God: Metaphor, Gender, and Religious Language', *The Journal of Religion* 89 (3), 2009, pp. 432–3.

Fiddes, Paul, 'Ecclesiology and Ethnography: Two Disciplines, Two Worlds?' in Pete Ward (ed.), *Perspectives on Ecclesiology and Ethnography*, Grand Rapids, MI: Eerdmans, 2012, pp. 13–35.

Flett, John, *Apostolicity: The Ecumenical Question in World Christian Perspective*, Downers Grove, IL: InterVarsity Press Academic, 2016.

Fox, Matthew, *Confessions: The Making of a Post-Denominational Priest*, San Francisco: Harper San Francisco, 1996.

Fresh Expressions, 'Developing Pioneers in Leicester Diocese', 29 October 2015. Available at http://109.104.89.222/news/dioceseofleicester [viewed 14 May 2019].

Frost, Michael and Alan Hirsch, *The Shaping of Things to Come: Innovation and Mission for the 21st-Century Church*, Peabody, MA: Hendrickson, 2003.

Frow, John, 'Michel De Certeau and the Practice of Representation', *Cultural Studies* 5 (1), 1991, pp. 52–60.

Gal, Susan, 'A Semiotics of the Public/Private Distinction', *Differences: A Journal of Feminist Cultural Studies* 13 (1), 2002, pp. 77–95.

Gallagher, Sally K. and Chelsea Newton, 'Defining Spiritual Growth: Congregations, Community, and Connectedness', *Sociology of Religion* 70 (3), 2009, pp. 232–61.

Gaventa, Beverly Roberts, '"You Will Be My Witnesses": Aspects of Mission in the Acts of the Apostles', *Missiology* 10 (4), 1982, pp. 413–25.

Gay, Doug, *Remixing the Church: Towards an Emerging Ecclesiology*, London: SCM Press, 2011.

Gelpi, Donald, 'Conversion: Beyond the Impasses of Individualism', in Donald L. Gelpi (ed.), *Beyond Individualism: Toward a Retrieval of Moral Discourse in America*, Notre Dame, IN: University of Notre Dame Press, 1989, pp. 1–30.

Gibbs, Eddie and Ryan Bolger, *Emerging Churches: Creating Christian Community in Postmodern Cultures*, Ada, MI: Baker Academic, 1995.

God in the House, 1995. Available at www.youtube.com/watch?time_continue =1&v=QQQbcb5YPBA [viewed 27 March 2019].

'Grace' – *God in the House*, 1996. Available at www.youtube.com/watch?v= d1FJIq2YvQU&feature=youtu.be [viewed 29 April 2019].

Greggs, Tom, 'Janet Martin Soskice, The Kindness of God: Metaphor, Gender and Religious Language'; Book review, *Scottish Journal of Theology* 64 (2), 2011, pp. 241–3.

Guest, Matthew, 'In Search of Spiritual Capital: The Spiritual as a Cultural Resource', in Kieran Flanagan and Peter C. Jupp (eds), *A Sociology of Spirituality*, Aldershot: Ashgate, 2007, pp. 181–200.

Gutierrez, Gustavo, *A Theology of Liberation: History, Politics and Salvation*, revised edition, ed. and trans. Sister Caridad Inda and John Eagleson, Maryknoll, NY: Orbis Books, 1988.

Harrold, Philip, 'Contextual Churches in History', in Michael Moynagh, *A Church for Every Context: An Introduction to Theology and Practice*, London: SCM Press, 2012, pp. 28–50.

Hawthorne, Gerald and Ralph Martin, *Philippians*, Nashville: Thomas Nelson, 2004.

Healy, Nicholas, *Church, World and the Christian Life: Practical-prophetic ecclesiology*, Cambridge: Cambridge University Press, 2000.

Healy, Nicholas, 'Ecclesiology, Ethnography, and God: An Interplay of Reality Descriptions', in Pete Ward (ed.), *Perspectives on Ecclesiology and Ethnography*, Grand Rapids, MI: Eerdmans, 2012, pp. 182–99.

Hess, Carol L., *Caretakers of Our Common House: Women's Development in Communities of Faith*, Nashville: Abingdon, 1997.

Hopkins, Neil, Pers. Comm. Available at http://members.tripod.com/neil_hopkins/docs/nos.htm [viewed 21 July 2014].

Howard, Roland, *The Rise and Fall of the Nine O'Clock Service*, London: Continuum International Publishers, 1996.

Hundred-Foot Journey, The, Universal City, California, DreamWorks Pictures, 2014.

Hunter, James Davison, *To Change the World: The Irony, Tragedy and Possibility of Christianity in the Late Modern World*, New York: Oxford University Press, 2010.

Hurst, Lincoln, 'Ethics of Jesus', in Joel B. Green, Scot McKnight and I. Howard Marshall (eds), *Dictionary of Jesus and the Gospels*, Downers Grove, IL: InterVarsity Press, 1992, pp. 210–22.

Hutchinson, Vivian, 'The Business of Complexity', in Vivian Hutchinson and the New Zealand Social Entrepreneur Fellowship (eds), *How Communities Heal: Stories of Social Innovation and Social Change*, New Plymouth, NZ: Florence Press, 2011. Available atwww.nzsef.org.nz/howcommunitiesheal [viewed 10 April 2019].

Ihimaera, Witi, *The Whale Rider*, Auckland: Reed, 1987.

Jones, Andrew, 'Together toward life: when The Shaping of Things to Come is much more bleak', April 15, 2014. Available at www.emergentkiwi.org.nz/archive/together-toward-life-when-the-shaping-of-things-to-come-is-much-more-bleak/#comments [viewed 15 May 2019].

Jones, L. Gregory, 'Traditioned innovation', Faith & Leadership, 2009. Available at www.faithandleadership.com/content/traditioned-innovation [viewed 11 April 2019].

Jones, L. Gregory, *Christian Social Innovation: Renewing Wesleyan Witness*, Nashville: Abingdon, 2016.

Julian of Norwich, *Revelations of Divine Love*, trans. Clifton Wolters, London: Penguin, 1966.

Keener, Craig, *IVP Bible Background Commentary: New Testament*, Downers Grove, IL: Intervarsity Press, 1994.

Late Late Service, *God in the Flesh* CD, Sticky Music, 1994.

Lyon, William John, 'Preaching at the Nine O'Clock Service: A Study of Shifting Meaning in a Published Sermon', in William John Lyons and Isabella Sandwell (eds), *Delivering the Word: Preaching and Exegesis in the Western Christian Tradition*, Sheffield: Equinox, 2012, pp. 231–45.

McDougall, Joy Ann, 'The Kindness of God: Metaphor, Gender, and Religious Language: Janet Martin Soskice'; Book review, *Theology Today* 66 (4), 2010, pp. 531–4.

McKie, John and Andrew Brown, '"Sex cult" leaves 150 in need of counselling', *The Independent*, 23 August 1995. Available at www.independent.co.uk/news/sex-cult-leaves-150-in-need-of-counselling-1597498.html [viewed 21 July 2014].

Mainstone-Cotton, Sonia and Iain and Clare Birch, 'Curating Uncluttered Spaces', in Jonny Baker (ed.), *Curating Worship*, London: SPCK, 2010, pp. 139–48.

'March 2006: Lent Bring Your Own Station', *Grace: Fresh, Vital Worship since 1993*. Available at www.freshworship.org/archive/services/2006/2006-03-lent.html [viewed 21 April 2019].

Marti, Gerardo and Gladys Ganiel, *The Deconstructed Church: Understanding Emerging Christianity*, New York: Oxford University Press, 2014.

Martin, Ralph, *Philippians*, London: Marshall, Morgan and Scott, 1976.

Minear, Paul, *Images of the Church in the New Testament*, Philadelphia: Westminster Press, 1960.

Mission-Shaped Church: Church Planting and Fresh Expressions of Church in a Changing Context, London: Church House Publishing, 2004.

Monmouth Diocesan Newsletter, Summer 2011. Available at www.churchin wales.org.uk/monmouth/news/newsletter/News198Pentecost2012.pdf [viewed 13 March 2013].

Morais, Richard C, *The Hundred-Foot Journey*, New York: Scribner, 2010.

Morgan, Richard, 'Q&A: Producer of Hundred-Foot Journey On the Food Behind the Movie', 6 September 2014. Available at https://news.nationalgeographic. com/news/2014/09/140907-hundred-foot-journey-indian-french-entertainment-ngfood/ [viewed 24 April 2019].

Moynagh, Michael with Philip Harrold, *A Church for Every Context: An Introduction to Theology and Practice*, London: SCM Press, 2012.

Moynagh, Michael, *Church in Life: Innovation, Mission and Ecclesiology*, London: SCM Press, 2017.

Noll, Mark, *The Rise of Evangelicalism: The Age of Edwards, Whitfield and the Wesleys*, Leicester: Apollos, 2004.

O Donnchadha, Gearoid, *St Brendan of Kerry, the Navigator: His Life and Voyages*, Dublin: Four Courts Press, 2004.

O'Loughlin, Thomas, *Celtic Theology: Humanity, World and God in Early Irish Writings*, London and New York: Continuum, 2000.

Packard, Josh, 'Resisting Institutionalization: Religious Professionals in the Emerging Church*', *Sociological Inquiry* 81 (1), 2011, pp. 3–33.

Packard, Josh and George Sanders, 'The Emerging Church as Corporatization's Line of Flight', *Journal of Contemporary Religion*, 28 (3), 2013, pp. 437–55.

Paas, Stefan, *Church Planting in the Secular West: Learning from the European Experience*, Grand Rapids, MI: Eerdmans, 2016.

Philips, Catherine (ed.), *Gerard Manley Hopkins: Selected Poetry*, Oxford: Oxford University Press, 1995.

Phillips, Ann, *The Faith of Girls: Children's Spirituality and Transition to Adulthood*, Abingdon: Routledge, 2017.

Pranger, Jan, 'Inculturation as Theology of Culture: Exploring Kathryn Tanner's Contribution to Intercultural Theology', in Rosemary P. Carbine and Hilda P. Koster (eds), *The Gift of Theology: The Contribution of Kathryn Tanner*, Minneapolis: Fortress Press, 2015, pp. 175–208.

Priorities for the Methodist Church: Report of the 'Where are we heading?' consultation process, 2004. Available at www.methodist.org.uk/downloads/ conf-priorities-for-the-MC-2004.pdf [viewed 29 April 2019].

Rabey, Steve, *In Search of Authentic Faith: How Emerging Generations are Transforming the Church*, Colorado Springs: WaterBrook Press, 2001.

Rack, Henry, *The Future of John Wesley's Methodism*, London: Lutterworth Press, 1965.

Rack, Henry, *Reasonable Enthusiast: John Wesley and the Rise of Methodism*, London: Epworth, 2002.

Richards, Anne and Mission Theological Advisory Group, *Sense Making Faith: Body, Spirit Journey*, Churches Together in Britain and Ireland, 2007.

Riddell, Mike, *Threshold of the Future: Reforming the Church in the Post-Christian West*, London: SPCK, 1998.

Riley, Adrian, *God in the House: UK Club Culture and Spirituality*, 1999. Available at www.btmc.org.uk/altworship/house/ [viewed October 2013].

Rodriguez, Ruben Rosario, *Dogmatics after Babel: Beyond the Theologies of Word and Culture*, Louisville, KY: Westminster John Knox Press, 2018.

Rogers, Eugene, *The Holy Spirit. Classic and Contemporary Readings*, Chichester: Wiley-Blackwell, 2009a.

Rogers, Eugene F, 'The Kindness of God: Metaphor, Gender, and Religious Language – By Janet Martin Soskice', *Modern Theology* 25 (3), 2009b, pp. 519–21.

Rogerson, J. W., 'The Lord is Here: The Nine O'Clock Service', in Martyn Percy and Ian Markham (eds), *Why Liberal Churches are Growing*, London: T&T Clark, 2006, pp. 45–52.

Roxburgh, Alan, *Structured for Mission: Structured for Mission*, Downers Grove, IL: InterVarsity Press, 2015.

Ryken, Leland, James C. Wilhoit and Tremper Longman III, *Dictionary of Biblical Imagery*, Downers Grove, IL: InterVarsity Press, 1998.

Schults, LeRon, 'Reforming Ecclesiology in Emerging Churches', *Theology Today* 65 (4), 2009, pp. 425–38.

'September 2005: Engage', *Grace: Fresh, Vital Worship since 1993*. Available at www.freshworship.org/archive/services/2005/2005-09-engage.html [viewed 21 April 2019].

'September 2006: New year', *Grace: Fresh, Vital Worship since 1993*. Available at www.freshworship.org/archive/services/2006/2006-09-newyear.html [viewed 21 April 2019].

Severin, Timothy, 'The Voyage of the "Brendan"', *National Geographic Magazine*, 152 (6), December 1977, pp. 768–97.

Shortt, Rupert, *Rowan's Rule: The Biography of the Archbishop*, London: Hodder and Stoughton, 2008.

Skreslet, Stanley H., 'Emerging Trends in a Shifting Global Context: Mission in the New World Order', *Theology Today* 54 (2), 1997a, pp. 150–64.

Skreslet, Stanley H., 'Networking, Civil Society and the NGO: A New Model for Ecumenical Mission', *Missiology* 25 (3), 1997b, pp. 307–19.

Skreslet, Stanley H., 'Impending Transformation: Mission Structures for a New Century', *International Bulletin of Missionary Research* 23 (1), 1999, pp. 2–6.

Skreslet, Stanley H., *Picturing Christian Witness: New Testament Images of Disciples in Mission*, Grand Rapids, MI: Eerdmans, 2006.

Skreslet, Stanley H., *Comprehending Mission: The Questions, Methods, Themes, Problems, and Prospects of Missiology*, Maryknoll, NY: Orbis, 2012.

Slee, Nichola, *Women's Faith Development: Patterns and Processes*, Aldershot: Ashgate, 2004.

Smith, James, *How (Not) to Be Secular: Reading Charles Taylor*, Grand Rapids, MI: Eerdmans, 2014.

Smolarski, Dennis Chester, *The General Instruction of the Roman Missal, 1969–2002: A Commentary*, Collegeville, MN: Liturgical Press, 2003.

Soskice, Janet Martin, *The Kindness of God: Metaphor, Gender, and Religious Language*, Oxford: Oxford University Press, 2007.

Spriggs, David, 'Christmas Angels Help to Get the Message Across!' *Christian Today*, 2006. Available at www.christiantoday.com/article/david.spriggs.christmas.angels.help.to.get.the.message.across/8864.htm [viewed 20 March 2019].

'Swindon's Angels', *Wiltshire Life*, n.d. Available at www.bbc.co.uk/wiltshire/content/image_galleries/swindon_angels_2006_gallery.shtml?2 [viewed 20 Mar 2019].

Swinton, John, *From Bedlam to Shalom: Towards a Practical Theology of Human Nature, Interpersonal Relationships, and Mental Health Care*, New York: Peter Lang, 2000.

Swinton, John and Harriet Mowat, *Practical Theology and Qualitative Research*, London: SCM Press, 2006.

Tamez, Elsa, 'Letter from James to the General Assembly in Seoul of the International Association for Mission Studies', *Mission Studies*, 34 (1), 2017, pp. 78–91.

Tangata Whenua, *Artefact*, Greenstone TV, Mt Eden, Auckland, 2018.

Tanner, Kathryn, *Theories of Culture: A New Agenda for Theology*, Minneapolis: Fortress Press, 1997.

Tapsell, Paul and Christine Woods, 'Social Entrepreneurship and Innovation: Self-Organization in an Indigenous Context', *Entrepreneurship & Regional Development* 22 (6), 2010, pp. 535–56.

Taylor, Charles, *The Ethics of Authenticity*, Cambridge, MA: Harvard University Press, 1992.

Taylor, Charles, *A Secular Age*, Cambridge, MA: Belknap Press of Harvard University Press, 2007.

Taylor, Lynne and Naomi Nash, *Learning from Innovation: Sharing Learning from Innovative Projects within the Uniting Church*, Parammatta, NSW: Uniting Mission and Education, 2018.

Taylor, Steve, 'A New Way of Being Church? A Case Study Approach to Cityside Baptist Church as Christian Faith "making do" in a Postmodern World', PhD thesis, Dunedin, New Zealand: University of Otago, 2004.

Taylor, Steve, *The Out of Bounds Church? Learning to Create a Community of Faith in a Culture of Change*, Grand Rapids, MI: Zondervan, 2005.

Taylor, Steve, 'Emerging, Established or Re-emerging? A Trinitarian Reflection on Church and Ministry Today', *Ministry Today*, 2006, pp. 24–34.

Taylor, Steve, 'Wanted Dead and Alive: UK alt.worship Communities', 12 April 2012. Available at www.emergentkiwi.org.nz/archive/wanted-dead-and-alive-uk-alt-worship-communities/ [viewed on 17 May 2019].

Taylor, Steve, 'The Complexity of Authenticity in Religious Innovation: "Alternative Worship" and Its Appropriation as Fresh Expressions', *M/C Journal* 18 (1), 2015. Available at http://journal.media-culture.org.au/index.php/mcjournal/article/view/933 [viewed 29 April 2019].

Taylor, Steve, *Built for Change: A Practical Theology of Innovation and Collaboration in Leadership*, Adelaide: Mediacom, 2016.

Taylor, Steve, 'Where Does Mission Come From? The Genealogy of Jesus as Deep Mission', *Australian Journal of Mission Studies* 11 (2), December 2017, pp. 28–35.

Taylor, Steve and Rosemary Dewerse, 'Researching the Future: The Implications of Activist Research for Theological Scholarship in Teaching and Learning', in Les Ball and Peter Bolt (eds), *Wondering about God Together: Research Led Learning and Teaching in Theological Education*, Sydney: SCD Press, 2018, pp. 87–104.

Thiel, John E., 'Foreword', in Rosemary P. Carbine and Hilda P. Koster (eds), *The Gift of Theology: The Contribution of Kathryn Tanner*, Minneapolis: Fortress Press, 2015, pp. xxi–xxiii.

Thornton, Andy, 'The Late Late Service', n.d. Available at www.andythornton.me.uk/?page_id=68 [viewed 27 March 2019].

Thornton, Sarah, *Club Cultures: Music, Media and Subcultural Capital*, Hanover, NH: University Press of New England, 1996.

Thurston, Bonnie B. and Judith M. Ryan, *Philippians and Philemon*, Collegeville, MN: Liturgical Press, 2005.

Till, Rupert, 'The Nine O'Clock Service: Mixing Club Culture and Postmodern Christianity', *Culture and Religion* 7 (1), 2006, pp. 93–110.

'Time & Space', St Helen's Church, 2014. Available at www.york360.co.uk/whats-on/illuminating-york) [viewed 19 March 2019].

Times of India, 'Health Benefits of Mustard Seeds', *Times of India*, 11 August 2017. Available at https://timesofindia.indiatimes.com/life-style/health-fitness/diet/health-benefits-of-mustard-seeds/articleshow/5912874.cms [viewed 3 May 2019].

Tindall, Mike, 'William Carey: Pioneer'. A paper presented at the Carey Conference, Swanwick, Derbyshire, UK, 2011.

Vannini, Philip, 'Authenticity', in Dale Southerton (ed.), *Encyclopedia of Consumer Culture*, Los Angeles: Sage, 2011, pp. 74–6.

Verter, Bradford, 'Spiritual Capital: Theorizing Religion with Bourdieu against Bourdieu', *Sociological Theory*, 21 (2), 2003, pp. 150–74.

Vincent, John, *Alternative Church*, Belfast: Christian Journals Limited, 1976.

Wallace, Sue, *Multi-sensory Prayer: Over 60 Innovative Ready-to-use Ideas*, Milton Keynes: Scripture Union, 2000.

Wallace, Sue, *Multi-Sensory Church: Over 30 Innovative Ready-to-use Ideas*, Milton Keynes: Scripture Union, 2002.

Wallace, Sue, *Multi-Sensory Scripture: 50 Innovative Ideas for Exploring the Bible in Churches and Small Groups*, Milton Keynes: Scripture Union, 2005.

Wallace, Sue, *Multi-Sensory Worship: Over 60 Innovative Ready-to-use Prayer Activities for Creative Churches*, Milton Keynes: Scripture Union, 2009a.

Wallace, Sue, 'Alternative Worship and the Story of Visions in York', in Steven Croft and Ian Mobsby (eds), *Fresh Expressions in the Sacramental Tradition*, Norwich: Canterbury Press, 2009b, pp. 9–15.

Walls, Andrew, *The Missionary Movement in Christian History: Studies in the Transmission of Faith*, Maryknoll, NY: Orbis Books, 1996.

Walsh, John, 'Religious Societies: Methodist and Evangelical 1738–1800', *Studies in Church History*, 23, 1986, pp. 279–302.

Ward, Pete, *Liquid Church*, Carlisle: Paternoster Press, 2002.

Ward, W. R., *The Protestant Evangelical Awakening*, Cambridge: Cambridge University Press, 1992.

Warner, Daniel, *Live Wires: A History of Electronic Music*, London: Reaktion Books, 2017.

Westerholm, Stephen, 'Clean and Unclean', in Joel B. Green, Scot McKnight and I. Howard Marshall (eds), *Dictionary of Jesus and the Gospels*, Downers Grove, IL: InterVarsity Press, 1992, pp. 125–32.

Whale Rider (DVD), Culver City, California: Columbia TriStar Home Entertainment, 2003.

'What is a Fresh Expression?' n.d. Available at http://freshexpressions.org.uk/about/what-is-a-fresh-expression/ [viewed 21 April 2019].

Williams, Rowan, *Resurrection: Interpreting the Easter Gospel*, London: Darton, Longman and Todd, 1982.

Williams, Rowan, 'Doing the Works of God', in *Open to Judgement: Sermons and Addresses*, London: Darton, Longman and Todd, 1994, pp. 254–66.

Williams, Rowan, *On Christian Theology*, Oxford: Blackwell, 2000.

BIBLIOGRAPHY

Williams, Rowan, 'Statement at first press conference, Tuesday 23rd July 2002'. Available at http://rowanwilliams.archbishopofcanterbury.org/articles. php/1809/statement-at-first-press-conference [viewed 13 April 2013].

Williams, Rowan, *The Dwelling of the Light: Praying with Icons of Christ*, Norwich: Canterbury Press, 2003a.

Williams, Rowan, 'Archbishop's Presidential Address – General Synod, York, July 2003', 2003b. Available at http://rowanwilliams.archbishopofcanterbury.org/articles.php/1826/archbishops-presidential-address-general-synod-york-july-2003 [viewed April 2013].

Williams, Rowan, Foreword to *Mission-Shaped Church: Church Planting and Fresh Expressions of Church in a Changing Context*, London: Church House Publishing, 2004, pp. vii.

Williams, Rowan, 'Stop doing that which is pulling us apart – Archbishop of Canterbury appeals in interview', *Global South Anglican Online*, 2007. Available at www.globalsouthanglican.org/index.php/comments/stop_doing_that_which_is_pulling_us_apart_archbishop_of_canterbury_appeals [viewed 28 May 2019].

Williams, Rowan, *Ponder These Things: Praying with Icons of the Virgin*, Norwich: Canterbury Press, 2012, reprint.

Witherington, Ben, *Women in the Earliest Churches*, Cambridge: Cambridge University Press, 1991.

Witherington, Ben, *Conflict and Community in Corinth: A Socio-Rhetorical Commentary on 1 and 2 Corinthians*, Grand Rapids, MI: Eerdmans, 1995.

Witherington, Ben, *The Acts of the Apostles: A Socio-Rhetorical Commentary*, Grand Rapids, MI: Eerdmans, 1998.

Zhang, Michael, 'Back in 1995, A 1MP Pro Digital Camera Cost $20,000', Available at https://petapixel.com/2015/07/17/back-in-1995-a-1mp-pro-digital-camera-cost-20000/ [viewed on 25 May 2019].

Index of Names and Subjects